ALL ABOUT PSYCHOLO
AND ASSESSMENT CENTRES

For a complete list of Management Books 2000 titles,
visit our web-site on http://www.mb2000.com

ALL ABOUT PSYCHOLOGICAL TESTS AND ASSESSMENT CENTRES

Dr Jack J R van Minden

2000

Originally published in the Netherlands by Business Contact, within a series of books under the group title 'Alles Over ...' 'All about ...' success in all aspects of job search, interviews and tests.

First published in 2004 by Management Books 2000 Ltd
Forge House, Limes Road
Kemble, Cirencester
Gloucestershire, GL7 6AD, UK
Tel: 0044 (0) 1285 771441/2
Fax: 0044 (0) 1285 771055
E-mail: mb.2000@virgin.net
Web: www.mb2000.com

Printed and bound in Great Britain by Digital Books Logistics Ltd

British Library Cataloguing in Publication Data is available
ISBN 1-85252- 458-8

Foreword

Psychological tests and the assessment centre method are personnel selection techniques that previously had meaning only for a handful of experts, but are now in every jobhunter's handbook.

This book is based upon years of research into the theory and everyday practice of tests and assessment techniques, as employed by selection agencies and large organisations. A great deal of information is also derived from the continual feedback given by test candidates.

Why write this book?

The impenetrable land of better jobs has strict entry requirements. The only passport acknowledged there is the test report. The barrier is only lifted for those with the 'passed' stamp. For this reason, the growing stream of clients to selection agencies would like to know what to expect when they are invited to a 'test' or an assessment centre. This book will offer those keen to move to the world of better jobs not only practical information, but also the chance to practise typical tests and assessment exercises at home.

The former US Minister for Foreign Affairs, Mr James Baker, is attributed with the quote: 'prior preparation prevents poor performance'. This book stands between succeeding or failing the test.

Who should read it?

This book is written for those who (sooner or later) experience tests and assessment centres, who wish to succeed, and want to prepare for this important milestone to the best of their ability. We are thinking of:

1. Senior and middle managers who are being assessed as part of an extensive selection procedure.

2. Personnel who are seeking a management position in the long term, or who for other reasons wish to be investigated in detail.

3. Commercial staff who must 'prove' their sales ability (ingenuity?) via role plays and other tasks.

4. All types of staff in large organisations, who must demonstrate what they are capable of – before they can be promoted. By this, we mean a so-called development centre.

5. Recent graduates who must undergo strict selection procedures in order to gain a place on a further training course.

6. Graduates who want to pursue a management-oriented career and who must know something about management and management selection.

7. Students of psychology, personnel and human resources and other people-oriented courses who wish to know about selection methods.

What can this book do for you?

This is what is offered to you:

1. It throws light on tests and assessment centres, principally as a means of selection. Think of increasing your knowledge in terms of the workings of an automatic coffee machine: drop by drop the coffee pot fills up. This book gives an overview of a large number of well-used tests and assessment tasks. Thus, you will gain an idea of what you can expect. You will encounter countless examples in the book. You have the chance to become familiar with a number of tests – some of which you can practice. You will therefore be much more self-assured, confident and relaxed on the test day itself.

2. It encompasses a plan to allow you to see in broad outline how your assessment centre could appear. You can convert your good intentions into actions, because you will be judged on them.

3. If you suffer from test anxiety (perhaps due to having been tested and rejected), this book will do you a good service. Your fear will melt away like ice cubes on a hot Summer's day.

4. It offers a number of mini-courses, on subjects such as leading a group discussion and problem solving. In a nutshell, you will learn how to approach these situations more effectively.

In short, this book contains a great deal of practical information. It is written for candidates who are about to undergo a test procedure. Reading it greatly increases your chances of success!

The 'tipbox' and the 'warning triangle'

> **TIP** In this book, you will see in various places grey boxes with TIP written in them. You will find all sorts of practical advice in these 'tipboxes'. Make use of them!

Selection procedures contain many dangerous situations which can lead you astray. Throughout this book, you will be warned about these via the warning triangles, which (how else!) will be symbolised as follows:

I would like to thank my colleagues at Psycom for the small and (sometimes inadvertently) large contributions they have made to the completion of this book. Further thanks also to diverse experts, institutions and selection bureaux who have read through this manuscript and given advice. And let's not forget the translator, psychologist Leanna Roscoe.

I hope that reading this book will deliver the desired result: **a job, a promotion or a training place!**

Contents

- Speed tests versus power tests
- Duration
- A day at the agency

- Some questions about preparation
- Suggestions to help you prepare
- Agencies don't like candidates who practise ...
- What are you being tested for exactly?
- Concentration in ten steps
- Physical and mental fitness
- Personal test problems

- What is intelligence?
- Intelligence is not unitary: the profile
- Diagrams
- The meaning of IQ
- Margin of error
- Boosting your IQ score
- Integral test versus 'sub-test'
- What is an analogy test?
- Two techniques for verbal analogies
- Antonyms
- 'Jumbled sentences'
- Syllogism test
- Similarities
- Numeracy test
- Numerical series
- 'Letter crunching'
- Timetabling problems
- Reasoning tests
- Inappropriate use of the IQ test

- Traits and personal competencies
- Objective personality tests
- Motivation and needs

- 'Big Five'
- Emotional intelligence
- What not to do on personality tests
- Inkblots, sketches and trees
- Evaluation

- Sales Comprehension Test (SCT)
- Sales Motivation Inventory (SMI)
- Sentence Completion Test
- Thomas Kilmann Instrument
- Integrity tests
- Attention and concentration
- Vocational interest tests

- What is an assessment centre?
- Uses of assessment centres
- Behavioural dimensions
- What types of tasks to expect?
- 'Integrated' assessments
- The ORCE model
- The assessors
- Time management
- Who are your opponents?
- Some critical points regarding the AC

- What to expect?
- Your own programme in seven easy steps
- How is your behaviour evaluated?
- Overall assessment rating (OAR)
- Disqualifiers
- How do you want to come across?
- Making requests

- Why have role plays?

- How it works
- Professional actors
- Nervous?
- Remember T.I.F.
- Creativity
- Hazardous pitfalls and nagging problems
- Using silence
- Dealing with difficult partners
- Ten tough evaluation questions
- The bad news talk
- Conflict
- Fact-finding: gaining information and making recommendations

- What is being measured? How are you evaluated?
- Outline of situation and task
- Three types of in-tray activities
- Three hours of sweat and toil?
- Time pressure and time management
- Any more questions?
- Standard versus specific
- In-tray advice
- Towards excellence

- Your role
- The group discussion
- Variations
- Positive comments
- The building task
- The meeting task

- What is being measured?
- Types of analytical tasks
- Different perspectives and systematic approaches
- How to approach the analysis task
- Presentations

- The post-assessment discussion
- Recycled reports?

1

Introduction

The book you see before you is an excellent preparatory tool: you will learn an exceptional amount about psychological selection and assessment. Preparation bears fruit, as the author can testify from his own experiences at his office in Amstelveen, the Netherlands, where at Psycom people take time out to practise before their 'test'. Every day, the value of Test-Training programmes is proven.

'*Most people try to speculate what is expected of them. Our experience is that often the speculations are incorrect. We therefore would advise you to be yourself*'. This is the 'tip' that one agency gives its candidates. We have a problem with this. What does 'be yourself' mean? When are you yourself? Can you ever not be yourself? And if you can, then who are you? What they are saying here is: stay ignorant and naive, because it makes it easier for us to assess you! The best advice is: prepare yourself, because then you increase the chances of leaving the psychological selection or assessment procedure with a job in the bag.

The psychological test as standard procedure

The largest British companies make use of psychometric testing methods, particularly for middle range and senior level jobs. These organisations don't want to take any chances and wish to inspect you from every possible angle. Sometimes, these companies do their own testing, and sometimes they contact a specialist agency to do it on their behalf. No matter how good you may be, rules are rules, and you will be faced with the tools of the psychologist's trade.

It may well be that you are the only remaining candidate. This means your future employer wants to be more sure about you. Maybe it is standard procedure to test every new employee. So, you are invited to spend a day being tested. Our experience has been that people take testing too lightly. Don't make that mistake! You can only be sure of landing this new job if you receive a positive recommendation from the testing agency. So don't run any unnecessary risk (the employer doesn't) and prepare yourself for this situation as much as possible.

This book deals with both psychometric or psychological tests and the assessment centre technique. For now, it suffices to say that tests measure your non-observable 'inside' (intelligence, personality), while the assessment centre examines your observable behaviour.

The odds are against you

It is highly unlikely that you will be the only one applying for a particular post. You will have a number of competitors, 'blots on the landscape'. If you and three others have made it to the last round, then you have a 25% chance of emerging as the winner. Or for the pessimists amongst you: you have a 75% chance of 'flunking'.

TIP If the future employer (for example, the personnel manager) says that you are the only remaining candidate and they still want to test you, try to get out of it. There is always the possibility that you will come out of the test less than positively. Avoid this risk. Give the employer another means of testing you. Perhaps a second interview with the MD, a day 'shadowing' your predecessor in the company to assess your actual behaviour or ask them to contact your referees. You could also consider a temporary contract. In short, try to get an employment contract without being tested!

Why pre-employment selection methods

Employers see a number of advantages to administering tests, some of which also clearly benefit jobhunters:

- the methods (that is, by far most of them) are objective
- when outsourced, they are saving valuable company time
- quality, since experts are involved
- speed (test report can be published in a matter of days)

- large amount of data available (personality, intelligence, behaviour, skills etc.)
- many data can be expressed in numbers
- relatively inexpensive
- risk avoidance ('insurance policy').

Is it possible to prepare?

When you call the testing agency in anticipation of your procedure and ask them what to expect, you probably get an ice-cold silence. *'Just be yourself'*, may be the reply. *'Preparation is not possible'*, is the conclusion of the phone call. Agencies prefer naive candidates, but they may also be a bit gullible. However, the author knows by experience – having trained thousands of people – that test preparation is effective. And there is independent scientific research to back up this claim: 'training can lead to an increase of 20 traditional IQ points in the numerical reasoning test ... The results were less impressive in the verbal reasoning test, but training still resulted in an increase of roughly 7 IQ points'. (Keen)

A brochure from a well-known agency reads: *'The question: to what extent are certain criteria trainable? is difficult to answer. Few details on this can be found in books and journals. If one accepts the strictly behaviourist approach, that all behaviour can be learnt, then one must also allow that all criteria can be taught'.*

Preparing for the in-tray and other assessment centre tasks is also quite possible. *'In-tray training had a significant effect on performance dimensions of this task ... Whatever is actually being measured in the in-tray task, be it psychological characteristics, situational capabilities or a mixture of the two, responds in every case to short, quick (test) training ... It would appear that skills are much easier to teach than characteristics.'* (Van der Flier, Jansen & Zaal)

Dishonest and deceitful candidates

Jobhunters do not always tell the whole truth when they have set their hearts on a job. Neither are employers strictly honest when they wish to enlist a particular candidate! They may have various reasons to be untruthful or to hide something.

Employers and selectors have two reasons for wishing to know about honesty.

First, the selector wants reliable results from his investigation. If a candidate is not speaking or writing the truth during a task, there already exists some doubt about his or her assessed capabilities.

Second, staff and management are not supposed to steal from the boss, cheat or have a high level of absenteeism ('time theft'). An umbrella term for this type of behaviour is 'transgression'. Stealing, pinching and pilfering is regrettably not confined to a single group in society.

Candidates do indeed conceal information, when they have good reason to do so, for example:

- getting sacked/being unemployed
- not possessing certain qualifications
- an alcohol problem
- an emotionally draining divorce
- having once been admitted to a psychiatric institution
- having a criminal record
- being (or having been) seriously ill.

In this age of 'recycled CVs', it is becoming increasingly difficult in the chess game called selection to discover the 'true value' of an individual. Neither tests nor assessment centre tasks can predict that Miss Peterson will steal £17 from her new employer over the next three years, or that she will in effect be a 'time thief'. But this form of theft is perhaps more a question of fitting in with the norms and customs of the work environment and organisational culture. Opportunity creates the thief. Or does the thief create the opportunity? The assessment centre can certainly check if the skills and capabilities which the candidate claims to possess are actually 'true'. However, honesty is notoriously difficult to predict.

The pre-assessment briefing

Before the candidate honours the selection agency with a visit, the professional psychologist must do some preparation with the recruiting company. There are four most important questions which they need answered.

- What is the job profile exactly? With a little luck, the psychologist will have a job profile available to him or her.
- Which qualities and skills is it imperative that the candidate possesses? And which ones must *not* be possessed?
- Must the candidate have a high degree of potential? In other words, must he or she have something in store for later – promotion!
- What type of organisational culture must the candidate fit in with?

In short, the psychologist needs a brief from the client.

> ***TIP*** Always ask the employer (as soon as possible) if a job profile or job description is available, and if it can be sent to you, because you want to make the right choice. The job profile 'helps' you to present yourself in the desired manner in the selection procedure.

Some organisations provide comprehensive information. All that remains is the assessment ... But more often, the psychologist is groping in the dark, and the assessment 'building' must be done from the bottom up. For that reason, an extensive checklist for the client's convenience (because he or she is always 'king') must be produced. The questions are then filled in with the client's help, so that a picture emerges of the job in question. One agency informs its clients that 'this briefing form is aimed at defining organisational parameters and job or function content, as well as establishing the requirements which the candidate needs for the job. If you could fill in the form as fully as possible, then you will greatly improve the quality of the psychological investigation (the assessment centre).

a. What's the job title? Which department is it? And what is the salary level?
b. How does the function fit into the organisation plan?
c. What is the aim of the function? Why has it been set up? What does it contribute to achieving the objectives of the department?
d. Work features, which the client must list in order of importance, like ability to work independently or result-orientation.
e. What are the most important components of the job (in order of importance) and how much time does each component take (in percentages)?

f. Which minimum educational qualifications are required? Just GCSEs, or must the future job-holder know the university system inside and out – and have a degree?

g. Have you ever heard of an occupational psychologist who isn't interested in the intelligence of his or her visitors? The 'soul searcher' wants to know how (under)developed the candidate's verbal, numerical and analytic reasoning is, and how his or her inventiveness and/or creativity is.

h. And if that isn't enough, they also ask about 'specific competencies', like technical, commercial, administrative or computing skills.

i. Naturally, the psychologist also wants to know with whom the person appointed will have contact (internal and external) and how much.

j. Every job has certain so-called 'critical points'. These are potentially dangerous situations. The employer may wish to flag these up, indicating his preferred method of dealing with them. Think of the friction between business and ethics: higher profits versus honest customer relations.

k. The psychologist also wheedles out of his client the desired personal characteristics, which he must quickly place in rank order.

l. To what extent must the candidate possess abilities like making judgements, or taking decisions, planning, leading, maintaining contact, persuasiveness, co-operative behaviour, oral communication, written skills, commercial ability. These are all behavioural dimensions, which will be defined and described later in this book.

m. When the vacancy is a management position: how many people will he or she be managing; what level of education do they have; and what do they do? Management style is also a question of organisational culture. What is allowed and what must happen? Is it motivation-oriented or results-oriented? People management or supervisory type management? Does the manager also have to be expert in a particular field (professional grommet hole convertor), or merely a facilitator, 'networker', 'mover & shaker', market-oriented, service-oriented, customer-oriented, product-oriented?

So, you are not the only one who has to do a great deal of homework.

Organisational culture and you

Every organisation, no matter how small, has its own distinctive culture, the norms and values of the group of people who together make up the company or institution. It will always have a mission (even though this might not be screamed from the rooftops), goals and certain issues that are deemed important.

It is essential for you to know beforehand one or two things about the culture in which you will be working, because you will also be evaluated on the extent to which you fit into the employer's culture. If you 'grew up' in a very results-oriented organisation, then you may well choose the 'wrong' approach in the role play if you are making the transition to Sleepyshire Country Products Ltd.

Organisational culture is something vague, but certainly not unimportant. In good assessment centres, you will find some assessors working for the (neutral and objective) selection agency and others for the employer. The latter will determine if the candidate is 'a chip off the same cultural block' as the company. Someone who scores well on all the behavioural dimensions, but does not fit in at all with the organisational culture will not get the job. ('*Sorry, but your profile doesn't match*', is the polite explanation.)

If you don't know what the company culture is of the organisation for whom you are being tested, then you have to try and find out. Do not despair – there are things you can do!

a. Request the company's latest annual report (only available for public limited companies – plcs) from the organisation itself, its website, a public library, a bank or the local Chamber of Commerce.

b. The PR department will often provide information packs. Give them a call.

c. Press reports (cut them out!) are a valuable source of information. You can read about the image of your future employer, and sometimes even what type of culture the company has. (But watch out – not all news is good news...)

d. Enlist the help of specialist publications, databanks and libraries.

e. Your potential employer (via the personnel manager who conducted your interviews) is also a good source of inspiration.

f. And finally, don't forget the 'grapevine'. You can sometimes pick up some fantastic snippets.

Organisations prefer to enlist 'our kind of people', who think and dress the way we do, who share our political views, practice our sports etc. The implication is that 'odd' candidates are rejected. That is a pity, because uniformity may kill corporate creativity. Political dictatorships quite often go under because of the 'yesmen', surrounding and advising the strongman. Employers should be aware of this phenomenon.

Management competencies

We will now examine a number of specific management skills, fairly broad competencies which the manager must have (or learn) in order to supervise a team or department for instance. (In professional terminology, the phrase 'interactive skills' is used – that means the manager interacts, influences others.)

Below is a list of skills that you must possess to a greater or lesser extent in order to manage. It is clear that you cannot possibly have all these skills. What you need will depend on the type of organisation you are hoping to work for, its size, the scope of your department's work, your authority ('power') and so on. This list is by no means exhaustive.

Inventory of management capabilities

Motivating (good/bad/average) employees
Delegating (responsibilities, work, projects)
Conducting (periodic) appraisals (positive or negative)
Discussing salary (positive or negative)
Handling workers' grievances
Overcoming objections to workplace changes
Interviewing (external and internal candidates)
Correcting employees' problem behaviour
Handling conflict between staff members
Setting and adjusting work standards and objectives
Training new workers
Supporting and instructing staff
Advising staff on career decisions
Supervising tasks and responsibilities
Making improvements to work activities
Negotiating   cont.

> Presenting (ideas, plans, products)
> Training staff
> Chairing meetings
>
> The manager must also possess a number of general communicative competencies in the following areas.
>
> To listen well (something many managers find hard to do!)
> Ability to observe
> Giving feedback to staff
> Putting oneself in the employee's shoes
> Writing (reporting)

Finally, we would like to outline **conceptual skills** that the manager should possess. This is a rather vague term, by which we mean that the manager is expected to be able to see how he (and his team) fits into the organisation, and how the organisation relates to the outside world. The manager is also expected to keep a broader picture in mind – not just what is important to him and his department, but also what's going on in the wider organisation and society at large (as far as it impacts upon the organisation).

> *TIP* Always try to assess which management competencies are important in your new job. You can find this out during the interviews with your future employer. You can use the list above as a point of reference.

Test anxiety – never again!

The psychometric testing procedure is often a great puzzle to many candidates, whether they have to deal purely with psychological tests or to participate in an assessment centre. Why are they worried and sometimes anxious?

1. They have never been tested before and have only heard what happens through the grapevine.
2. They have already been tested – and were rejected. This can be a

very painful, even traumatic, experience for some people, which can still bother them years later.

3. The testing procedure is the last hurdle before they can be assured of the new job. So much is dependent on the psychologist's final report!

Agencies don't do a lot to allay test takers' anxieties. A letter here, a note there – that may be sufficient. But is it? The agencies see hordes of candidates, day in day out – it's their daily job – and have lost sight of what these examinations mean in the eyes of their 'visitors'. They don't take into consideration that some people have a long history of test anxiety, going back to their early school days, suffer from fear of failure or just feel very uncomfortable when investigated thoroughly.

TIP   'Test yourself' before others will do that. Get familiar with tests. See the practice tests at the end of this book. When you know what to expect and after having had a close look at tests and assessment exercises, you may feel more relaxed when it's time for you to perform.

An employer's view of selection problems

Evaluating people is a difficult task, whether new people or appraising the present staff. The problem becomes even worse when managers must be selected for important positions, trying to predict the future behaviour of key organisational players. This may generate three problems:

1. As the employer, how can you be sure that you have taken on the right candidate? What is the likelihood that you have rejected better applicants, because of your reliance on poor selection methods, for example? There is little research in this field because it is so difficult to find out what happens to rejected candidates. They won't appreciate being asked to participate in 'scientific' research with the organisation or agency that's just rejected them.

2. Employers have another worry: it costs time and money to train the newly appointed manager. The more senior the position, the longer it takes for the new 'boss' to learn the ropes, and get to know the company

culture. This means that you can only really evaluate the new employee after about a year with the company. That's a long time. And what if he or she doesn't quite 'suit'? Do you have to start the selection process all over again? That could be an expensive business!

3. Getting rid of an employee is not a simple task. (We can use euphemisms – outplacement, early retirement, voluntary redundancy, downsizing, rightsizing, but basically they all mean getting rid of people.) It's particularly expensive and time-consuming if the redundant employee sues for unfair dismissal, or if a golden handshake is involved.

Employer and employee are joined in marriage, so a divorce is also possible. But it's fair to say that divorce is painful. It exposes the employer's weak points. For many, management means 'risk management'. So, the work of the hired psychologist can be seen as a sort of *insurance policy* for the company.

It is important for both parties to make a good choice. The employer has little use for a new manager who leaves after a short time, or who starts looking around for something better after a few weeks. It is just as frustrating for the employee – to have to undergo another long-winded selection procedure. Excitement and uncertainty once more – at work and at home.

The right person for the job?

A common objection to preparation is: 'What if I prepare fully for the testing procedure, and my competitors do not. I pass with flying colours – and they offer me the job. How do I know that I am really the right person for the job?' The answer is simple: neither you nor the employer knows this for sure. What you do know is that if you manage to get through to the final round of the recruitment process – and the 'test' is the last hurdle you have to overcome – you and your competitors are roughly equally as good as each other as regards the main points of the job. But maybe you are more ambitious, more driven, more motivated: at least you have taken the time to prepare.

How important is the test procedure?

The most sensible answer to this question is: the procedure is only as important as the weight attached to it by the employer. Cryptic? Yes and no. If the prospective employer uses testing to gain more information about a prospective employee, then it is only one of many factors that have a part to play in the total evaluation process. It is on a par with the 'insight' gained during several interviews, references, and the 'intuitive' opinion of the many evaluators.

But sometimes what can happen is that the employer uses tests like a judge (and a jury). If the candidate's report ends with a 'We do not recommend this candidate on the basis of his/her test scores', then the employer feels free to give the candidate a 'thumbs down'.

So you cannot tell in advance precisely what level of importance the testing procedure is afforded. Is it merely a source of extra information or the final verdict? Tests are viewed by many applicants as a crucial part of the selection procedure, although they may be actually less important than the applicants believe them to be. A bad test result doesn't automatically mean a rejection!

> ***TIP*** Psychologists are always employed in an advisory not a decision-making capacity. They are contracted to conduct a selection procedure, not to make the final decision on your future - although it may look like that. If you have any queries or problems, you are better going straight to the employer.

Rejection

Of course, it's nice to be in the running for a medal in the selection procedure. But silver or bronze isn't good enough – gold is the only colour you want.

Rejection is always difficult to face – whether you're rejected by an employer or by a lover. But honours can only go to one person in the selection race. It's a question of how well you and the employer 'match'. If you didn't get the job this time, then you may well succeed next time. You now have the added advantage of experience. Experience that should reap dividends. Because the more you are tested, the better you perform, the higher your test results and you will outstrip the competition yourself. Naturally, the three parties involved (you, the employer, and the agency, where applicable) must be absolutely sure that the appropriate selection instruments are being utilised, which may not be the case.

Discussing your test results

All those involved in the testing procedure know that psychological tests are not perfect instruments. Even within their own professional circles, many psychologists recognise this, although reluctantly. (Some psychologists tried to prevent the author from broadcasting the fact that test quality is disappointing.)

The more doubts the employer has, the easier it is for you to discuss the test results with him. The objections you raise may hit home! You have to take the initiative yourself and have an objective when 'negotiating'. For example, a retest with another agency, or only being tested in relevant areas, or not taking the test results into account any further in the decision-making process, etc.

How to determine a test's quality

Quality: what is it and how can you determine it? We will briefly outline what quality means with reference to psychological tests generally, focusing on those categories which specialists use to evaluate tests. You can distinguish five components in test quality:

1. **Aim of the test:** What objective lies behind this test? What is it measuring? What is the theoretical background to the test? Is it closely related to a particular theory, or is it 'obvious' what the test is about?

2. **Test materials and scoring:** Are the test items (the questions and exercises), the scoring and instructions standardised? Is the scoring system objective? (The less need for human interpretation – and therefore the more the computer can do the scoring – the more objective the scoring system.)

3. **Norms:** Do the test publishers and authors provide norms, standards, against which the candidate can be compared with similar people? Thus, a pilot's score must be compared with scores of other pilots, rather than with musicians' or agricultural workers' scores.

4. **Reliability:** Do the results remain consistent over time? Does a person tested today get (roughly) the same score three months (years) later? It is a well-known fact that, if your intelligence is tested several times during a one year period, your IQ score gets higher. In other words, it is an unreliable test.

5. **Validity:** Does the test measure what it purports to measure? Does it measure the candidate in the way it was intended? For example, does a 'sales test' measure someone's sales knowledge, sales ability, sales insight or is it measuring something else entirely? Remember that tests are used to predict – at least, that is the intention.

Dutch psychologist Hofstee is not a diehard optimist. He wrote: 'for personnel selection, the validity of the selection procedure is rather low, about .30. When selecting at higher levels, you can expect higher levels of validity, about .40. Naturally, at this level, they are nothing more than clues ... A validity of .30 is so low that you can barely see it'. By this he meant for instance that we are not certain that someone's numerical ability score is due to his or her ability, a lot of it could be due to other factors. Does this reassure you?

TIP Suppose that you're unhappy about your report, and you want to know how good the applied psychometric tests really are. You can get an idea of their quality as regards reliability and validity amongst other factors through professional books. This will give you some ammunition to back up any complaint you have. But be careful - this qualitative data says nothing about the interpretation of the test or about the relevance of the tests used to the job you're applying for.

2

An Endless Variety of Tests

For many people, psychometric tests are a bit mysterious, untouchable. Is that because of the word 'psycho', or perhaps that some feel that psychologists can look right through them? Or because the end result of a procedure has potentially far reaching implications? Or simply because they don't know enough about them and have never seen them in action?

Tests come in all shapes and forms and measure an incredibly huge number of traits, skills, competencies, attitudes, etc. To mention a few, and not in any particular order: concentration, leadership, honesty, interests, intelligence, stress tolerance, critical thinking, eye-hand co-ordination, creativity, administrative skill, brain damage, political conviction, accuracy.

In this chapter, we present a rather practical division of tests, (the more scientifically based categorisations are of no use here) so that you get familiar with their 'look and feel' and find out what they really are. Quite often, ordinary pieces of paper ...

The previous chapter has made it clear that selection is, generally speaking, not a piece of cake. If a word processing typist (because you only have to record her typing speed and number of errors per 500 words, for example), a musician or a carpenter can be easily assessed, this is certainly not the case with people working in a supervisory or managerial position, sales staff or other complex professions. So it makes sense for employers to call upon outside help to deal with the difficult selection task, traditionally the recruitment agency or psychologist. Agencies make use of a large number of tests and methods in order to evaluate prospective candidates' abilities. We will cast a brief glance over these various methods and inspect them in more detail in the following chapters.

Maximum versus typical performance tests

The crudest division is between tests that measure maximum performance (quantity-oriented, like intelligence tests – you cannot score higher than what is supposedly your 'ceiling'), and those that assess your typical performance (quality-oriented). These tests don't have correct or incorrect answers, like in personality tests.

Written tests

Most tests by far are of the paper-and-pencil (or digital) variety, and the huge majority of these are multiple-choice, comparable to school exams. Some request you to write an essay, or complete sentences. Others urge you to draw a tree, a person or something else, that may reveal your 'true' personality. (These old-fashioned tests will be briefly discussed in chapter 5.)

Obviously, the multiple-choice test is the favoured weapon of the psychologist. However, there are certain disadvantages:

- no room for creative answers
- some highly intelligent people may come up with the wrong answer because the right choice seems too simple (perhaps they are smarter than the test author!)
- the alternatives turn the test into a guessing game (recommendable when you can't reason yourself towards the correct answer).

TIP When you are suffering from dyslexia, a concussion, eye problems, etc. you may want to request - prior to your test day - to have oral tests administered to you instead of the written variety.

Oral tests

Since these tests require personal involvement of a psychologist or assistant (time is money) they are being phased out of procedures. They are also sensitive to subjective influences, either way. In case you may not be aware of this, the best known oral test is the interview with the psychologist. The Rorschach inkblot test – now in disrepute – is another example of an oral instrument. Sometimes marketing and business cases are 'thrown in' during the interview. They can be considered to be oral tests. (See chapter 14.)

> **TIP** Be aware that in oral tests it not only matters what you say, but also how you say it. Therefore, be cautious and take your time in your replies.

Computer-aided tests

Modern technology has also influenced psychometric testing (more so than ACs). In principle, every paper test can get converted into bits and bytes, by way of disks, CD-ROMs, DVDs, websites or other digital means. Speed (of processing the results and reporting) and (thus) costs are the main reasons behind the increasing popularity of digital tests. Added benefits are quality control (skipping an item may not be possible), strict time control (the built-in clock turns the screen black when your time is up) and 'playing' with norms (of any particular group of candidates, 'top score' of the day, etc.) A relatively new development is adaptive testing; see below. In theory, the entire test day can be computerised, thereby eliminating human contact altogether. So far, this has not been a very fruitful approach.

Adaptive testing

Some intelligence tests are rather time-consuming. Instead of asking the candidate to do the entire test, a computerised test can be programmed in such a way that only a handful of items can quickly determine someone's ceiling. Here is how this is done: the computer selects an item of an average degree of difficulty. If the test taker's response is correct, a tougher item is picked. If not, the computer then selects an easier item. This procedure is repeated a few times, until the candidate's peak is reached, for instance after two consecutive wrongly-answered items. More and more tests are made suitable for adaptive testing.

Reaction times, concentration and accuracy

The 'psychological computer' can also be put to use in different ways. Quick reactions, important for pilots, can be tested by pressing a screen button, mouse, joystick or foot pedal as fast as possible after a green light ('press the button on your right'), or a red light (left side button) flashes on your screen. These tests can get more complicated, like detecting certain blots (fixed or moving) on the screen together with the green and red light, or adding numerical series that need to be solved at the same time, or interacting with a nagging actor who is supposed to be your buddy in this combination of computer test and role play. Experienced 'gamers' may do well on these tests.

Observational tests

Quite a variety of methods belong to this category and what they all have in common is that how you work, your style, is being investigated. You may be watched directly, by an assistant sitting in front of you, or be spied upon through a camera or one-way (see-through) mirror. What to expect? A few examples:

- Are you technically skilled? The Wiggly Block Test lets you assemble the nine pieces of this wooden cube. Do you start straight away, or do you devote a few minutes to think about the best approach? How do you correct mistakes? Regardless, your way will be generalised to your daily work behaviour (rightly or not).
- How do you handle stress? You may be confronted with a more sophisticated apparatus that checks your eye-hand co-ordination under time pressure.
- Small wooden or plastic blocks or cards that have to be handled according to certain instructions also belong to this category.

Test assistants may observe candidates' non-test related behaviour and brief their bosses. For example, does the visitor mingle with other candidates, at the beginning of the day or at lunch? Does he recognise the receptionist as a person, or treat her like a totally insignificant human being?

Remember, although observational methods are classics in the psychological practice, the validity of these methods is often questionable. (Put differently, the behaviour demonstrated during the investigation may not predict your future work place behaviour accurately.)

Speed tests versus power tests

Speed tests have a clear time limit. The candidate's time is up, whether all test items have been made or not. All intelligence tests are speeded. Power tests don't have a time limit. The test is over when all items have been finished, the testee gives up, or when – subjectively, or based on experience – the test user decides to end the test. 'Timeless' tests like personality and attitude scales, are not power tests but typical performance tests. Speed tests are usually of a simple nature – but they contain too many items. (E.g. basic calculus.) Power tests are more complex. (E.g. data interpretation.)

Duration

Tests may take anywhere between a few minutes (accuracy test) and three hours (in-tray basket). Test developers are very much interested in the optimal length of a test. Long tests get boring (that is, for the candidate) and decrease the motivation and concentration of the test taker. Ultimately, the person may fall asleep ... A short test (consisting of a couple of items) is unreliable. Somewhere in the middle lies the developer's paradise.

Many well-used tests change over time. Items may be modified to make them more in tune with the times. Sometimes tests will be shortened, after is has statistically been discovered that the shorter version is just as strong as the original longer one.

A day at the agency

Agencies don't just use one test, but a so-called test battery – a combination of at least two tests. Which ones are applied depends upon the job in question, the employer's requirements and the agency's own preferred way of working, sometimes based on scientific research, sometimes on experience, or simply on subjective preference.

You will certainly be subjected to a minimum of two of the categories below:
1. Intelligence tests
2. Personality measures
3. Vocational interest tests
4. Management and commercial tests – and case studies
5. Other tests (including tests for creativity, concentration, etc)

6. Assessment centre (AC)
7. Interview

We will briefly describe these tests and methods and explore their scientific credentials. We will also look at their effectiveness in practice, too, because selectors will want to know their practical value above all else!

1. Intelligence tests

Scientifically speaking, intelligence tests are the 'soundest' tests there are, according to many psychologists. For now, it suffices to say that they measure all kinds of abstract reasoning, usually through 'puzzles' that may have very little to do with realistic problems. IQ tests, as they are called in popular parlance, form an almost integral part of each psychometric selection procedure, although one may question their added value, if the testee's level of formal education is known. (See chapter 4.)

2. Personality measures

Personality tests are designed to unveil one's 'true' personality. People may lie about their self during an interview, but the truth will come out after having rated a number of written statements or self-descriptions. That, at least, is the rather shaky assumption. Chapter 5 will let you in on objective and projective tests and will advise you how to handle these devices.

3. Vocational interest tests

Sometimes, agencies utilise vocational interest tests, because they provide an indication of (the extent of) your motivation for the job. For example, if you are being tested for a sales manager's job your no.1 areas of interest must be (yes, you guessed it) in the supervisory and sales fields. If, however, your interests are administration and art, then they (rightly) think that your true nature doesn't correspond with that of a sales manager. You prefer to do other things rather than supervise sales staff. See chapter 6.

4. Management and commercial tests – and case studies

An enormous number of tests have landed in this category. How many? No-one can provide an answer. Every agency has access to a large quantity of management tests (whether so called or not), some of which could be of dubious quality…

You may need to demonstrate how assertive you are, the quality and speed of your business calculations, how politically involved or sensitive you are, etc. Information on the quality (including validity and reliability) of these tests is scarce, rarely publicly published, therefore their value must seriously be questioned. This also applies to management and commercial tests. (See chapter 6.)

Case studies are quite often presented in procedures involving managerial and commercial jobs. Many organisations create their own cases – for their exclusive use. Thus, there is no public scrutiny, as regards to their content, quality or predictive value. Some commercially oriented cases require number crunching, as in Practice test 3, others are more prosaic as in chapter 13, where we will you prepare for them.

5. Other tests

This category comprises all those tests which may be used for selection but which don't fall into the other categories and include tests for creativity, cognition, concentration, clinical and many others.

6. Assessment centre (AC)

In contrast to psychological tests, assessment centres measure someone's actual behaviour. It is a collective name for a number of widely varying transparent behavioural measures, in all shapes and forms. In contrast to many psychological tests, there is no hidden agenda: the candidate knows what is expected of him, e.g. sell a product or service in a role play. Chapter 7 presents the details.

Although research has been carried out on the effectiveness of this selection method, it shares the same faults as psychological tests. That is, its validity and reliability are generally unknown, and there is a problem with norms, if they exist at all. The AC technique has, however, what psychologists call a high degree of 'face validity'; in other words, it gives the impression of being a good predictor of behaviour.

7. Interview

The interview can be regarded as a type of test. You will find several mentions in the book to be on your guard. Many selectors set traps for you during the interview. They regard the interview as a good (although unreliable) source of information. Rightly so. It is a pleasant way of getting to know more about you in a short space of time.

From a scientific viewpoint, it is a rather weak selection instrument. The interviewer can be put off by a number of things that have nothing to do with your capabilities, such as: prejudice, verbal fluency, sexual charms, signs of tiredness, 'social skills'. In short, the interviewer is only human. The interview will be discussed extensively in chapter 14.

It was precisely because psychologists recognised how subjective the interview is that they designed psychometric selection methods, objective instruments, giving every candidate an equal chance.

3

How to Prepare for the Test Day

The magical powers, which had been attributed to psychometric tests, have melted away like freshly fallen snow on a warm day. Whereas previously candidates saw themselves as helpless victims, awaiting 'divine judgement', now their 'questioning disbelief' is growing. Many take matters into their own hands and practise for the test. Quite rightly, too, as a lot is riding on the result! After all: you prepare for your driving test, don't you?

Preparation is important, because you have to perform at your best on the day itself – you rarely get a second chance. Furthermore, even if you get through the test, this doesn't necessarily mean you'll get the job. The test is only part of the recruitment process. The test report recommendations may be followed (as often happens) but can also be ignored.

You probably realise that agencies are not always overjoyed to see candidates who really know their way around these tests. Unlike what happens in education or work, when it comes to psychometric tests, knowledge and experience can count against you. But there is no need to be despondent.

We advise you to find out which exact attributes and/or aptitudes are being investigated by the employer. Sometimes, the standards set are higher than you realise. Basically, you must perform at the required level on the Big Day. In this chapter a number of conditions of the test day will be dealt with. Physical and mental fitness and other general pieces of advice, including how to improve your concentration during the test day are home to this chapter. Test-specific details will be covered in the following chapters.

Some questions about preparation

'Can one really prepare for the psychometric test procedure?' In the past, people thought that this was not at all possible. One went to the

psychometric test like a lamb to the slaughter, but nowadays people's attitudes are changing. The possibility does exist and does lead to tangible success. The author of this book, and the founder of Test-Training™, has shown that anyone can prepare for the test experience – and get good results! Moreover, professional occupational psychologists have only hinted but never stated categorically that you cannot prepare for a test.

'Can a psychologist see right through you?' Many people still believe this, but it's absolutely untrue! Psychologists are people just like you. They are also affected by all types of subjective impressions that they pick up from the candidates. There is also the question of how good a judge of character the psychologist is.

'Is it possible for a psychometric test to pick up dishonest answers?' Personality tests can determine if someone is supplying consistent answers. This means that the candidate must be aware of giving the same (sort of) answers, or else he will be seen to be 'lying'. It is therefore a question of good preparation and logical thought! The psychologist also wants to know in the interview whether or not you are answering honestly. (We will return to this point later).

'What is the best way to prepare for a test?' To undertake some specific individual training. Moreover, you are well advised to read one or more books about psychometric tests. Lastly, you can learn a lot by doing some practice exercises – in this book or on the various websites. (For example, with number series, analogies, etc.) and, naturally, be mentally geared up well before the day itself.

Good preparation may also involve taking part in a test beforehand. It is a well-known fact that the more often you are tested, the better you perform. You can learn a lot that you can use later on. So, apply for a job where testing is a pre-requisite. See this procedure as a learning experience. (You never know, you may get the job and find you like it! No-one knows what your original intentions were!)

The key to test success lies in practice, i.e. something totally under your own control. Psychologists have a good reason to be worried about so-called practice effects. They are aware that you perform better after every test you take. This is why the agency is curious to know if you have been tested before, where, when and for what job. They may also enquire if you have used books or other publications to prepare.

Our advice: never let them know you've been tested before, if at all possible. Unless you darkened their door three weeks earlier – then, glossing over previous experiences can be a very precarious business. In any case, let sleeping dogs lie, if you can!

'Agencies and psychologists may not like you to have read books about selection procedures, or to have undertaken training. How do they react to this?' The fact that some agencies and psychologists have a problem with test preparation testifies to their success! The greatest complaint you will hear is that these methods make it more difficult to distinguish between various applicants. They are admitting that skilful preparation can throw a spanner in the works!

As far as personnel managers are concerned, the following may apply. Firstly, HR people are more critical of the use of psychometric tests in the selection process. Secondly, they don't have a problem with candidates preparing for the test procedure. Many of them think that it shows motivation, ambition and commitment. These are qualities which are good to see in a new employee! Thirdly, if test anxiety is removed, then you can optimise your performance on the test day itself. HR managers know that your performance is then actually a true picture.

'Can the test user find out if I've been practising or if I've read books on the subject?' No, that is impossible – however, we'd advise you not to mention that you've undergone training, or read several books on psychometrics. There is no way of knowing exactly what they will do with your information, but it probably will not have positive results for you.

Suggestions to help you prepare

1. **Be tested in your own good time.** What do we mean by this? The invitation you get from the employer to come for a soul-searching session still sounds like a diktat. You will usually have little time beforehand to prepare, you have to arrive on a certain date and time, but that may not be the best day for you.

    ● So ensure that you always have sufficient time between the invitation and the test day itself for some mental preparation. You can use this time to get hold of some useful books, speak to colleagues and friends who've been tested, organise a training session, etc.

- If you can't get out of it, then, make sure they test you at a quiet time for you. If you are running all over the place, have your family visiting unexpectedly from Australia, have to decide whether or not to buy a new house, get married, have to manage an important business contract, then you will certainly not be able to concentrate on the testing procedure.

- This also applies to any periods where you feel physically below par. Avoid times when a flu epidemic is raging, you have a cold, your period or are coming down with something.

- The date the employer or agency chooses is not cast in stone. It is only a suggestion, nothing more and nothing less. Our experience is that candidates, regardless of the job they are applying for, assume that the test date is a given fact and cannot be altered. Naturally, the date can be changed to fit in better with your schedule. If you are still unsure, then contact your future employer. Be honest in your reasons for seeking another date. If you have no valid excuse, you can always call in sick – remember, you only get one chance, so use it!

2. **Agencies observe your behaviour.** Sometimes, they will tell you upfront, as in the assessment centre, sometimes they will keep it a secret. One word of warning: the receptionist in a small practice may also be in on the plot. She may give another point of view on you ...

    If you know that you will be spied on, then you should prepare for it as follows:

    - In your way of working. (Should you think first before acting, or do you jump in with both feet? How do you use the test materials, systematically, orderly, neatly? Do you use your rough paper?)

    - Non-verbal communication. (Does this correspond to your verbal behaviour, your use of language? If your non-verbal and verbal behaviour do not correspond, they may draw the conclusion that you are a different person from the person you portray, or that you are dishonest, etc).

3. **How you are dressed and your appearance** also play an important role. Do they match up with the job you are being tested for? Are you neat and tidy? Always wear the right clothes!

4. **Present yourself as an actor would.** By this we mean paint a consistent picture of yourself. Your answers on the test (especially on the

personality questionnaires) need to be consistent. But the image on paper must also correspond to your image in the interview and throughout the whole day.

If the selector notices inconsistencies, then he or she will become nervous and tremble. His or her mental image of you is under attack. 1 + 1 don't appear to make 2. Your job is to explain why. Maybe you will see the words 'dishonest', or 'unreliable' in your test report. A good selector will make your life difficult, in any case. He or she wants to get *'the truth'* out of you!

5. **Many applicants misjudge the role of the selector** (sometimes the psychologist). We're not referring to all his 'invisible' activities, such as getting to know the employer's organisational culture, selecting tests, and soon, but we mean the interview you will have with him. You won't only get 'psychological' questions, but also questions to do with the job. (*'You said you had a good job, so why do you want to leave?' 'How do you know if you are really motivated for this new job?'*) Moreover, the psychologist may also want to know if what you say corresponds to what your qualifications and CV say about you. We will cover this more fully in chapter 14.

Aside from some standard interview techniques, you will find a number of questions which many candidates find extremely tricky and difficult as well.

You don't have to fall into any of the traps during the interview – practice helps here, too. Think about some of the difficult questions the psychologist may ask you. Role play with a friend or partner – video it. Look at your own behaviour in the mirror. Be critical of yourself.

6. **Immerse yourself in the testing procedure.** Close your eyes and try to imagine what might happen on the day itself. What do you envisage?

- There are probably people in your direct environment who have been tested in recent years. Talk to them; ask them what happened. (They'd do the same with you, right?)
- If you are busy with an actual recruitment procedure, then you can contact the relevant employer or agency. Remember that you can always ask them too many questions, but never too few.
- Maybe there is someone in Personnel in the company where you are applying or working, who can help you access more information.

7. **Find out as much as you can** about the job and the organisation you are being tested for. Read about the organisation, study their advertisements, annual reports, etc. Get hold of as much information as possible. You will be amazed what is available to the general public!

Agencies don't like candidates who practise ...

Agencies dislike knowledgeable applicants. They prefer to work with so-called naive subjects, who haven't been tested before and who don't ask critical or difficult questions. These candidates swallow anything and can be easily caught out.

Psychologist Roe claims that discouraging knowing applicants from distorting their answers is a lost battle. He believes that it is almost impossible to protect personality tests in particular from dishonest responses. The first line of attack is to make the tests non-transparent for the candidate. Roe rejects this on ethical grounds. (It is often not difficult to see which way the wind is blowing ...)

A second possibility is the principle of forced choice. But, quoting Roe, 'it appears here, too, that the effects are limited. You cannot avoid distortions in answers totally in this way'. But there's even more. Roe also suggests that the instructions given to the candidate can also be adapted: 'apart from the invitation to the candidate to respond as honestly and openly as possible, there is often also the 'added' explanation that distorting your answers can invalidate the tests and increase the chance of poor decisions'. Not only is such an explanation unpleasant – it is also untrue. Applicants should make sure that they don't fall into such a simple trap with eyes open wide. Roe mentions another aid: norms which are later adapted to the candidate. This would only happen if the agency thinks the applicant isn't being totally honest, open and spontaneous in his or her answers. It is clear that the subjective opinion of the psychologist may well play a role here.

Roe also has some worries about candidates' experiences with tests and practising for them: 'if the candidate comes across tests in the selection procedure which he has already done before, this gives him a clear advantage, at least if he remembers the items correctly. Something similar applies to the practice effect, particularly with certain types of items'.

> ***TIP*** If asked if you have ever completed a career/vocational interest test, then you should say 'no'. Why? Because the borderline between selection and occupational choice can be very fine. It may give the selector an excuse to ask you why you felt it necessary to go to a career counsellor anyway... Without your telling him, the selector would never have known if or where you were tested previously.

What are you being tested for exactly?

'Of course I know what I'm being tested for', you will say. That's the whole point of the testing procedure. But what you must be aware of is that you may be being tested for another reason entirely. To give an example:

> Dutch airline KLM doesn't only select its pilots for their flying abilities, but also on their ability to become a captain. For this, they don't just need to be able to navigate, but also to demonstrate the necessary management skills. The pilot therefore has to show that he can lead people, particularly in times of crisis. One flying school trainer puts it like this: 'In days gone by, if a problem arose, the captain would say 'I'm in charge – the rest of you shut up'. Consequently he soon became a nervous wreck. We now know that this isn't the best way of doing it. So now the captain lets someone else do the flying and he sets about managing the problem. What information does he need? Where does he get it? How much time does he have? We call this resource management. Consulting the co-pilot is important. But if it is a real emergency, then the captain has to adopt the usual authoritarian leadership style'.

The unsuspecting aviator must therefore have more going for him than he may at first realise. In large organisations, candidates are regularly selected for positions higher than the one they are actually applying for. Selection requirements may therefore be set higher than expected.

Concentration in ten steps

As you know, the test is a one-off happening, Therefore, it's all about delivering a peak performance on the Big Day. Not a day earlier, nor a day later. It is important to be able to concentrate on the day itself and ensure that your full attention is focussed on the tests. (Your concentration and attention as such may be tested by the agency as well.)

1. Concentration means paying attention. If you are attending to one thing, then you can't also be attending to something else at the same time. So, direct your attention to one single issue (problem, question, solution, etc).

2. Cut off all possible distractions, from the environment around you or from inside your own head (all types of thoughts, which may be about the test, or your next holiday, or unpaid bills).

3. If you have a choice as to where to sit in the room, then choose a spot where you are least likely to be distracted. This means away from a door, or a corridor (people passing may irritate you), away from windows (you'll keep looking outside), and away from pictures and drawings, which may stop you focussing.

4. Look for a well-lit spot, so that you have no problems reading the text. If you feel it is too warm or too cold in the room, if it smells unpleasant or there is some other 'climatic' imbalance, then ask someone for help. But don't keep doing it, that's bad for your concentration!

5. If there is a lot of noise around you (phones ringing, people walking to and fro, loud conversations) notify an assistant. Your complaint will be taken seriously; after all, you are the client! They are honour-bound to do everything possible to enable you to produce your best performance. Complain quickly so that you are not unduly bothered by the noise.

6. There's no harm bringing back-up supplies from home – two pens instead of one, a calculator for certain tests, yellow 'post-its', etc.

7. Time is an important consideration. Most tests state the maximum time allowed. If this isn't the case, then ask an assistant how long you have. If you are refused an answer, then ask how much time he or she thinks someone would need to complete this test.

    If a test comprises several sub-sections, it is often a good idea to figure out in advance how much time you need to spend on each of these. (You will find some tips about how to divide your time amongst certain sub-sections elsewhere in this book.) This reduces anxiety and stress about not finishing on time. This is obviously very detrimental to your concentration.

8. Always take a (stop)watch with you. Or even more useful, a watch with an alarm. Set it so that it goes off about five minutes before the test is due to end. You won't then be unpleasantly surprised and will have enough time to go through any unfinished items and make a stab at some you don't know. This is an efficient way of using your time. You will create a professional impression (although other candidates in the test room may be put off by you ...)

9. You have read the items and know more or less what you are required to do. You may find that there are things you don't want to forget, but that are not relevant at this moment. (These may be issues that you want to raise during the interview with the psychologist.) Jot them down on a rough piece of paper, so that your mind isn't distracted by what you shouldn't forget.

10. A lot is riding on your performance in the test. But don't make yourself unnecessarily nervous. The worst that can happen is that you don't get this job. There will be other chances, maybe better ones ... If you don't come out top of their list, then you are still one very important experience better off than before. You will find that you will do even better next time!

Physical and mental fitness

It has been mentioned before – during the test day, you have to deliver a peak performance. Not only twice for ten minutes, or for one hour, you will be inspected inside out for anywhere between six and eight hours. It is virtually impossible for anyone to stay in 'phase red alert' for so long, yet that is what is requested of you (or else...). Therefore:

● Make sure you go to bed early the night before.
● Shy away from heavy and rich food and alcohol the night before the Big Day.
● Get up at a reasonable time, so that you don't have to hurry. Avoid time pressure, you will get plenty of that at the agency's!
● In order to avoid congested roads and parking problems, you may consider spending the night before in a quiet hotel, near the agency.

Personal test problems

One can think of various reasons why your test performance may not be up to standard. If you fall into one of the categories below you are well advised to inform the agency ahead of time, and preferably through a formal letter, of your suggestions. You may not have any impact with your complaint after the show is over.

- Are you suffering from dyslexia? Get objective evidence from a specialist and subsequently request from the agency an extended test day.
- Your verbal English is almost perfect, but not in writing. (Because you have spent so much time abroad, or English is not your mother tongue.) Perhaps you can be partially tested in another language, or alternatively, norms can be adjusted for your particular language handicap.
- You will be tested from behind the computer screen, but you are a computer illiterate, or are suffering from computer anxiety. Ask for paper-and-pencil tests; this should not be a major problem.
- You are suffering from a concentration disorder, perhaps caused by a recent traffic accident. Request an adjusted programme. (One important consideration: will this problem influence your job performance? If that is the case, you may prefer not to bring up this touchy subject.)
- Your physical problem may make it virtually impossible for you to sit still in a chair for a long time, or to walk from one department to the next. Inform the agency of your handicap, so that appropriate measures can be taken prior to your arrival.

4

IQ Tests

No mortal on this planet has ever seen, heard, touched, smelt or tasted intelligence. Intelligence is intangible. Yet, everyday, the cognitive capacity of people is measured. Is this a good thing? Fact: intelligence forms one of the key components in any selection procedure involving psychological testing. This has lead to considerable debate, not only in the scientific community, but also in the social, political and educational spheres. Feelings run high once more when some expert digs up the old theory that intelligence is mainly inherited. The meaning is clear: you are set at a particular level and you are stuck with it for the rest of your days. Opponents of this view state that intelligence is learned. So, there is hope after all, if you wish to improve your scores on the intelligence test!

This lengthy chapter will give you a good insight into intelligence and IQ. You will get a taste of some popular instruments, like analogy tests, and some lesser known intelligence tests. And you will benefit from a number of tips, so that you will enter the agency fearlessly – but with just a little excitement! If you can gain some insight into the underlying principles behind these tests, you can relax and treat them like interesting 'puzzles'. You won't become any more intelligent, but you will score better and thus appear more intelligent. And that's smart.

Intelligence testing is still used to predict someone's success in later life. It appears that your parent's wealth is a better indicator of this than intelligence … as much as anyone can predict something as vague as success in society!

What is intelligence?

The word 'intelligence' comes from the Latin, and encompasses, amongst other concepts: information, knowledge, insight, cognitive ability, cleverness. Try to equate intelligence with being smart, and you still don't know what intelligence actually is!

Some definitions are:

- the ability to solve problems
- the ability to assimilate knowledge/facts, and to apply them
- the capacity to think rationally (logically).

Many psychologists admit these definitions to be rather worrying. So, they prefer to accept the following definition: ***intelligence is what is measured by an intelligence test ...***

Of course, things are not quite as bad as all that, because intelligence is related to other things which have nothing to do with the test itself. So, an intelligence test predicts which pupils will belong to the top 20% in terms of classroom performance. This prediction corresponds closely with the teacher's. If there would be no relationship or a very poor one between high IQ and a high level of academic achievement, then the IQ test would have become extinct a long time ago!

Intelligence is measured in the recruitment process, because:

- it defines someone's intellectual level. (Is the candidate with average 'O' level results actually *thinking at this level?*)
- it says something about how fast someone can learn and solve problems. Can the candidate pick up a lot of new facts quickly?
- it can predict someone's potential within the organisation – at least that's what is being claimed ...

There are also other, more modern, views of intelligence; like the way one solves problems in a practical, common-sense fashion.

Why are IQ tests so popular? They are an objective way of comparing people on their reasoning and problem-solving abilities. (Someone's 'reason' captured in a single figure – that's very useful. They are also good predictors of a person's success (at school, at work) and they are easy to administer. These are all plausible reasons, but what about what happens *in reality*? That's where the assessment centre comes in. (See chapter 7.)

Intelligence is not unitary: the profile

In the 1930s, the famous American psychologist Thurstone claimed that the whole concept of intelligence was 'tainted'. So, he did two things. Firstly, he distanced himself from the concept and began to talk instead of 'primary mental ability' (or 'capacity'). Secondly, he suggested that intelligence comprises a number of largely independent parts. Someone's 'intellect' would have the following components:

1. Verbal meaning
2. Number
3. Spatial perception
4. Word fluency
5. Memory
6. Reasoning
7. Perceptual speed

In 1938, Thurstone unveiled his new test, which is still used in places to determine children's intelligence. He has had a number of successors who have divided intelligence into smaller components. How many different parts is intelligence supposed to have? Everyone has a different view. The American psychologist Guilford believed it consists of 120 separate parts, of which he and others (as yet?) were only able to track down a limited number.

It all means that someone's intelligence can be expressed as a profile. The IQ figure itself tells us very little. What is important is your strong and weak points. You should be told exactly how your intelligence is constructed. For example, your numerical ability may be poor, compared to your verbal intelligence.

A distinction can be made between 'general' and 'specific' intelligence tests. The former usually includes time-consuming tests, consisting of many different components – for example Thurstone's afore-mentioned test and the DAT, which will be discussed in a little while. 'Quick tests' fall into this category as well. By 'specific' is meant tests which measure only one or two specific areas of intelligence. Agencies may take one or two sub-tests from a 'general' test and use them as specific tests.

Other measures of 'g' (for general) intelligence include the Raven Matrices and Cattell's Culture-Fair Intelligence Test (the IPAT).

Raven Matrices

This test was developed by the British psychologist Raven, during the Second Word War. He wanted to measure intelligence without having to assess someone's ability with language. Such a test is called 'culture-fair', because it can be applied in any country, regardless of the language spoken, educational system, or local customs, and with all minority groups in society, whose grasp of English may be poor.

The matrix test takes between 20 and 45 minutes to complete. The candidate is presented with a large number of abstract figures (matrices) with increasing difficulty, as illustrated below. In each one, a part of the figure is missing. You have to decide which of the six or eight alternatives completes the figure. In the 1990s, a much tougher version, called the 'Advanced Matrices' was published.

Raven matrix

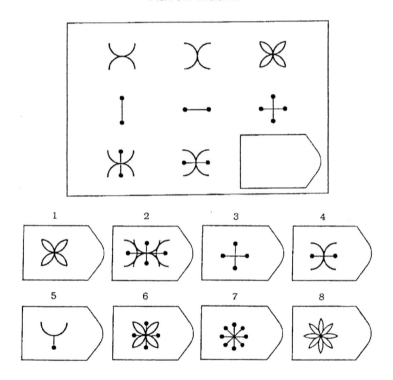

Correct answer: 2

TIP If you are stuck, start thinking in a more abstract way. Or close your eyes (don't fall asleep...) and try again. Perhaps now you see something new. A line? A circle? A corner? This may point you into the right direction.

IPAT

This is another example of a culture-fair test. (The name is rather confusing, because IPAT stands for the American Institute for Personality and Ability Testing. The official name of this test, which dates from 1950, is 'Test of g: culture-fair'.) You are allowed 12 ½ minutes to complete 46-50 items. Two examples:

Which box (a-f) can be placed into the empty box on the left?

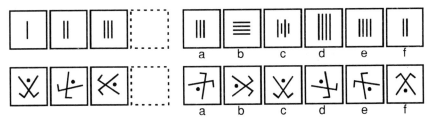

Correct answers: 1: e   2: e

> **TIP**   Always try to think what the link is between the row of figures: what do they have in common, or what is the logical reason behind their order? Then make an educated guess as to what figure comes next. See if the selected figure matches any one of the figures you have to choose from. If you can't see a match, then proceed to the answer block again and spot the nearest approximation.

Diagrams

Various tests feature different types of diagrams, all measuring the recognition of logical rules behind sequences of symbols, shapes, sizes, colour changes and the like. The test taker has to follow these changes. Flowcharts also fall into this category, as well as following sequences of figures. One illustration:

Correct answer: A

The meaning of IQ

IQ is short for 'intelligence quotient', and is nowadays a household expression. Quotient suggests division – and that is indeed the case. IQ tests were originally intended to determine how 'clever' French schoolchildren were. The final outcome of this old-fashioned type of test was a figure which yielded the mental age of a child. But school officials were not only interested in the child's mental age – they also wanted to know which children performed better than average *for their age*, and which were below average. In order to determine this, they had to know the child's actual age (in jargon: chronological age). To dispense with clumsy fractions, the outcome was later multiplied by 100 (mental age divided by chronological age x 100).

Applied psychologists thought it would be easy to understand to have the average IQ (arbitrarily) set at 100 . Most general IQ tests have an average of 100 for the whole population. So, an individual IQ of 130 is high, compared to the rest of the population.

Imagine that you have a law degree and have applied for a job as a company lawyer. You know that you are '30 IQ points better' than the rest of the population. What does that mean? Your future employer is not really very interested in this. He wants to know if you are *more intelligent than other company lawyers*. If the average business lawyer scores 135 on this test, then you belong to the group of 'less intelligent' lawyers. If the average is 120, you start to look good! Now you can see why test norms are important.

Margin of error

An agency can never state 'your IQ is exactly 120', because there is always a margin of error, usually15 points above or below the figure stated. So, in reality, an IQ of 120 could be anywhere between 105 and 135. Therefore, the score is an estimation of the level of intelligence. Why would that be? Because this crude instrument can be regarded (theoretically) as an amalgamation or sample of all possible test items. By definition all drawn samples suffer from error.

Boosting your IQ score

So you want to improve your IQ! Is that fair to the agency, the employer, the other candidates? Absolutely! Everyone has the right to prepare for the test. And why can't you be cleverer than the next person?

1. Using your brain is tiring, especially when you have to deliver a peak performance. Be absolutely sure to be mentally and physically fit for the test day.

2. Time management is very important. If in a particular test you have 40 minutes for 40 items, you only have one minute per item. But you also need to know that most are in order of increasing difficulty. The first question is supposed to be the easiest ... and the last one the hardest. Therefore, it is a proven strategy to complete the first ten questions in, say, eight minutes, leaving you some spare time to tackle the real brainteasers. (Don't forget to bring your (stop)watch.)

3. Train yourself with the practice tests of this book, visit relevant websites and purchase test books and CD-ROMs.

4. Almost all IQ tests are of the multiple-choice type. Get familiar (again) with this examination technique. If still in doubt about the concept of multi-choice questions, watch *'Who Wants to Be a Millionaire'*!

5. If you are unsure of the correct answer, take a guess (contrary to what the agencies advise). In a test with four alternative answers to choose from, you have a 25% chance. Come up with an educated guess. Start with eliminating the really unlikely answers. This way, you increase your chances.

6. Three pieces of general advice.

   (a) Read the instructions carefully. A very important word that sometimes gets overlooked is: 'doesn't', for example: 'which word (symbol, figure) doesn't belong in this sequence?' So, it is a question of finding the exception.

   (b) Many IQ tests start with warming-up items. Don't skip them.

   (c) Be accurate. Some people solve the problem, but tick the wrong box. An unnecessary and sometimes 'expensive' mistake. (Too much pressure? Carelessness? A vision problem?)

Integral test versus 'sub-test'

WAIS-III

The Wechsler Adult Intelligence Scale – III refers to the 3rd update, published in 1997. The full scale IQ has a mean of 100, as do the Verbal and Performance IQs. The WAIS consists of 14 sub-tests and takes 75-110 minutes and also comes in a shortened form – that is, 11 sub-tests (60-90 minutes) and shortened sub-tests.

- **Information**: covers facts that one can learn, e.g. 'What month comes right before December?' (No technical or scientific questions are asked.)

- **Digit Span**: a test of one's short-term memory. A test assistant reads out numbers between three and nine digits that have to be repeated by the candidate. A second list (different digits) asks for the reverse order.

- **Vocabulary**: the candidate has to define 40 increasingly difficult words.

- **Arithmetic**: basic calculations must be worked out without the help of paper.

- **Comprehension**: these items question and assess what you would do in certain circumstances; why certain practices and customs exist; the meaning of sayings and phrases. You must use your common sense here.

- **Similarities**: see the 'similarities' section in this chapter. The quality of one's answers are awarded.

- **Picture Completion**: write down what is missing in cards depicting people or objects (e.g. part of a face is missing).

- **Picture Arrangement**: a random series of pictures (3-6 pieces per item) must be arranged in such a way that they will tell a logical story.

- **Block Design**: the candidate receives a number of three differently coloured blocks (all of the same size): red, white and red & white. The paper model has to be copied in three-dimensional blocks.

- **Object Assembly**: whole figures must be constructed from individual pieces, e.g. you must make a cardboard person from legs, arms etc.

- **Digit Symbol Coding**: nine symbols must be matched with nine numbers.

- **Matrix reasoning:** incomplete gridded patterns that need to be completed by picking one from five alternatives.

- **Symbol Search:** 60 paired groups of symbols. The test taker needs to tell whether the target symbol can be found in the search group.

- **Letter-Number Sequencing:** testing the candidate's memory and attention by ordering a series of letters and numbers that are orally presented.

DAT

The Differential Aptitude Test (fifth edition) was developed in the USA, came to the British market in 1948, and holds the 'middle ground' between an IQ test and a scholastic achievement test. It consists of eight sub-tests, which can generally all be covered in one session: Verbal Reasoning, Numerical Reasoning, Abstract Reasoning, Perceptual Speed and Accuracy, Mechanical Reasoning, Spatial Relations, Spelling, Language Usage.

In practice, the candidate will only be faced with a couple of these sub-tests. The DAT can be taken by anyone over the age of twelve, regardless of educational background, but is not generally used for graduates, since they find the test too easy.

This battery can be administered as a screen test and in a CAT version: computerised adaptive testing, whereby the candidate only takes a few items which are appropriate for his or her level.

Verbal Reasoning: expect a synonym test.

Abstract Reasoning: the ability to think logically is translated into double analogies. (Five double alternatives to choose from.) Try your hand at these two examples:

1. **? : water :: eat : ?**
   A. Continue-drive
   B. Foot-enemy
   C. Drink-food
   D. Girl-industry
   E. Drink-enemy

2. **? : night :: breakfast : ?**
   A. supper-corner
   B. gentle-morning
   C. door-corner
   D. flow-enjoy
   E. supper-morning

Correct answers: 1: C   2: E

Numerical Reasoning: the ability to manipulate numerical concepts is measured by way of numerical series, of which samples are presented later on in this chapter.

Perceptual Speed and Accuracy: as exemplified in the following box:

'Each item on the test paper consists of five combinations of two letters and/or numbers. On the answer sheet, for each item, you will also see five possible letter or number combinations. Mark down for each item the one combination that does not appear on the actual test paper'.

Test paper item	Answer sheet item
1. AC AE AF AB AD	BA AC AD AE AF
2. 4H 4N NH N4 H4	N4 NH 4N HN 4H
3. 1s 13 31 3s s3	13 S1 31 3s 1s

Correct answers: 1: BA   2: HN   3: S1

Spelling, Language Usage: these two sub-tests each take 30 minutes to complete, and examine your knowledge of English. Is the underlined word correct? Two examples:

1. The suspect refused to say <u>anything</u>.   Correct/ incorrect?
2. Your <u>bicicle</u> is too big for me.   Correct/incorrect?

Correct answers: 1: Correct; 2: Incorrect.

Spatial Relations: the candidate has to 'manipulate' 60 three-dimensional sketches in 30 minutes, differently stated: visualise how certain 'objects' can be folded or rotated. If you are good in design, technology or architecture, you will enjoy this test. See the box below for an example:

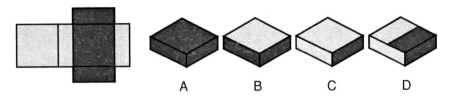

A   B   C   D

Correct answer: C

Mechanical Reasoning: you will be presented with 65 drawings on basic applied physics. In one drawing one sees two men carrying a heavy object on a board. The object is close to one end of the board. So, one man must compensate to reach a balance. Which one? Pictorially, we offer the following example:

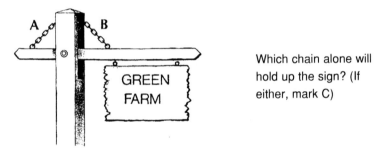

Which chain alone will hold up the sign? (If either, mark C)

Correct answer: B

General Aptitude Test Battery (GATB)

This test (USA, 1958) is rather extensive and takes quite a long time: fifty minutes for the group tests and twenty minutes each for the four individual 'apparatus' tests. (The others are paper and pencil tests.) So, it should not come as a surprise that generally only a few of the twelve components are taken.

What does the GATB measure? **General Learning Ability** (general intelligence), **Verbal Aptitude** (knowledge of grammar and vocabulary), **Numerical Aptitude** [together: Cognitive]; **Spatial Aptitude, Form Perception, Clerical Perception** (administrative capability) [together: Perceptual]; **Motor Co-ordination, Finger Dexterity, Manual Dexterity** (hand-to-eye co-ordination) [together: Psychomotor].

You have already guessed that not all sub-tests are equally important for each and every selection procedure. Two examples of the vocabulary test (Verbal Aptitude) follow, where the test taker must identify the 'closest' synonym from the five alternatives given:

A. **Topography = ...?**	**B.** **Cadaver = ...?**
1. Tree surgery	1. Turkish cupboard
2. Study of population growth	2 Enormous appetite
3. Location	3. Corpse
4. Re-allocation	4. Knave
5. Study of soil samples	5. Type of lute

Correct answers: A: 3   B: 3

Experienced candidates may have a sense of 'deja-vu', as the GATB is really a blend of other tests. Reason for not discussing it further.

What is an analogy test?

As de Zeeuw stated: 'A good analogy test is one of the most reliable predictors of general intelligence available'. That's why analogy tests are widely used to determine the level of intelligence. An analogy can be broadly described as a relationship between two objects, two concepts, etc. The advantage of an analogy test is that it doesn't take long and most practitioners believe you can't practise for it in advance. (Untrue!) We can distinguish between the following types of analogy, which will be covered here:

A. Verbal (single and double)
B. Non-verbal (numerical and geometrical)

A standard analogy is always expressed as:

A : B as C : D

Or, put in words, 'A is to B as C is to D'. In a standard analogy, one of the four terms is missing. Almost all analogy tests are of the *multiple choice* type. Moreover, there are so-called 'double analogies'. Here, two of the four words (e.g. A and D) are missing. You have probably already realised that double analogies are more difficult. (Note that a double colon :: is often used instead of 'as'.)

A. Verbal analogies

In verbal analogies, you are trying to establish a relationship between the meanings of words. For example: the relationship between an apple and an orange. Both could be classified under the category 'fruit'. This is a simple example, but analogies can be presented in numerous ways, and often are not as easy to solve as this one. Try to come up with the right answer before you read the explanation.

Single analogies
Single analogies (as in the Miller analogies below; widely used in the USA to select students for university admission) are most common:

1. Synonyms or similar concepts

DELIVERANCE : ? :: EXERCISE : PRACTISE
A. rescue   B. oration   C. freedom   D. liberate

Explanation: The given terms in this analogy consist of a noun and two verbs. The verbs, to exercise and to practise, are synonyms. Therefore, the missing word must be a noun, with the same meaning as deliverance, in this case: rescue.

2. Antonyms (Opposites or contrasting concepts)

? : FRIENDLY :: CHASTE : LEWD
A. virulent   B. hostile   C. amicable   D. moralistic

Explanation: Chaste and lewd are both opposites, so the missing term must be the opposite of friendly, therefore hostile.

3. Cause and Effect

HEREDITY : ENVIRONMENT :: ? : RUBELLA
A. infectious   B. pneumonia   C. haemophilia   D. contagious

Explanation: In this analogy, the cause and effect relationship is easier to spot when you look at the second and fourth terms as the given word pair. A virus in the environment causes rubella (German measles). The same applies to the sex-linked gene which causes haemophilia (a blood disorder, which can lead to excessive blood loss).

4. Part to whole

LEAF : TREE :: KEY : ?
> A. lock   B. door   C. typewriter   D. car

Explanation: The first two terms are related in that a leaf is a small part of a whole (tree). A key is used to open a car door or any other door, however the only word that has a key as a small part of the whole is C (typewriter).

5. Part to part

FATHER : DAUGHTER :: GILL : ?
> A. fish   B. fin   C. lung   D. twig

Explanation: Father and daughter are each part of a family. Gill and fin are each part of a fish.

6. Purpose or use

PEN : WRITER :: BRUSH : ?
> A. paint   B. ink   C. painter   D. portrait

Explanation: The purpose or use of the terms are quite clear. What you must be careful of, however, is selecting the right answer. All alternatives have some relationship with 'brush', but C is the correct answer. (A writer uses a pen to write – a painter a brush to paint.)

7. Action to object

PITCH : FIRE :: ? : GUN
> A. coal   B. ball   C. sound   D. slope

Explanation: You may well be tempted to look for a synonym relationship in this analogy as pitch and fire both mean to throw with force. However, none of the give alternatives is a synonym for gun, so you must look for another relationship. On closer inspection, we can see a relationship between the second and fourth terms. This should lead to the realisation that fire is an action taken with a gun, just as pitch is an action with a ball.

8. Object to action

SPRAIN : ? :: BITE : ITCH

        A. ankle B. tape C. twist D. swell

Explanation: You have to unravel whether the terms are being used as nouns or verbs. When you realise that sprain and bite are nouns in this analogy and itch as a verb, then you have to find another verb, which bears the same relationship to sprain as bite does to itch. (Swell, as the itch comes after the bite, as swell comes after the sprain.)

9. Place

PARAGUAY : BOLIVIA :: AUSTRIA : ?

        A. Afghanistan B. Germany C. Czech Republic D. Slovenia

Explanation: Paraguay, Bolivia and Austria are all land-locked countries, just as Afghanistan and the Czech Republic. In order to complete the analogy, you must specify the relationship between the given terms. Paraguay and Bolivia are land-locked South American countries, who share a common border; Austria and the Czech Republic also share a common border in Europe.

10. Association

MOZART : MUSIC :: MOORE : ?

        A. painting B. architecture C. sculpture D. dance

Explanation: The Austrian composer Mozart is associated with music, just as Henry Moore is associated with sculpture.

11. Sequence or time

SAIL : STEAM :: PROPELLER : ?

        A. aeroplane B. engine C. jet D. wing

Explanation: Ships were first propelled by sails then by steam. There has been a comparable development in aeroplanes; first driven by propeller and later by jet engines.

12. Characteristic or description

? : PIERCING :: CRY : PLAINTIVE

        A. scream   B. ear   C. shrill   D. vocal

Explanation: A cry could be described as plaintive, in the sense of woeful. A scream may be described as piercing, meaning loud and shrill.

13. Degree

WARM : HOT :: BRIGHT : ?

        A. dark   B. dim   C. genius   D. brainy

Explanation: Warm is a lesser degree of temperature than hot. Bright is a lesser degree of intelligence than genius. Remember, the relationship between terms must be the same on both sides of the analogy.

14. Measurement

ODOMETER : ? :: CLOCK : TIME

        A. speed   B. distance   C. pressure   D. temperature

Explanation: A clock is a device measuring time, just as an odometer assesses distances travelled. If you don't know the term 'odometer' then you are at a disadvantage. But by eliminating other possibilities you could solve this analogy. (For example: you measure temperature using a thermometer – so this answer cannot apply).

15.Grammatical

BROKE : BROKEN :: ? : FLOWN

        A. fly   B. flight   C. flew   D. flung

Explanation: Broke and broken are respectively the past tense and past participle of the verb 'to break'. Flew and flown are the past tense and past participle of the verb 'to fly'.

16. Worker to tool

DOCTOR : ? :: ACTUARY : STATISTICS

        A. hospital   B. patient   C. surgeon   D. X-rays

Explanation: An actuary applies statistics as a tool to calculate insurance premiums. A doctor applies X-rays as a diagnostics tool with a patient.

17. Non-semantic

OE : ROE :: THOUGH : ?
        A. rough B. flood C. flow D. how

Explanation: In this example, the terms are related by sound. The only answer that sounds the same as the other three terms is C (flow).

Double analogies

Just to refresh your memory, here you have to find two answers instead of one. You pick the first answer from the top row (numbers); the second answer from the row below (letters).

? : knowledge :: training : ?
        1. study 2. wisdom 3. school 4. attempt 5. ignorance
        A. schooling B. friend C. practice D. competence
        E. transpiration

Explanation: First, clearly establish the relationship. What type of analogy is it? Which answers offer the best alternative? In the top row, answers 4 and 5 can be immediately eliminated. The first three terms look promising, since study, wisdom and school all have a relationship with knowledge. What you need to do next is to determine which term has the strongest relationship. On closer inspection, study seems the best alternative. So, you come to step two. Study leads to knowledge, as training leads to .... competence is the right answer.

Two techniques for verbal analogies

To help you solve analogical puzzles, it is advised to apply the following two techniques:

The sentence technique

Formulate a short but well-formed and logical sentence from the available concepts. There is always one option which follows the relationship of the original word pair. An example:

PLAY : AUDIENCE :: BOOK : ?
        A. writer B. publisher C. plot D. reader

Step 1. Formulate a short sentence using the first two concepts, e.g. play is intended to entertain the audience.

Step 2. Now replace the first term with the third term, but leaving the rest of the sentence intact. By generating four possibilities, you can see to what extent the relationship between the concepts remains unchanged.

   A. 'Book is intended to entertain the writer.' *(This may well be the case, but that is not a book's prime intention).*

   B. 'Book is intended to entertain the publisher.' *(Such a book is likely to be of limited value.)*

   C. 'Book is intended to entertain the plot.' *(This does not make any sense.)*

   D. 'Book is intended to entertain the reader.' *(This sentence sounds logical and is in line with the original sentence. So,* 'reader' *is the only correct answer).*

The category technique

Make a list of possible logical relationships between the concepts. This list must be comprehensible so that you can describe how words relate to one another, but it must also be restrictive enough to be useful.

Some other tips

- If a double analogy test demands two answers per item, one (correct) answer will not suffice.

- Unsurprisingly, since analogies are by definition about similarities between different words, in different modalities, the phrase 'just like (or as)' may be helpful to check whether your answer is correct. An example: a person's skin is comparable to the peel of an orange. Both are, although in different modalities, outer, protective layers. 'Just as a person has a skin, an orange ...'

- If you can express a term in an analogy in numbers, then do so, because it lets you land on the exact word. For example, a year is not only 'more' than a season, it is four times as many.

B. Non-verbal analogies

Non-verbal analogies request the relationship between numbers or figures, rather than words:

Numerical analogies

12 ½% : ? :: 16 2/3% : 1/6

A. 1/4   B. 1/5   C. 1/8   D. 1/3

Explanation: Percentages are by definition fractions, whose denominators are always 100. Therefore, 12½% is 12½ divided by 100, which equals 1/8. Similarly, 16 ^{2}/$_3$% is 16 ^{2}/$_3$ divided by 100, which equals 1/6. This is one example of a 'straightforward' numerical analogy. In other tests, you may come across more difficult items, reminding you of your schooldays.

Geometric Analogies

For these analogies spatial insight may come in handy. You need to identify different figures in order to see the relationship between them. Two examples:

A

$\square$: $\square$ = $\triangle$: ?

1 $\triangledown$ 2 $\triangleright$ 3 $\bigcirc$ 4 $\triangle$ 5 $\square$

B

$\square$: $\bigcirc$ = $\triangle$: ?

1 $\square$ 2 $\triangle$ 3 $\bigcirc$ 4 $\square$ 5 $\bigcirc$

Correct answers: A: 1   B: 2

Antonyms

'Which word is the closest in opposite meaning to ...?' This is usually the start of an antonyms test. Such a test is considered to be more stretching than a synonym test. It helps to have a good feel for English and a broad vocabulary. Let Practice test 4 help you to further develop the appropriate skill. One example for now:

CONGREGATE:

       A: assemble B: renounce C: disbelieve D: scatter E: relax

Correct answer: D

'Jumbled sentences'

The various 'jumbled sentences' tests put your knowledge of English under the microscope. All the words in these sentences are jumbled together. There is one rule: the underlined word must always go at the beginning of the correct sentence to be formed. You need to circle or tick the last word of the new sentence. Although not overly difficult, this test still (as always) needs to be completed at a fairly fast pace. Some examples:

A. <u>To</u> your shoes in the rain waterproof keep you go out should not.

B. With the population they have aliens <u>half</u> the believes that had contact.

C. He had you a lift the appointment <u>if</u> to in time only would have made given it.

    Correct answers: A: rain B: aliens C: time

For certain jobs, where writing (reports, memos, instructions, legal documents) is an integral part of the job, it must be very important to do well on this verbal test

Syllogism test

A syllogism [from the Greek, meaning together ('sun') and reasoning ('logos')] is an argument built on two assumptions or assertions. You must draw a logical conclusion from these two assumptions. If you don't do that, you may find that your conclusion is (almost) identical to one of the assumptions. You haven't made optimal use of the information provided.

Like analogies, syllogisms are intended to tap into your capacity for logical thought. To what extent can you combine the available information to draw a sensible conclusion? Moreover, you must ignore the nature of the assertions themselves, and whether they sound plausible or not (for example, 'all women are green').Time for an example.

1. No bird is an insect.
2. All swallows are birds. So:

    A. No swallow is an insect.
    B. Some birds aren't swallows.
    C. All birds are swallows.
    D. No insect is a bird.

The right answer is (A) because birds don't belong in the insect category, and under the heading 'birds', we can include all swallows. You have noticed that you need to think hard and use your logical thinking ability to come up with the right answer! We will give you a couple more examples.

A.1. All salesmen are agents.
  2. No agent is a shopkeeper. So:

    A. No shopkeeper is a salesman.
    B. Some shopkeepers aren't agents.
    C. Some agents are salesmen.
    D. No shopkeepers are agents.

B.1. No ABCD is 1234.
  2. Some 1234 are efgh. So:
    A. Some ABCD are efgh.
    B. Some efgh aren't ABCD.
    C. Some efgh aren't 1234.
    D. Some 1234 aren't ABCD.

Correct answers: *1: A   2: B*

TIP   If you still can't see the answer, then take a guess. Two of the four answers can probably be easily eliminated, giving you a 50% chance, because they don't contain information from both statements.

However, before you embark on a guessing game, there are a few rules you should know:

1. You need to reduce both statements until A=B and B=C appear.
2. The right solution will be A=C, or C=A. In other words, the non-corresponding terms in both statements will always lead to the right conclusion.
3. There will sometimes be words in a conclusion that resemble those in the statement. These are rarely correct. (For example, in the statement the word 'ball' and in the conclusion 'round things'). Beware!
4. What if you have more than one conclusion remaining? Then look at the terms 'all', 'some' or 'no'. If both statements begin with 'all' or 'no' the right conclusion will also begin with 'all' or 'no'. If one of the statements begins with 'some', then the conclusion will also begin with 'some'. But first try to apply logical thinking to solve the syllogisms! (We refer to Practice test 2: syllogisms.)

Similarities

One type of test that is closely related to analogies and syllogisms is the similarities test, like in the WAIS intelligence test (and the WISC, the 'sister' intelligence test for children). Your task is to find out the similarity between two objects. Example:

What do oranges and apples have in common?

Possible open-ended answers: both are fruit, edible, round, have pips, grow on trees, have a sweet-sour taste.

The poorest answers include: 'both weigh something', 'grow on land' – both these answers can apply to many other objects and therefore tell us very little indeed. 'What have radio and newspaper in common?' Both are means of communication. What have messenger boy and beast of burden have in common'? Both are carriers, and so on.

Numeracy test

In numeracy tests, you must make a number of calculations within a certain time limit. These are basic mathematical operations (e.g. multiplication, addition, subtraction, etc.) Your knowledge of fractions is also being tested here, as well as your ability to solve simple equations.

In principle, you can easily practise this type of test at home. What is crucial is to learn how to complete these tests quickly. Below are 10 examples:

1. $0.667 - 0.019 =$
2. $0.16 \times 0.75 =$
3. $\frac{3}{4} \times 8/9 =$
4. $6/3 : 4/5 =$
5. $8/9 : \ldots = 10/9$

6. $27 : 3/8 =$
7. $3x + 5x = 12 \quad (x = ?)$
8. $14x + 4 = 60 \ (x = ?)$
9. $0.07 - \ldots = 0.057$
10. $\ldots - 0.02 = 0.28$

Correct answers: *1: 0.648* *2: 0.12* *3: 4/6* *4: 2.5*
5: 4/5 *6: 72* *7: 3/2* *8: 4*
9: 0.013 *10: 0.3*

Numerical series

Your numerical aptitude can also be measured by means of numerical sequences. For each set you must select one from five (or four) alternatives. Two examples:

A. 54 81 18 27 6 9 ?   2 3 4 12 15
B. 5 3 8 9 11 27 ?   54 13 38 14 18

Correct answers: A: 2 B: 14

Always start attacking these sets of figures by using the simplest approach. For example, assume there is a simple relationship between two successive numbers. If this is not the case try a more complicated pattern, e.g. skip every other element. (Put differently, there are two independent sub-series, or concurrent relationships.) You may also want to try adding up the first two figures, in order to arrive at the third, etc. Do you want to build up confidence? Practice test 1 will give you plenty of opportunity.

A (harder? easier?) variation is showcased below:

```
A.  2-6    5-9    3-7     7- -?
B.  4-8    2-4    6-12    7- -?
C.  16-4   64-8   9-38    1- -?
```

Correct answers: A: 11 B: 14   C: 9

'Letter crunching'

This type of test is rather out on a limb, as you will see. Originally developed to aid the selection of computer programmers, its application to other areas soon spread. You have to multiply letters rather than numbers – and as quickly as possible. In order to simplify matters:

- you only need to tick the 'correct' or 'incorrect' box, giving you a 50-50 chance when guessing.

- You are provided with a small explanatory table, that states that for this test, A =1, B= 2, C=3, etc.

Here are a couple of examples to help you. (Try the last three items yourself.)

Item		Correct?	Incorrect?
D x B	= H	yes	
C x F	= AE		yes
1. B x J	=AD		
2. AAA x E	= EEF		
3. AB x C	= CF		

Correct answers: 1: Incorrect 2: Incorrect 3: Correct

Timetabling problems

Sometimes, timetabling and logistical problems are included in the procedure. Your job: to draw up a workplan. The following problem will act as an example:

Two doctors hold sessions in a clinic from 9.00 am to 12.30 pm. Appointments are made 30 minutes apart. The patients must be seen by both doctors, separately. In addition, each patient must spend half an hour with the physiotherapist and they are then ordered to rest for one hour. During their visit to the physio, the patients must spend 30 minutes doing gymnastic exercises. But there are only two pieces of apparatus available.

(Now you must do some mental gymnastics!)

Please realise that your plan can be as simple as a table with seven half-hour time slots along the top (horizontally) and the two doctors, the physical therapist and the rest times along the side (vertically).

Reasoning tests

Many different data interpretation tests draw on one's reasoning ability, the capacity to think logically, critically and abstractly. (In fact, most intelligence tests do.)

The Watson Glaser Critical Reasoning Test generally takes 40 to 60 minutes to complete. (No time limits are set). You will certainly need every minute because the test is difficult, as the examples below will show. The shorter form consists of five components: Inference, Recognition of assumptions, Deduction, Interpretation, and Evaluation of arguments; a total of 80 items.

Test 1 – Inference

You have to draw the correct conclusion from a number of actual or presumed facts. The conclusions have already been drawn for you. You 'only' have to state whether the given conclusions are correct, incorrect, probably incorrect or whether you haven't got enough information to form an opinion. Example:

'The first American newspaper was published by Ben Harris and appeared on 25th September 1690 in Boston. The governor, Simon Bradstreet, forbade publication of the paper on the very same day. The long fight which followed to allow the publisher to continue printing and to be able to print whatever he desired marks an important episode in the continuing battle surrounding the free press in America'.

These are the conclusions:

1. The publisher of the first American newspaper died some days after

his newspaper was forbidden on 25th September 1690.

2. One copy of the first edition of Ben Harris' paper was brought to Governor Bradstreet's prompt attention.
3. The publisher of this paper wrote articles criticising Governor Bradstreet.
4. Ben Harris was a persistent man, because he stuck to his own aims and objectives.

Now you have to weigh up these four conclusions for their validity. Remember: there may be more than one correct or incorrect conclusion! (The answers are found at the end of this section).

Test 2 – Recognition of assumptions

You will find several assertions in this section, each followed by a number of different assumptions. It is your job to identify which assumptions follow logically from these statements. (It doesn't matter whether or not the rationale is correct in itself. That's another story...). Example:

Switzerland is a great place to live – it has the lowest taxes.
1. Efficient government leads to lower taxes.
2. An important consideration of a place to live is avoidance of high taxes.
3. The majority of Swiss people are satisfied with their present government.

> *TIP* You may find that you also have to state whether you are certain or uncertain of your answer for each item. If you are sure of your wrong answer, you may lose points...

Test 3 – Deduction

Every item contains two assertions, followed by a number of possible conclusions. You decide if one of the conclusions follows from both assertions. Example:

If someone is superstitious, then he won't believe in fortune-tellers.
Some people don't believe in fortune-tellers, therefore ...

1. If someone isn't superstitious, then he won't believe in fortune-tellers.
2. Some people aren't superstitious.
3. If someone believes in fortune-tellers, he is superstitious.

For more information on this type of test, we suggest you read the 'syllogisms' section in this chapter.

Test 4 – Interpretation

Once again you have to choose between alternatives: 'conclusion follows' or 'conclusion doesn't follow', after having read the 'story'. For all intents and purposes assume that the text is correct. Be careful that your knowledge of the real world doesn't influence your choice.

You have to decide whether or not the conclusions after the text follow logically – and without any reasonable doubt – from the information given in the text. Example:

In one academic year, 230,000 pupils out of a total of 800,000 chose to take A-level physics and 140,000 chose A-level mathematics.

1. Some schools in this academic year did not make A-level maths or physics compulsory.
2. One important reason for the fact that about half of all the A-level students did not take physics and mathematics was that they had already done these subjects the year before.
3. Some students from this year studied neither maths nor physics.

Test 5 – Evaluation of arguments

Here you have to state how strong or weak an argument is. An argument is weak if it bears no direct relationship to the question – even though the statement itself seems valid to you. Alternatively, there may be no relationship with the question at all: Example:

Should militant groups in this country be allowed to make unlimited use of the free press and media to criticise the government?'

1. Yes: a democratic state thrives if it allows free and unrestricted debate, which provides for the possibility of criticism.
2. No: those countries who oppose our form of government do not allow our opinion to be voiced in their countries.

3. No: if one gives complete media freedom to opposition groups, then this could lead to serious internal troubles which could ultimately lead to the loss of our form of democracy.

Correct answers: Test 1: 2   Test 2: 2   Test 3: 2   Test 4: 1
                     Test 5: 1

Inappropriate use of the IQ test

If an organisation is looking for, say a manager to lead a sales department, a multinational division, or the personnel department of a hospital, then they are looking for someone who must fulfil a number of concrete behavioural criteria. He or she must possess delegating skills, for example, recognise conflicts and be able to defuse them, give presentations to other members of staff and external company contacts, and so on. Someone's intelligence quotient doesn't really tell us much about these qualities.

If your potential employer wishes to know something about your intelligence (what is he actually going to do with this information?) then your qualifications should give him some clue. After all, IQ is really just an indication of ... well, what exactly? Yet, the intelligence test still remains one of the most widely used psychological tests, even for management selection.

5

Personality Tests

Personality tests still have a lot of credit with the general public. Sometimes even, they are revered because of their power to come up with personality descriptions that are quite good in the eyes of the test taker. These tests also generate interest on websites, CD-ROMs and the like (and at parties!). Critics however, are less friendly. They hold these tests responsible for breaking into one's bedroom, mark them as harassment, and pity their well-meaning victims.

Personality questionnaires are divided into so-called objective and projective tests. Projective tests are based on the concept that you project your ideas, dreams, fears and visions on the test material. If you are invited to tell what you see in black and white or coloured inkblots (the Rorschach test), or how you interpret vague, or old-fashioned drawings (as in the Thematic Apperception Test) then the psychologist must subscribe to the theory (it's no more than that!) that intimate sides of your personality, which generally remain hidden, can be brought to the surface. Scientifically speaking, these projective tests (for this, read 'subjective tests') are nightmares.

These problems are not new – they were identified a long time ago. It has led to the development of so-called objective 'paper and pencil' personality tests, where you must answer a number of written questions, which are supposed to throw a light on your personality. In a short space of time, your 'true nature' is revealed. In principle, you have no need for the intervention of a psychologist to implement, score and interpret personality tests. The whole procedure can be computerised and quite often is. The candidate crosses a few boxes on the screen and some time later, the computer spews out a compact or an elaborate personality report. We will lead you to various personality tests.

Is there such a thing as an 'ideal' personality? The answer is short and simple – no. Every organisation sets specific requirements for its employees. However, successful managers seem to score particularly high on the following dimensions: persuasive, leading (what else?), extrovert, inventive, relaxed, thick-skinned, optimistic, critical, energetic, competitive and decisive.

> *TIP* Assume that you will be confronted with more than one personality test and that your results may be compared with the way you come across during the interview.

Traits and personal competencies

The idea behind these tests is that people have stable personality characteristics or traits. If this were not the case, then every individual would change from one minute to the next. Only one minor detail: we have to find out what these (universal) traits are … Psychologists rather forget that people easily adapt to (new) situations (e.g. at home or at work). Furthermore, filling out personality questionnaires – especially with a known and desired outcome – may not be an altogether honest affair.

All modern personality tests are designed to 'catch' people's personality in a limited and fixed number of traits, be it five, ten or 15, as in the EPPS. Each item contributes to one and only one trait and all items (statements or questions) are then totalled per trait and compared with the relevant norm, if available. So a person might belong to the top 15% of male introverts.

A rather modern term that seems to be loved by HR specialists is competence (often seen as 'competency'). Competences are work-related, in contrast to personality traits. There are many definitions, and they all seem to have something to do with a cluster consisting of knowledge, skills, behaviour, tendencies, abilities, insight and attitude that are deemed necessary to carry out a job. Competences can be (partly) measured in assessment centres.

Objective personality tests

We now turn to a variety of multiple-choice tests.

GZTS

The Guilford-Zimmerman Temperament Survey, going back to 1949, yields ten traits: **restraint, general activity, ascendance, emotional stability, friendliness, sociability, objectivity, thoughtfulness, personal relations** and **masculinity**. In a report, these terms may be mentioned – or the opposites – depending on your scores. Statements like 'Often you are in a bad mood', or 'You are annoyed when you see somebody clean his nails in public' have to be rated on a 'Yes', '?', 'No' scale.

EPPS

The Edwards Personal Preference Schedule is another oldie, from the 1950s, and consists of 225 paired statements, of which the test taker has to select (forced choice) one favourite sentence per pair. There are 15 scales on which your personality will be anchored, among them **achievement, deference, exhibition, affiliation, dominance** and **aggression**. An example of paired sentences:

  a. I love travelling and trekking.
  b. I like planning my work well in advance.

Authorities Anastasi and Urbina state that: 'in spite of its simplicity and noteworthy features, the EPPS is in need of revision to eliminate technical weaknesses related to item form and score interpretation.'

> Personality tests have no time limit. You have sufficient time, regardless of what the agency personnel might tell you. So take your time for careful reading and don't rush into your own test grave.

OPQ

The Occupational Personality Questionnaires is a widely used personality test in the UK. Actually, it is a series of five questionnaires, each measuring 30 personality dimensions. Based on this test, a number of specialised scales have been developed, among others for **leadership, selling** and **team types**. Here are a few dimensions of the basic model, as developed by the British group SHL:

Relationships with people

Assertive
- **Persuasive**   Enjoys selling, changes opinions of others, convincing with arguments, negotiates.
- **Controlling**   Takes charge, directs, manages, organises, supervises others.
- **Independent**   Has strong views on things, difficult to manage, speaks up, argues, dislikes ties.

Gregarious
- **Outgoing**   Fun loving, humourous, sociable, vibrant, talkative, jovial.
- **Affiliative**   Has many friends, enjoys being in groups, likes companionships, shares things with friends.
- **Socially confident**   Puts people at ease, knows what to say, good with words.

Empathy
- **Modest**   Reserved about achievements, avoids talking about self, accepts others, avoids trapping of status.
- **Democratic**   Encourages others to contribute, consults, listens and refers to others.
- **Caring**   Considerate to others, helps those in need, sympathetic, tolerant.

An example of OPQ items:

You are given blocks of four statements and your task is to choose the statement which you think is most true or typical of you in your everyday behaviour (=M). Then choose the one which is least true or typical of you (= L).

I am the sort of person who...
- Has a wide circle of friends
- Enjoys organising people
- Relaxes easily
- Seeks variety

- Helps people with their problems
- Develops new approaches

- Has lots of energy
- Enjoys social activities

- Has lots of new ideas
- Feels calm
- Likes to understand things
- Is easy to get on with

The OPQ scores can be used to estimate the test taker's well-known Belbin's team type profile (often used for team building). Belbin differentiates the following types:

- **Co-ordinator**: setting team goals and defining roles.
- **Shaper**: the leader who makes things happen.
- **Plant**: the team's source of ideas.
- **Monitor-evaluator**: the critical analyst.
- **Resource investigator**: the salesperson and diplomat.
- **Completer**: the detail person who sees projects through.
- **Team worker**: 'in charge' of group harmony.
- **Implementer**: turns decisions into concrete tasks.

> *TIP* A personality test can only measure what it is designed to measure. If you know which traits together form the instrument, you have a rough idea about how you will be described in your report.

LIFO

LIFO (an abbreviation for Life Orientations) is a theory about human behaviour which assumes that someone's normal, productive behaviour is carried over to difficult situations, but in an extreme form. Therefore, a manager who is used to giving his workers as much support as possible will quickly decide to avoid problems if he has a conflict on his hands. The LIFO method is a training course, based on an intake questionnaire, which produces a number of possible styles. Various organisations administer this questionnaire for external and internal selection purposes.

LIFO's possible styles are: supporting/giving; controlling/taking; conserving/holding; adapting/dealing. The questionnaire consists of statements, each with four possible answers. You have to state 'to what extent these answers apply to you. Refer to actual behaviour, not desired behaviour. The answer that most applies to you scores 4, and the one that least applies to you scores 1. Example of a statement:

In a disagreement with someone, I can achieve more by:
1. trusting in the other person's sense of justice
2. scoring points off the other person or throwing him off guard
3. staying calm and rational, but sticking to my point
4. being open to and influenced by the other person's views.

Remember – in selection procedures, they are usually looking for your negative side, possibly unproductive and ineffective behaviour!

LPC

LPC stands for Least Preferred Co-worker and is a test that has been developed from a very well researched background, namely Fiedler's Contingency Theory. We will not bother going into the details of this theory but go straight into discussing the actual questionnaire.

The LPC goes under a variety of names and comes in many shapes and sizes: the actual questions, the number of questions, and the accompanying instructions may vary a little here and there.

Think of someone whom you would *least* like to work with. It can be a person with whom you've worked recently, or someone who you worked with some time ago. It doesn't necessarily have to be somebody you dislike, but it has to be someone who you found very difficult to work with in order to complete a task. Describe this person as you think he or she is by circling one of the numbers. Don't miss any items out.

Are the instructions clear? Then have a look at the following examples.

Enterprising	1	2	3	4	5	6	7	8	Unenterprising
Hard working	1	2	3	4	5	6	7	8	Lazy
Rude	1	2	3	4	5	6	7	8	Polite
Unreliable	1	2	3	4	5	6	7	8	Reliable
Unenthusiastic	1	2	3	4	5	6	7	8	Enthusiastic
Unsystematic	1	2	3	4	5	6	7	8	Systematic
Focused	1	2	3	4	5	6	7	8	Unfocused
Able to delegate	1	2	3	4	5	6	7	8	Unable to delegate
Good planner	1	2	3	4	5	6	7	8	Bad planner

With the aid of the LPC, your leadership style can be established. That lies somewhere between 'task-oriented' and 'socially motivated'. The first concept means that you place 'task completion' at the top of your priority list. Perhaps they call you 'hard' or 'authoritarian'. If you are socially motivated, you attach great importance to maintaining good working relationships with your colleagues.

Extensive research has discovered that 'task-oriented' managers perform best in (fairly) well controlled work environments. The opposite is true for 'socially motivated' managers: they do their best in more flexible work environments. So, the task is to find how controlled the work situation is and what the dominant culture is.

Survey of interpersonal values (SIV) – and of personal values (SPV)

Often these tests are used in conjunction with each other, to really put candidates through their paces. The SIV measures things that people feel are important in their daily lives and to which they give priority. If you know a person's values, then the reasoning is that you know what motivates him or her, why he or she behaves in such and such a way. The SIV is primarily interested in social intercourse, as the name 'interpersonal' suggests. The SIV measures the following six factors, or values, and luckily it is easy to spot which characteristic is being measured from the list of values:

- **Social support**: being encouraged, being treated with understanding.
- **Conformity**: following the rules, doing what is socially acceptable.
- **Recognition**: enjoying recognition and admiration.
- **Independence**: being free to take one's own decisions.
- **Benevolence**: being compassionate towards others.
- **Leadership**: being in charge, taking the lead.

The SIV, released in the USA in 1966, consists of thirty so-called triads (three statements). Pick the most and least important statement and leave one box always blank – the value that you find neutral. This takes about 20 minutes. Some examples are provided below:

IMPORTANCE

	MOST	LEAST

	MOST	LEAST
● To be free to do what I choose		
● To find that others agree with me		
● To make friends with those who have been very unlucky		
● To socialise with famous people		
● To devote my full attention onto the matter in hand		
● To exert a great deal of influence		
● To be able to live my life exactly as I choose		
● To do my duty		
● To know that others will treat me compassionately		

If you bear the six afore-mentioned values in mind, then you will probably guess which way the wind is blowing in each of these triads. Have you also noticed that there is an overlap between the statements used in these different triads?

The SIV scoring system works as follows: the 'most important' answer gets two points, the neutral value gets one, and your least important scores nil. Therefore, the maximum number of points per value is thirty. This makes you a top scorer. For 'hard-nosed' managers, it is important to score fairly high on leadership, independence and recognition. Scoring high on altruism (benevolence) is not regarded highly. That is, for managers. Obviously, though, this all depends on the organisational culture (i.e. the Red Cross or McDonald's).

The purpose of 'sister' test SPV (Survey of personal values) is 'to measure certain critical values that help to determine the manner in which individuals cope with the problems of everyday living'. The critical values are: **commercial orientation, motivation, variety, decisiveness, independence, order and neatness, goal-orientation**. The structure of the SPV is similar to the SIV. Again three examples, so that you have some idea of what you may get.

	IMPORTANCE	
	MOST	LEAST
● Working on something difficult		
● Having a clear goal in mind		
● Keeping my things neat and tidy		
● Having clear goals in mind		
● Planning my time in advance		
● Being sure in my dealings with others		
● Tackling a difficult but fascinating job		
● Visiting different new places		
● Having a clear objective to work towards		

> **TIP** Of course, your values, what 'drives' you, will not only be established by using written tests. Make sure that you also discuss these issues during the interview.

PAPI

PAPI stands for 'Perception and Preference Inventory' and is a 'workplace personality' questionnaire. Norms, validity and reliability for this test are not known – or at least not published. (But you can be sure that quality in these areas leaves a lot to be desired.) The results are always discussed later with the applicant, who may provide some supplementary information. The PAPI is regarded as a versatile instrument, and, as worded by a headhunter: 'the interviewer gets more information on the candidate than through the more traditional interview'.

The PAPI consists of 180 statements, divided into 90 pairs. The candidate must choose one of two statements which best describes his or her working situation. In this way, preferences can be broken down into twenty factors, among others: **need to change, need to achieve, need to be supportive,**

role of the hard worker, need to control others, leadership role, organised type, integrative planner, need for rules and supervision, ease in decision-making, emotional restraint, need to belong to groups, need to relate closely to individuals, need to be noticed, need to finish a task, concept thinker. These factors are then sub-divided into seven dimensions: **seeking to achieve, active dominance, conscientious persistence, openness to experience, sociability, work tempo,** and **agreeableness.** (Are you still with us?) This test, which takes roughly 15 minutes and aspires to know almost everything about you, leads to a profile, as illustrated below:

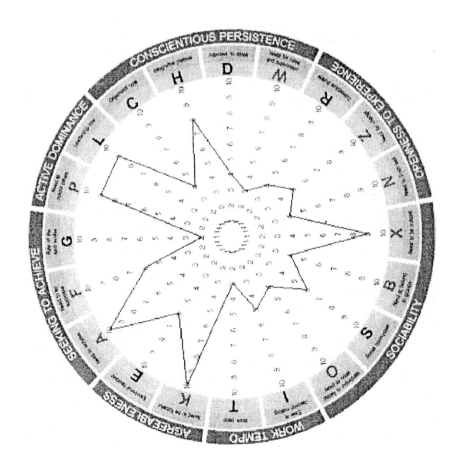

Two sample statements:
- I am a hard worker
- I am not moody

- I like to try out new things
- I prefer working with others than alone

Myers-Briggs Type Indicator (MBTI)

The MBTI is a somewhat older and in recent years resurrected American personality test, which dates from the Second World War, and is utilised more and more for management selection. Why is this test doing so well? The secret probably lies in the handy short forms of the sixteen types it identifies and its four scales:

- **Extroversion/Introversion**: the so-called **EI** scale.
  An extrovert is someone who is oriented towards the outside world, the environment, and other people. Introversion is the opposite: more oriented towards oneself, to one's inner world.

- **Sensing/Intuition**: the **SI** scale.
  Sensing here means that someone uses his or her senses effectively, which is easier if you have to deal with everyday reality. We are talking about practical and realistic people here. Another way of gathering information is to use your intuition. This means you can be finding new relationships, doing things in a different way, etc.

- **Thinking/Feeling**: the **TF** scale.
  Thinking here means a preference for logical reasoning, analysing, etc. Feeling: you make decisions based on how you feel (emotions) about things.

- **Judgement/Perception**: the **JP** scale.
  Judgement here refers to one's preference for a well-planned, orderly route through life and work, routine and control over one's activities. Perception: a more flexible, spontaneous way of living and working. Perceptive people try to understand things, rather than to control them.

The Myers-Briggs test has more than one hundred questions – you must state your preference for each one. Your answers are then processed and you are categorised according to one of sixteen types.

Sensing types		Intuitive types		
With thinking	With feeling	With feeling	With thinking	
ISTJ	ISTP	ISFJ	ISFP	Introverts
INFJ	INFP	INTJ	INTP	
ESTP	ESTJ	ESFP	ESFJ	Extraverts
ENFP	ENFJ	ENTP	ENTJ	

Can you understand all the types denoted in this table? We will help you with the first one, ISTJ. This stands for introvert, sensing, thinking, judging. ISTJs are (according to the test makers): *'serious, quiet, earn success by concentration, and thoroughness. Practical, orderly, matter-of-fact, logical, realistic, and dependable. See to it that everything is well organised. Take responsibility. Make up their own minds as to what should be accomplished and work toward it steadily, regardless of protests or distractions'.*

These types are used in the USA to come up with a concise, but clear profile (at least clear to those 'in the know') of a future employee. *'Our new advertising director must be a ENTJ'*. That means the ideal candidate is an extrovert, uses his or her intuition, but thinks things over and doesn't lose sight of the broader picture. (A full outline of this type is beyond the scope of this book).

More recently, the Myers-Briggs test has surfaced in the States in personal ads: *'Female ENFP is looking for a male INTJ'*. Is that the future for this serious test?

GPP/GPI

The American psychologist L.V. Gordon has developed two tests which are often combined if a manager's personality is under investigation. They are deemed to be particularly effective in the workplace environment. The instructions state: *'This booklet contains a number of descriptions of human characteristics. These descriptions have been grouped together in four categories. You should study each category and decide which description fits you. You should then denote this by pencilling out the small box alongside this description. Then, look at the remaining three categories and decide which of them is least applicable to you. There are no right or wrong answers; you only have to try and find those descriptions that give the fairest picture of you'.*

The Gordon Personality Profile and Gordon Personal Inventory, as they are jointly known, have 20 + 18 items – 38 in total. Here are a couple of examples:

	Fits most	Fits least
● Has very original ideas		
● Is rather slow and laid back		
● Tends to be critical of others		
● Takes a long time to think about decisions.		
● Doesn't easily get angry with others		
● Dislikes complex and difficult problems		
● Would rather go to a rowdy party than have a quiet evening		
● Feels tired and listless by the end of the day		
● Tends to make hasty and ill-considered judgements		
● Doesn't bear grudges		
● Is very hungry for knowledge		
● Tends to act on flashes of inspiration		
● Has a lot of energy and stamina		
● Only trusts people who have proven their reliability		
● Enjoys problems that require a great deal of thought		
● Doesn't need much company		

You can probably see which answers don't suggest a dynamic, brilliant and creative manager!

This test has no time limit, but experience suggests that you should finish in around 20-25 minutes. It measures altogether eight personality traits:

1. **Cautiousness**: Are you someone who avoids risk and weighs things up carefully before coming to a decision? Or are you just the opposite? You behave impulsively, respond to the moment, make hasty decisions and enjoy risks.

2. **Original thinking**: You love working with ideas and enjoy solving complex problems and philosophising. The other side of the coin: you

don't go into things deeply, you're not good at original, creative or intellectual thinking.

3. **Personal relations**: Trusting others, understanding them, and being tolerant and patient. On the negative side, critical of others and annoyed by them.

4. **Vigour**: You score highly on this personality trait if you are energetic, work quickly and do more than other people. The less vigorous amongst us work slowly and tire easily.

5. **Ascendancy**: Playing an active role in group situations, being self-assured and self-confident with others. Decision-making is an individual process and you can happily defend your own opinions. As you would expect, this type of person can easily influence others. The opposite pole: someone who plays a passive role, who would rather be on the sidelines than on the field, rather not be the leader and finds it easy to agree with others.

6. **Responsibility**: These folks take their responsibilities seriously, finish everything they begin. Someone who scores highly here is persistent, a stayer. Reliability is also characteristic of a high scorer. The low scoring candidate finds it hard to concentrate on uninteresting work. You can't rely on someone like this. Fickle and sometimes irresponsible.

7. **Emotional stability**: The words say it all: balanced, carefree and calm. (The ideal son-in-law?) People who score low on this factor are rather nervous, over-sensitive and easily worried. Very low scores suggest certain neurotic tendencies.

8. **Sociability**: The extent to which someone enjoys company and likes to work in a team, finds it easy to make friends and enjoys parties and get-togethers. The non-sociable person is rather reserved in contacts and doesn't find it easy to deal with others. They often have very few (but very good!) friends.

Broadly speaking, we would say that a balanced profile looks roughly like this:

- On cautiousness, an average score (it's okay to take small, calculated risks).
- Be somewhat of an original thinker, but not a theoretician.

- Score high on personal relations, you get on easily with others (colleagues).
- Be energetic, you can do a mountain of work.
- Have the ascendancy over others, but don't be a dictator. (That is, when leadership is an issue.) We still live in a democracy: participation and having one's say are achievements that are not easily relinquished.
- Obviously, the ideal candidate understands his responsibilities and must come across as reliable.
- This applies equally to emotional stability. (An employer will have a heart failure if he sees you described as an 'neurotic wreck'.)
- And naturally, the ideal person must be sociable, a group animal, who knows that work only gets done with the help of others.

16PF

This originally American test measures 16 Primary Factors, hence its name. 187 questions are eagerly waiting for an answer on one of three alternatives. (Very strange: one of the factors in this personality test is '**abstraction**', measuring intelligence through number sequences and analogies.) Some of the other factors are: **outgoing, emotionally stable, self-assured, trusting, imaginative, group-oriented.** 16PF items look like this.

- On social occasions, I
  - a. readily come forward
  - b. in between
  - c. prefer to stay quietly in the background

- Money can buy almost everything:
  - a. yes
  - b. uncertain
  - c. no

- I feel terribly dejected when people criticise me in a group:
  - a. true
  - b. in between
  - c. false

Motivation and needs

MQ.M5

This SHL test assesses, in their own words, 'the energy with which a person approaches tasks and what situations increase and reduce individual motivation'. The test is mainly applied at managerial level and measures the following 18 dimensions of motivation: **level of activity, achievement, competition, fear of failure, power, immersion, commercial outlook, affiliation, recognition, personal principles, ease and security, personal growth, intrinsic interest, flexibility, autonomy, material reward, progression, status.**

The test taker is offered 144 statements, all describing work-related situations, for which the degree of how this will influence his motivation has to be rated on five-point scales. Make sure you score relatively high on intrinsic motivation (interest), meaning you care a lot for the work as such, more so than the material rewards that go with it.

MNQ

The Maslow Needs Questionnaire is based on the self-actualisation theory of Abraham Maslow. 70 items need to be rated on a five-point importance scale (from not important to very important). Three sample questions, either on paper or on cards:

- I would find it (degree of importance) in a job if I could work according to my own ideas.
- I would find it (degree of importance) in a job if everybody would arrive on time.
- I would find it (degree of importance) in a job if they would accept my decisions.

The purpose of this test is to assess your work needs, in any of these four categories: **security, social, recognition, self-actualisation.** The highest score points to your dominant need. What is it that you are looking for in a job? And does that match with your future employer's?

'Big Five'

Personality questionnaires are often more or less based on a personality theory. If one would collect all underlying scales, one would see that all have their own 'pet traits', an incredible wildfire. Psychologists have been aware of this, but were apparently not in a position to do something about it. That is, until Costa and McCrae came along and found out that most tests seem to recognise (although under different labels) five fundamental traits:

- Extroversion (and introversion)
- Agreeableness
- Conscientiousness
- Emotional stability (and neuroticism)
- Intellect and openness to experience

Playing around with these labels leads to the following easy-to-remember acronym NEOAC (Neuroticism, Extroversion, Openness, Agreeableness, Conscientiousness). Based upon their extensive statistical work, they developed the NEO-PI-R test, containing these five personality dimensions. (A shortened form is called the Five Factor Inventory, FFI). Here are a few sample statements of this widely used test, which need to be rated on a five-point agree-disagree scale:

- I rarely feel lonely or sad.
- I keep my things tidy and clean.
- I rarely feel strong emotions.

Emotional intelligence

The claim to fame of emotional intelligence ('EQ') is that it in a way offers an 'alternative' to cognitive intelligence. How a person deals with his or her own emotions, and handles other people's is just as important as someone's rational side. The most serious and best known test is the Bar-On EQ-I test (after its developer, Bar-On), basically a personality test, measuring the following aspects:

- **intrapersonal** (including emotional self-awareness and assertiveness)
- **interpersonal** (including empathy and social responsibility)
- **adaptability** (including reality testing and flexibility)
- **stress management** (stress tolerance and impulse control)
- **general mood** (optimism and happiness)

EQ is measured on these five dimensions, by rating how true each of 133 statements is on you. Some examples:

- It's fairly easy for me to express feelings.
- It's difficult for me to stand up for my rights.
- I have good self-respect.
- I don't get enjoyment from what I do.
- Others find it hard to depend on me.

What not to do on personality tests

1. Make sure you don't answer positively on questions that try to measure if you are physically or mentally ill, neurotic, dissatisfied (with yourself, your work, your life) or a complainer.
2. Tests have built-in checks. Try to give consistent answers.
3. If you describe yourself as the most honest and noble person the world has ever known, you are not to be believed …

Inkblots, sketches and trees

In 1922, the Swiss psychiatrist Hermann Rorschach came up with a very simple (to some, brilliant) idea to assess personality – through folded inkblots. He was 38 when he died (one year after the launch of his test) but his spirit is still around – or at least his test.

The concept behind this projective technique, as it is called, is that people will express themselves freely, when confronted with vague material, in this case inkblots. There is no pressure, one's own creativity sets the ceiling. The instruction may go like this: *'people see all kinds of things in these (10 black and coloured) pictures. Please tell me what you see in them, what it reminds you of'*. (Follow-up questions are: *'what else do you see'?*)

Reactions to these pictures are compared with the norms, followed by an interpretation. When you describe the total picture, instead of the details, this will be interpreted as abstract thinking. Coloured (versus black and white) reactions refer to emotions. 'Moving' answers point to intelligence, adaptation, stability. Original (uncommon) answers point in the direction of creativity and fantasy.

Up to the 1960s, the Rorschach was widely applied, but not anymore. However, in clinical sessions (or when the psychologist is puzzled or suspects mental problems) this test is dusted off.

TAT

A related test is the TAT, Murray's Thematic Apperception Test, going back to 1935. 20 rather ambiguous sketches are presented. What does the candidate see in these pictures? A story is expected to follow, in writing or orally.

Tree tests

You get ten minutes to draw a tree (universal, dream, fantasy, or fruit tree). Your sketch is believed to be representative of your personality, at least according to Koch (another Swiss), who developed this interesting idea. In case you have to show your artistic talents at the agency, keep the following points in mind:

- a thick stem corresponds with a stable personality.
- will your job require an eye for details? Make sure you draw recognisable branches and leaves.
- sketching a dying or leafless tree may indicate a mental problem ...

RISB

The Rotter Incomplete Sentences Blank consists of 40 sentence stems: *'complete these sentences to express your real feelings. Try to do every one. Be sure to make a complete sentence'*. Each completion is rated on a seven-point adjustment-maladjustment scale (according to the models in the manual.). Other sentence completion tests operate along the same lines. A few examples:

- It annoys me that ....
- If I would be the boss ....
- Men .... Women ....

If you want to leave a favourable impression:

- avoid negative terms, jot down as many positive and optimistic words as possible
- put humour and warmth in your reactions
- offer a neutral and bland answer every now and then
- tend to stay on the conservative side – no political statements.

Evaluation

As measuring instruments, projective tests are useless in the occupational practice, and they are also dishonest: the candidate is being led down the garden path and kept in the dark about their purpose. And even worse, the psychologist's interpretations and conclusions are indisputable. A negative conclusion – no matter how it has been made – can be fatal. *'Perhaps the candidate has problems with his sexuality'*. This phrase can never be positive. Are you able to refute it? Do you want to refute it? And will they listen to you? Psychologists who use projective tests (happily only a very small number nowadays) regard them as a type of X-ray: a look at the candidate from the inside. Let's go one step further: just as an X-ray only makes sense to the medical specialist, so too does the projective test to the psychologist.

The scientific basis of modern psychology began in 1875, in the world's first psychological laboratory, in Leipzig. Since then, psychology has developed a great many theories, carried out millions of experiments and helped to solve many practical problems. It is a useful science – no one disputes that. But, if psychologists really believe that they can determine someone's personality by asking them a number of, often, simple questions (187 in the 16PF), then they are displaying an undeserved arrogance. Or naiveté. Or is it just that psychologists have too much faith in their own products?

The human personality is complicated. Psychological theories in this area have helped a little, but really they are still in their infancy. Selection psychologists' pretensions are quite often unrealistic, despite the wonderful statistical smoke screens that surround these tests.

6

Sales and Some Other Tests

Before moving to the assessment centre part of this book we conclude with several 'commercial' tests and others, namely integrity (getting more loved in the U.S. by employers), concentration and vocational interest tests. (Tips on how to concentrate as a test taker have been presented earlier.)

Sales Comprehension Test (SCT)

The SCT, going back to 1949, was developed by Martin Bruce, a well-known American test constructor, and is available in several versions. The test aims at establishing an individual's *'understanding and appreciation of the fundamental sales principles'*. In other words, it doesn't matter what type of selling experience you have or how old you are. We have a few doubts about this, but we won't go into them further here and will stick to the actual test questions.

This test consist of 27 questions, and each question has a choice of four answers. But beware! Each answer is awarded plus and minus points, ranging from -8 to +11. There is no way of knowing how many points each answer may get you. But, as you can see, the difference between a good and a bad answer vary widely. (The scores on the entire test range from -136 to +119). For most questions, there are several good – and bad – answers. One answer may be 'more' correct than the other. You will get no points for questions you miss out. In all cases, it is a real gamble to deliberately leave blanks, to reduce the risk of being wrong. Only use this strategy if you are convinced that you have answered most of the questions correctly and are stumbling in the dark for the right answer on one or two remaining questions.

There is no time limit on the SCT, so you can take as long as you want. In practice, 'commercial' candidates take about 15-20 minutes to complete the test.

Since you may be desperate to see some actual test questions, we have selected three and, for each, we will give you the number of points you can gain or lose. (At the end of the chapter.) We will not explain why these correct answers get this number of points. That is left to the wisdom of the test constructor...

Question 1: Which of these options should a salesperson use generally in order to increase his or her sales?

    A. Invite a customer for dinner.
    B. Read the latest publications about his/her products.
    C. Take a course in psychology.
    D. Study economic theory.

Question 2: What do you do when faced with a reticent customer?

    A. Don't talk as much yourself.
    B. Ask the customer some questions to open him or her up a little.
    C. Begin talking about a subject which you know particularly interests the customer.
    D. Give your presentation in the usual dynamic, chatty fashion you use for all your customers.

Question 3: You are the marketing manager and must sell a whole new range of pharmaceuticals. How would you approach this?

    A. Approach a doctor, whom you believe would use this new drug.
    B. Gather a group of doctors together, give a talk and give them a few samples to try out.
    C. Try to convince a famous doctor to prescribe the drug.
    D. Send a trial sample to all eligible doctors.

There are norms to be used with this test, allowing your score to be compared with the relevant group of salespeople. (Your score can also be compared against scores from non-salespeople). It appears possible to use this test to differentiate between people with commercial understanding and those where it is lacking. But it is not possible to distinguish between good and exceptional salespeople within the same company.

What exactly is the SCT measuring? Statistical research indicates the following:

- general sales understanding, knowledge and experience (despite what the test constructors would like us to believe, experience does help!)
- responding to problems and setbacks in the sales process itself and within the customer relationship
- persuasiveness, tenacity and, as it is called in this test, 'sales dynamism'
- sensitivity in customer relationships
- 'hard sell'.

So what is the secret of this test? How can you best answer? The test author and the selection agency expect the salesperson to be:

- persuasive
- persevering, not to give up to quickly
- able to put him or herself in the customer's shoes
- service-oriented, really wanting to help the customer
- loyal to his or her job, products, firm
- constantly trying to improve his or her performance, be ambitious.

The Sales Motivation Inventory (SMI)

This test, also developed by Bruce, originated in 1976, and consists of 75 groups of 4 activities. The candidate must select one of the four activities in every group, which he prefers above the others. There are no right or wrong answers. The test only determines to what degree the applicant is interested in and motivated for a sales function. The questions are therefore rather transparent. Clearly, if the salesperson must answer a question on teaching, he should choose teaching a commercial subject rather than geography, biology or science. The SMI resembles a vocational test, and it is often used precisely for this aim.

There is no time limit on completing this test. But most people have this test 'licked' within 20 minutes. For each answer you can score -1, 0, or +1. The groups of activities listed below show you how the test looks.

State which activity out of the four listed you prefer above all the others.
- working with politicians
- working with doctors
- working with decorators

- working with librarians

- building your own house
- selling a house
- making up blueprints for a house
- designing a house

- becoming a psychologist
- becoming a biologist
- becoming a stockbroker
- secoming a statistician

You should be able to see how you can do well on this one and similar tests. Pick answers which show that you like working with others, that you enjoy going out and being in company, that you want to 'sell' to people etc.

Sentence completion test

Sentence completion tests have been discussed in the preceding chapter. Here is an example of a commercial variety (there is no time limit imposed for filling in your answers):

Fill in these sentences so that your answers reflect your true feelings. Do not miss any sentences out and complete each phrase fully.

1. People who say they have no money......
2. One way of making selling easier is to ......
3. If you are faced with more competition,........
4. A customer may be frightened.......
5. A satisfied client......
6. In my free time,......
7. Advertising........

How can you pick up marks for this test? The test makers have classified all possible – at least all probable – answers into between 5 and 9 categories. Your answer will be placed in one of these categories.

Thomas Kilmann Instrument

The task faced by many managers is conflict avoidance. But if a conflict does arise, then the manager's duty is to keep it under control or to resolve it. One way of finding if the manager can handle it is to do a role play (Chapter 9). Another method is to use a written test, as exemplified in the Thomas Kilmann Instrument.

The test is simple, first read the instruction: *'Think about those situations when your wishes clashed with someone else's. How do you usually react in this type of situation? The next few pages contain statements which describe possible behaviours in these situations. Circle either A or B to denote which statement most closely describes your own behaviour. If neither A nor B is really characteristic of your behaviour, please choose the one which is closest to your own behaviour.'*

The test contains thirty of these A/B statements, where you are forced to choose. The following statements, generated from this Instrument, give you a fair idea of what to expect.

A. Sometimes I let other people take the responsibility for solving problems.
B. Rather than negotiating over issues we disagree on, I try to emphasise those issues that we do agree on.

A. I consistently ask for others' help when working out a solution.
B. I try to do whatever is necessary to avoid unnecessary stress.

A. I am determined in pursuing my objectives.
B. I try to find a compromise.

A. I try to meet others halfway.
B. I really push the other person to get my point across.

A. If it makes the other person happy, I give into his point of view.
B. I will acknowledge some of his views, if he acknowledges some of mine.

Do you have some idea which answers suggest you are a good manager, someone who knows how to deal with (potential) conflicts? Do you also see which answers show that the person filling in the questionnaire is a 'hawk' and not a 'dove'?

> ***TIP*** Be aware that the Thomas Kilmann Instrument contains some overlapping statements. If you read through the list carefully, you will soon see where the shoe pinches. If in doubt, go back to the earlier statements.

Your conflict profile is measured on the following five conflict handling characteristics:

- **Competing**: *self-assured and non-co-operative*. His or her self-interest is of paramount importance, even at others' expense. Key concepts are power, argument, and financial sanctions. This person always wants to win.

- **Co-operating**: *self-assured and co-operative*. Someone who wants to reach the right solution together with others. Both parties' interests must be met. Thus, the problem must be thoroughly researched. No stone is left unturned in the search for alternatives.

- **Looking for compromises**: *self-assured and co-operative – but to a lesser extent*. Someone who always wants to come up with acceptable solutions for both parties. Attempts to overcome differences, make concessions, choose the middle ground

- **Avoiding**: *neither self-assured nor co-operative*. Conflicts are diplomatically avoided, subjects are postponed or one withdraws from a threatening situation the easiest way possible.

- **Adapting**: *not self-assured but certainly co-operative*. Self-interest is put aside to make the other party happy. Self-sacrifice. Charity. Obedience. Giving into the other's wishes.

How should you answer? Firstly, it is important to possess a good blend of qualities, so you shouldn't be an extreme 'compromiser'. Moreover, you need to adapt your style to the organisational culture. Is it a fairly authoritarian environment that calls for a firm hand, or are problems discussed endlessly in meetings? You can appreciate once again how important it is to have good information on your future employer.

Integrity tests

In the US, the popularity of written (and other) integrity tests is clearly on the rise. Reasons behind this trend are the increasing alcohol and drugs use on and off the job, workplace violence, and (retail) theft. The test developers (or sellers) claim that their integrity tests (which sounds better than honesty or lie tests):

- have a high degree of both validity and reliability
- are not transparent (applicants cannot hide).

Test instructions inform the applicant that lying is not possible at all, and cheating is always discovered and will lead to an abrupt end of the entire procedure. In reality, these tests are just as weak, perhaps even less robust than personality tests...

Integrity tests are based upon the following assumptions that less honest people:

- report more dishonest behaviour
- tend to find excuses for dishonest behaviour rather quickly
- tend to offer more reasons for theft
- think often about theft
- accept dishonest behaviour more often
- tend to punish themselves and others more heavily.

Typical test questions are:

- Offenders need to be punished harder.
- I don't want to think about having enough money to spend.
- It is quite understandable that people steal, when it is without any risk.
- Basically, almost everybody wants to cheat.

Attention and concentration

Earlier, you have met the DAT sub-test Perceptual Speed and Accuracy. In a way the Bourdon test (1902!) is comparable in that a fair outcome also requires attention and concentration. The ten minute Bourdon (after the French designer) consists of 50 lines with, on each line, 25 compositions of three, four or five dots. (See the figure below.) Your objective is to detect and mark all (for instance) compositions of four dots – as quickly as possible. You are being observed by an assistant who also times your speed.

⠒⠒ ⠦ ⠿ ⠐ ⠈ ⠙ ⠒ ⠐ ⠈ ⠒ ⠐ ⠐ ⠐ ⠈ ⠐ ⠒ ⠦ ⠐ ⠈ ⠒ ⠐ ⠒ ⠈ ⠒ ⠦
⠐ ⠒ ⠈ ⠦ ⠿ ⠐ ⠒ ⠐ ⠒ ⠦ ⠐ ⠿ ⠒ ⠐ ⠈ ⠒ ⠐ ⠈ ⠒ ⠈ ⠒ ⠐ ⠒ ⠐ ⠐
⠦ ⠒ ⠐ ⠿ ⠐ ⠒ ⠒ ⠦ ⠒ ⠿ ⠒ ⠦ ⠒ ⠐ ⠦ ⠦ ⠿ ⠐ ⠐ ⠈ ⠒ ⠐ ⠒ ⠒ ⠒
⠒ ⠦ ⠦ ⠐ ⠐ ⠒ ⠈ ⠒ ⠿ ⠒ ⠦ ⠒ ⠈ ⠒ ⠐ ⠦ ⠒ ⠦ ⠐ ⠒ ⠿ ⠐ ⠒ ⠦ ⠐
⠦ ⠒ ⠒ ⠒ ⠦ ⠈ ⠒ ⠐ ⠈ ⠒ ⠦ ⠦ ⠈ ⠒ ⠐ ⠒ ⠈ ⠒ ⠦ ⠦ ⠿ ⠒ ⠐ ⠐ ⠒

> ***TIP*** A normal, average performance requires roughly ten seconds per line, an equally dispersed number of seconds per line (no lapses), on average less than one omission per line and a maximum of three errors.

Vocational interest tests

Some organisations try to find out if your vocational interests correspond to those of the group to which you belong or want to belong. This is really rather misleading, as they are not measuring how well-suited you are for the job, but whether your hobbies and interests match those of others in your professional group – and **how motivated** you are. Well-known tests in this arena are:

SII

The Strong Interest Inventory (SII) consists of 317 items grouped into eight parts. The respondent shows his or her preference by indicating 'like', 'indifferent' or 'dislike'. (This test can only be scored by a computer.) The summary ('snapshot') report shows General Occupational Themes (investigative, realistic, conventional, artistic, social and enterprising), Basic Interest Scales (e.g. medical) and Occupational Scales (e.g. dentist).

KOIS

The Kuder Occupational Interest Survey is the latest of the many Kuder versions. Scores are available for 109 specific occupational groups. It provides occupational scores and broad homogeneous interest scores. Out of three activities per item, you choose which ones are most and least favourable.

SDS

The Self-Directed Search was designed as a self-administered, self-scored, and self-interpreted vocational counselling instrument and is used by (educational) professionals and laymen. Its coded 'themes' (professional clusters) overlap with the SII. They lead to a number of occupations of which many in all likelihood are far away from your expectations and will make you laugh (or cry...). Optimists may find the jewel in the outcome of the test.

The STC answer assessment

	Item 1	Item 2	Item 3
A.	-1	-8	-5
B.	+4	+3	+5
C.	-1	0	+2
D.	-4	-2	-2

7

The Assessment Centre

The shortcomings of the traditional psychometric investigation are becoming increasingly evident. Is someone who scores highly on a numerical reasoning test also good at making decisions? Can someone who scores 100% on analogical reasoning quickly grasp the finer points of delegation? Are the committee skills of the candidate who professes to have mastered these so well, really top class? Traditional psychological research cannot answer questions such as these.

Another growing problem: the classic 'questionnaire method' appears to be inappropriate for ethnic minority candidates. Although some psychometric tests claim to be 'culture-free', minority applicants tend to score lower than their level of education would lead one to expect. The assessment centre (AC for short) is often put forward as a 'cure' for this. One decides exactly which qualities are needed to be successful in a particular job and then measures them using behavioural simulations.

Evaluating personnel, especially those involved in 'abstract' tasks such as sales and management, is difficult. But when the employer must select candidates for these functions – that is to say, people of whom he has no prior knowledge whatsoever – then it is even more difficult to reach a considered judgement. Employers' requirements continue to increase. (International) competition is growing rapidly and more and more work must be done by fewer people. Therefore stress levels are also climbing. And not every individual can withstand it. The AC is more effective than other methods at finding out which people make the most resilient, flexible, motivated, dynamic (read: hardworking), socially competent and loyal workers. 'Missing the mark' in selection is becoming more and more expensive, for organisations and candidates alike, financially as well as emotionally. And the disappointed employee does not usually find a new job quick as a flash.

A totally different reason for the growth in ACs is that occupational psychologists have discovered that they can earn more money by adopting this method, than they do from traditional psychological testing. But, merely adding a 'pinch' of role playing and a 'dash' of presentation to a battery of personality and aptitude tests, together with an interview with a psychologist, does not make such an enterprise a true AC.

The AC has its roots in the UK's War Office Selection Boards, who wanted to improve their selection of officers during the Second World War. Their discovery was quickly taken up by the American Office of Strategy Service (OSS), which – amongst other things – had to select spies. One of the psychologists involved, MacKinnon, wrote thirty years later: *'Every candidate had to create a school, where he had lived and worked, although none of it was in fact true'*. (Then, the candidates had to lie, but not now!)

But it was not until 1956 that the American telecom firm AT&T, used the method for other purposes. In the 1960s, big American companies, such as IBM, General Electric and retail chains Penny and Sears, introduced the AC-method for managerial selection. Around 1980, the method really took off. At present, some 90% of organisations in the UK are estimated to use the AC method. The AC enjoys its greatest notoriety as a management selection tool in commercial companies and to a lesser extent for the Civil Service, but it is broadening its use to more and more other functions.

What is an assessment centre?

The best means of selection is naturally a 'real' evaluation on the 'shopfloor'. Offer each applicant a job ('practice assessment') for a few months, weeks or days, and observe his or her behaviour thoroughly. But, that is not an achievable goal. It means chaos for the organisation and a long period of uncertainty for the candidate. An applicant will find it difficult to announce to his or her present employer: *'I must do a bit of practice work with our largest competitor, and, if I'm rejected, I'll end up back here again'*. A director who wishes to move on cannot let the market know so early that s/he is going to transfer.

An AC means that *your behaviour in the working environment* is placed under scrutiny. Psychometric tests only measure your behaviour 'on paper', so to speak, whilst the AC is like spending a whole day with your future employer.

The 'impossible reality' described above is best approximated by the AC method. Here, use is made of 'hard' behavioural assessment techniques, whereby an attempt is made in a systematic way, through group and individual exercises, tests and simulations, to establish those qualities which are essential for the effective performance of a given function. The term AC encompasses a large number of working methods and approaches. Perhaps we should place them all under one heading: 'work sample tests'. As the old saying goes, 'actions speak louder than words'. Here's a good example. Suppose that you've applied for a job as director for a wholesaler with several warehouses in the UK. You will be asked to complete a number of exercises, which are, to a greater or lesser degree, related to the job, and you will be evaluated on your behaviour, using pre-determined behavioural dimensions. We will be showing you examples later.

Recruitment agencies claim that the AC scores of candidates are more valid and reliable that those from psychological tests. The method is transparent, for both parties, because the candidate performs tasks which are very like those carried out in reality – sometimes even the same. Candidates are said to describe the AC method as fascinating, informative, honest, challenging and exciting, and appreciate the fact that there is no hocus-pocus with dubious psychological questionnaires, from whence sometimes unrecognisable and incomprehensible conclusions are drawn.

By far, most ACs take more or less a full working day, from 9 am to 5 pm, with time off for lunch. In some cases, both agency and/or client discover that a half day is enough – a good thing for the budget. Executive job seekers get away with it less easily. They are sometimes asked to bring their overnight bag with them, because they must 'sing and dance' at the AC over a 36 hour period. It is not beyond the bounds of possibility that even their calorie intake is studied during this time. What are their table manners like? How elegantly do they hold their coffee cup?

Uses of assessment centres

ACs are principally utilised by occupational psychologists but a number of large employers (think of multinationals) also use ACs in-house. Even the mafia and teenage gangs 'test' the behaviour of potential members, in order to gain their loyalty, heart and soul.

But the AC has countless other applications. We find ACs employed for **pre-selecting candidates for training**. For example, an organisation will specify that only those candidates with a positive AC result may put their names down for a certain course, training scheme or place on a management development programme. Only afterwards does the actual selection procedure take place.

AC's are being increasingly used for **specifying the training and educational needs** of personnel (so-called 'needs analysis'). From here, it is only a short step to use the same 'test' for training evaluation – to see if it achieves the desired result.

To a lesser extent, the AC is used to **explore career choices**. The question which must be addressed is: does the image that someone has of a job match the 'reality' as demonstrated by the test? We can see that the AC is used to manage **career development** in organisations. The strong and weak points, as well as the shortcomings of personnel are revealed. That this discovery has something to do with a large-scale reorganisation in the company should not surprise you …

How well does a member of staff give **presentations**? This can be a criterion, for example, for admittance to an ad hoc work group or when being considered for a transfer. Give the candidate a standard presentation task, let him or her prepare and perform the presentation, and then evaluate the presentation on previously established criteria.

Is the manager a **team-builder**? Give him or her a standard team-building task and again evaluate performance using pre-formulated criteria.

In principle, if the system is already in place, every type of AC task can be applied in this simple way to test one or more skills. So, if you have been accepted on the 'inside' once, this does not necessarily mean that you will be not be tested by your employer again sometime in the future!

ACs are also utilised as an **aid in outplacement**. The most suitable functions for the candidate (who has at this point either lost or is about to lose his job) are mapped out on the basis of his scores.

TIP Always try to find out if you are to be faced with a 'pure' AC (this means simulations, tasks etc.), or a series of psychometric tests together with a role play, or a mixture of assessment tasks and psychometric tests. Important for focusing your preparations!

Behavioural dimensions

Some people describe the AC as a technique that measures the candidate's strong and weak aspects in terms of pre-determined behavioural dimensions. A behavioural dimension is a specific and perceptible form of behaviour, which can be classified logically and reliably. If an observer can perceive a certain behaviour, then you must presumably be aware of this behaviour. Because after all, it's your behaviour! If an observer can see or hear (or smell?) your behaviour, then it can be measured. This means: classification and numbers in boxes. So, a '1' could be bad, for example, and a '5' excellent. Why reliable? Because you will (probably) behave the same way again next time, as that is the nature of the beast. (We will show you how to improve your behaviour later.)

Sometimes other dimensions are used, such as the five meta-dimensions or 'powers' (Jansen, 1991), which we will describe below, with examples:

1. **Cognitive power** (thinking): examples – logical thought, creativity, sensitivity to organisation.
2. **Social power** (feeling): examples – listening, empathy, persuasiveness.
3. **Action power** (doing): examples – supervisory ability, management control, eye for costs/benefits.
4. **Willpower** (wanting): examples – taking the initiative, completion, energy.
5. **Balance** (the balance between the 'four' powers: examples – self insight, maturity, control.

Another method of classification is into competencies, combinations of behavioural dimensions. For example – one agency defines the competency 'impact' as 'dynamic manner, flair, easily able to begin conversations and keep them going, able to argue effectively, and with natural persuasive abilities'. This competency consists of the following behavioural dimensions: **oral presentation, persuasive ability, sociability** and **attitude**. But of course you've guessed that already.

Our emphasis is on selection. But often the candidate's future skills are under investigation. So, KLM, for example, selects future pilots not only on the basis of their flying skills (although that's nice to know), but also on their potential to become a captain. This means that these professional aviators must possess leadership qualities.

> ***TIP*** In an AC, try not only to complete all the tasks and exercises, but always show that you have even more to offer, that the organisation will get value from you in the long term.

As promised, there follows a long list with behavioural dimensions, divided into categories, with a brief explanation of each (definition is too strong a word).

a. Individual Behaviour

Adaptability: ability to remain 'goal-oriented' by adapting effectively to changes in work environment, task, responsibilities or people. Willing to change. The level of performance remains at a high level, in spite of setbacks and pressure. (This is a good dimension to look for if you wish to do well in a turbulent organisation).

Ambition: strives to go higher and higher in the organisation; wants to build a career, and be successful. Goes to the trouble of developing his/herself in order to achieve this.

Scope of interest: generally well informed; has a great deal of factual knowledge across a wide subject area.

Decisiveness: able to take (fast) decisions by making judgements and/or undertaking actions. Takes the long and short-term consequences into account. Can defend any decision taken. (A manager who doesn't dare to make decisions is talking himself into redundancy ....)

Conformity: conforms to the organisation's politics, philosophy and procedures. Goes to the right people for approval.

Creativity: able to come up with original solutions to problems which fall within the scope of the job. Can think up totally new ways of working to replace existing methods and techniques. Innovative.

Discipline: ready to fit in with the organisation's management and/or procedures. Seeks confirmation with the right authorities, when changes occur.

Nerve: able to take risks to gain a certain advantage.

Flexibility: able to change one's own behaviour to reach a stated goal.

Drive for power: exercising influence or power is important to personal well-being.

Ethical stance: able to maintain generally accepted social and ethical standards when carrying out job-related duties.

Manual dexterity: able to put objects quickly into the correct order, without being awkward or messy.

Resourcefulness: resourceful when the situation demands. Reacts to unforeseen developments in an appropriate manner.

Integrity: follows social and ethical standards, as far as they relate to work, the organisation, the office, etc.

Irritability: avoids getting annoyed or resentful.

Attention to detail: able to work effectively with detailed information, over a long period, without losing sight of the bigger picture.

Organisational ability: able to use available time and resources effectively in order to perform his/her own function and reach the desired goal.

Problem analysis: effectively identifies problems; looks for the relevant details; recognises important information and tracks down possible causes. Also aware of the way different factors may influence one another.

Risk-taking: wants to gain an advantage from (potentially) risky situations. Dares to take calculated risks.

Ability to withstand stress: performs effectively under time pressure, or in the face of setbacks, disappointment, opposition and stress. Doesn't get irritated, or anxious, but stays composed. Adapts his or her behaviour to suit the new situation.

Tolerance: understands and accepts other opinions, standards and values. Can get on well with people from other cultures, and of different ages.

Determination: carries out decisions with conviction, and keeps a cool head in the face of setbacks.

Tenacity: sticks with a particular problem or view until it's over or a particular goal is reached.

Perfectionism: sets high standards for him or herself and for other people (colleagues/subordinates), and makes it known. 'Adequate' is not good enough.

Sense of responsibility: clearly feels wholly responsible for the results achieved, even if he or she has only made a partial contribution.

Loyalty/affiliation: believes in his or her own function or role within the organisation, and its value. Goes the extra mile for the company, even if it doesn't coincide with his or her own agenda. ('He who pays the piper, calls the tune').

Friendliness: stays cheerful in all circumstances – even under pressure, or in difficult situations.

Self-discipline: sets his or her standards and sticks to them. Makes it clear he or she is responsible for own behaviour and its consequences.

Independence: can work on his or her own. Decides when 'the boss' needs to be consulted.

Self-confidence: demonstrates faith in his or her own performance.

b. Interpersonal (relational) behaviour

Assertiveness: forceful in dealings with others; can take the lead (if desired); is decisive and will take risks, even when only in possession of limited information.

Customer-orientation: tries to identify customer needs and centres his or her subsequent sales behaviour on these.

Leadership/person-oriented: directs and guides colleagues in their job performance and further development.

Listening: can pick up important spoken information. Asks questions. Focuses on responses, and analyses them. (As the management expert Levitt said: 'The true manager develops the ability to hear what others do not say'.)

Ability to express oneself: can clarify ideas and opinions in understandable language, with the correct intonation. Also, takes the trouble to listen to others, which includes amongst other things making eye contact.

Oral presentation: expresses him or herself clearly and uses the necessary means in order to present ideas and facts. Does this enthusiastically and animatedly. Tailors the content of his or her story to the audience.

Appearance: makes a good first impression on others and can maintain this.

Persuasiveness: can convince others of a certain viewpoint in order to gain co-operation and agreement for particular plans, ideas or products. In a conflict, he or she uses his or her personal influence. Flexible and 'negotiates' in order to reach a compromise.

Co-operation/team spirit: can function as a fully fledged team member, and make effective contributions, especially when the group is working on something in which he or she has no direct personal interest. Enjoys co-operative working and takes the needs and wishes of his or her colleagues into account.

Written communication: presents ideas, opinions, plans, proposals etc skilfully, using correct grammar and in plain English. Formulates his or her thoughts intelligibly and convincingly in report form.

Sensitivity/empathy: proven awareness of (the feelings) of other people, of the environment as well as his/her own influence on them. Behaviour shows recognition of the feelings and needs of others. Demonstrates understanding, without being intrusive. Can put himself/herself in their shoes.

Sociability: doesn't find it difficult to get on with other people. Approaches others easily and mixes well in company.

Teamwork: able to participate in a team, even when not in charge. Makes effective contributions, even when the group is concerned with something of no direct interest.

c. Managerial Behaviour

Ability to stay one step ahead: can think ahead and thus take situational changes into account.

Organisational awareness: can see beyond internal problems and possibilities and therefore adapt to them. Also, takes account of consequences for fellow workers, customers, suppliers, and so forth.

Commercial skills/market orientation: demonstrates insight into commercial situations, with as much customer-oriented behaviour as possible.

Supervision: oversees subordinates' tasks and activities effectively, and reacts appropriately when goals change.

Delegation: can divide his or her own tasks, decision-making capabilities and responsibilities correctly amongst staff, to get effective involvement. Aware of the level at which a decision can be taken. Sets up and monitors procedures and processes.

Leadership/group orientation: can get ideas accepted. Stimulates individuals and groups when performing tasks. Disciplines subordinates when necessary. Takes the initiative on essential actions, and team relationships. Initiates activities and makes use of helpful sources. Uses the correct style to attain group goals. Keeps track of progress, and evaluates. Motivates, gives vision and inspires. Develops the skills and competencies of his or her colleagues.

Management identification: can identify with the concerns and problems of management.

Community awareness: interested in various social and community problems, developments and issues. Well-informed on these subjects, particularly in business matters, and makes use of this knowledge effectively in his or her own job or for the company.

Independence: undertakes actions based on his or her own convictions rather than on pleasing other people. Willing to divert from the 'official' line. Goes his or her own way.

Entrepreneurial spirit: looks for possible openings with existing as well as with prospective customers. Will dare to overstep the mark to achieve this.

Organisational sensitivity: aware of the influence and effect of his or her own decisions and activities on other sectors of the company. An awareness of how decisions come about in the organisation. Able to make a good assessment of what is (or is not) possible within the organisation.

Planning: can set priorities effectively and demonstrate (via an action plan) what actions are necessary for other people to perform in order to attain a particular goal (within a particular time-frame), using the manpower and resources available. Takes care of preparation, co-ordination and execution.

Stimulation: encourages subordinates (and others) to develop their competencies further, and gets excited about certain plans, ideas, tasks etc.

Supervision of progress: appears to be aware of the necessity to monitor progress; supervises the progress of tasks and processes; undertakes necessary actions.

d. Motivational Behaviour

Energy: can be effective over a long period to a high standard, when the job demands it. Can work hard; has stamina, and vitality. A self-starter. High output.

Initiative: can spot chances and take them. Would rather be active and influence situations, than passively wait.

Performance motivation: sets high standards for his or her own work and that of others; dissatisfied with an average performance. Makes full use of time and resources. Completes a task, no matter what barriers are in the way. Believes in 'self-management'.

Zest for work: seems as though work is essential for his or her well-being. Wants to exert himself or herself, and be actively busy in his or her job.

Work tempo: keeps up a quick pace for long periods.

e. **Intellectual Behaviour** (Some intellectual behavioural dimensions are 'brain teasers'.)

Analytical reasoning (numerical analysis): can identify problems and gather relevant information. Can process numerical (financial; statistical) details accurately, and come up with sensible interpretations. Makes decisions based on logic.

Short-term memory: capable of storing a lot of (relevant) information in the short term.

Critical thinking: can reason logically, draw reasonable conclusions from the facts, identify options, distinguish between weak and strong arguments.

Capacity for learning: capable of picking up new (and complex) information quickly, and applying it effectively. (Useful, if your new organisation finds itself in a fast-changing environment).

Making judgements: capable of weighing up details and possible courses of action, in light of certain criteria, and coming up with a realistic evaluation.

Problem solving: can develop different solutions for problems. Weighs up which one is the best solution, keeps an eye on alternatives, and feasibility.

Numeracy: can perform mental calculations quickly and without errors.

Strategic perspective/vision: possesses the intellectual capacity to uncover the broader picture from details. Looks at this from a 'distance' (the so-called 'helicopter view'). Sees possible implications. Takes these into account as well as the sensitivities of those inside and outside the organisation, before proceeding with planning or taking action.

Professional knowledge: appears to have essential professional, technical and commercial information at his or her disposal. Innovative behaviour: willing to offer new solutions, insofar as this is relevant to the job in question.

TIP When the employer requests your attendance at an AC, ask for a list of behavioural criteria (or 'qualities') against which you will be evaluated. You will therefore already know what to take into account …

Read the behavioural dimensions through carefully and take them in well. Otherwise, you will come across terms in your report that make you think: Oh no, something else to learn … You don't want to be caught out!'

What type of tasks to expect?

You will have to carry out various exercises. There are group and individual simulations. A typical group task is for example the group discussion.

Every agency has its own typical exercises, the way it evaluates candidates and its norms can also differ. For you, this can mean that your way of tackling a task may be evaluated as 'good' one time, but as 'inadequate' a second time.

Role play

The role play constitutes a standard component of almost every AC. Why? Because, in a well designed role play, the candidate can demonstrate a wide range of (managerial) skills. So, someone's manner of judging, their decisiveness, speed of thought, flexibility, sensitivity, listening ability, persuasiveness and persistence can all be evaluated. The assessors will also see how well you know the 'social codes'. In other words, how do you get it on with others? How do you approach them and speak to them? What type of people do you enjoy working with and which ones do you find more difficult to get along with? Everyday people, or real extraverts? Are you a democratic leader during the role play or a dictator? How do you come across? And does this correspond with the job's requirements?

The Bad News Talk is a form of specialised role play, whereby you first receive information about a department and a staff member. After a (sometimes short) preparation period, you must 'speak' to the member of staff about: dismissal, transfer, salary cut and so on. How would you do this in practice? See chapter 9 for a detailed discussion.

Fact-finding

You must give advice on a particular problem, about which you have earlier received little information. How do you go about this? How do you structure it? Does it have a logical structure? Do you outline one solution, or several alternatives? Which solution would you recommend? Dare you stick your neck out? Or do you let the other person decide?

Analysis/Presentation

On the basis of too little or alternatively too much information, you have to give a presentation, after preparation, on a particular plan or problem, e.g. a new marketing or investment plan. Perhaps, you must present your plan to a board of 'directors'. (See chapter 12).

Coaching talk

Can you develop your team? You will be observed to see how you handle your staff and if/how you delegate. Which tasks do you teach your staff?

What's the reasoning behind this? Do you let them set their own limits on what they can do?

Planning task

In this simulated management task, you must plan activities for a number of staff members. For example you will be given a large amount of company information, and your task is to plan an in-house move, where you must take account of holidays, sickness and personnel turn-over.

Interview simulation

In this role play, you are on the other side of the desk, interviewing someone. And your aim is to get to know as much about the other person as possible, using effective questioning and listening. An example: you are mediating a conflict, whereby you must find out about the causes and background to the dispute. Another example: an interview – where you are of course NOT the applicant! Obviously, this last role play is used primarily for personnel managers, but this is also a possibility for line managers with far-reaching staff responsibilities.

'Business game'

In a business game, a broad commercial problem is simulated, usually by a computer. You are director of a company (or marketing manager, or another key player). The market situation (e.g. purchase of materials, competitors' prices, extensive advertising campaign by leading competitor, etc) is changing rapidly. With little time to prepare or think, you must respond fast. A small error one way or the other, and your company could go bankrupt. Management games are often conducted on a group basis. We will not be looking at this task in more depth.

 Many candidates fluctuate from fear to hope (two basic human emotions) when invited to an AC. What are YOU afraid of? Seeing the new job slip away from you? Getting stuck in a career rut? Becoming or remaining unemployed? Missing out on a promotion or training? Afraid of failing in front of colleagues or bosses? Fear is a nasty companion. Hope is a better friend. It offers you a view into the future; a higher salary; a better life. Your fear is easily sensed. Don't let it get that bad. Stay optimistic, because the price of fear is rejection.

How you are evaluated will depend largely on the type of role play it is. A bad news talk taps into different behavioural dimensions than an advisory talk. Read more about this in chapter 9.

> *TIP* It is a good idea to read a lot about role plays. Even better: practise, train and get information about the standard required. Then you can match your behaviour accordingly.

The advisory talk

You must present a recommendation to one of your superiors. How do you approach this task? How do you structure your response? Can you produce a logical 'story'? Do you offer one solution or several? Which solution do you favour? Or do you let the other person to choose?

Provocation and blame

You are apparently provoked, challenged. You are attacked in either a professional or personal sense. They are trying to find out how you cope with stress. You are accused of having performed a project badly. You have messed up. Do you blame your boss, another colleague, the supplier, poor materials, or are you someone who can accept full responsibility – and all the consequences? And moreover: do you tussle over the question of blame or do you try to solve the problem by doing something about it? The latter approach scores highly with the assessors.

The in-tray exercise

The aim of the most well-known and most used AC component is to pinpoint a number of different skills: **planning and organisation; ability to delegate; management control; judgement; setting priorities; decision-making; problem analysis; initiative; written communication; organisational sensitivity; independence,** and **administrative capability.** Chapter 10 will help you achieve a 'good' in-tray!

> ***TIP*** When evaluating your performance in this exercise, they are particularly interested in your planning and organisational abilities, your decision-making ability (and the quality of those decisions) and how you delegate. They also want to know how you deal with time pressure and too little information. After this exercise you will probably have to justify your decisions in an interview!

Writing notes

Management applicants can expect the note-writing task. One possibility is that you will have to produce something after analysing and interpreting written material (e.g. reports, balance sheets, etc). Some details are perhaps unclear, too detailed or confusing. Or essential information is missing ... Have you noticed what's missing?

Group exercises

ACs make use of various group exercises – some examples of which are provided below.

Meetings

The candidate either plays the role of an ordinary attendee or (more often) the chairperson, in a meeting with his future colleagues. (We recommend that you refer to specific books on how to behave in meetings if you wish to know more about this subject.)

What kind of meeting can you expect? You may get the 'soft option'- they'll ask you to lead a 'normal' meeting, the type that takes place daily in your new organisation. But don't be overly surprised if they ask you to defend a particular standpoint, in the face of opposition from everyone else there! Be careful not to be too conciliatory, because you may well come across as a weak manager, someone who cannot reach his own objectives. But the other extreme also poses dangers: if you force your arguments down others' throats, then you will be labelled an autocratic (or dictatorial) manager. Most organisations prefer democratic managers. You can see that you must match your manner to the organisational culture.

Budgets

Another popular group exercise is setting a budget for a commercial or 'non-profit' organisation, and dividing up duties. Together with the group, you have to reach an optimal decision (compromise). A variant is the committee meeting. You are on a committee which must share out dividends from previous year amongst different departments. Obviously, you want the lion's share for your own department. But your colleagues have already sussed you out! Your task: to come up with a solution together with the other committee members which is clever, flexible and convincing. (Remember that you want to reward your department's efforts, but that you don't want your colleagues to lose face. Basically, everyone must leave the committee meeting as winners.) We are talking about so-called 'win-win' negotiations here.

Promotion

You must discuss a list of possible candidates with your colleagues and defend your choice.

Group games

These activities demand a certain division of labour. The group must solve the problem (under your leadership.) Sometimes, the activity requires a certain amount of physical effort, – such as assembling a machine. Remember that, generally, they are trying to establish if and how you assume leadership of a team. Can you delegate tasks? Can you co-ordinate? Can you motivate people?

Planning

In a management simulation exercise, you may be asked to plan the activities of several staff members. In some cases, it may be necessary to revise your plans in light of sickness, holidays, or staff turnover. You may also be asked to draw up a staff rota.

Leaderless group discussion

Sometimes roles are clearly defined and you are given a certain part to play, but on other occasions you have 'complete freedom. The underlying objective of the group discussion will affect your 'playing'- do they want to see your co-operative behaviour or how you manage a group (conflict).

The leaderless group discussion dates back to pre-AC days. The underlying idea is that 'natural born leaders' will come to the fore in every situation – in the group discussion, as well. This logic seems reasonable but is flawed, however. People can learn how to become leaders!

In the leaderless group discussion, the assessors are looking for several things, amongst others.

- Who become(s) the leader(s)?
- What type of leadership does he or she demonstrate?
- How do you help the group to reach decisions?
- How are problems amongst members solved? (How do you convince others?)
- Can you set realistic and clear goals?
- How is consensus reached in the group? (How willing are you to reach a compromise?)
- Which techniques does the leader use to manipulate others? (How do you negotiate?)

'Integrated' assessments

The AC can be seen, and is often presented, as a battery of individual tasks, which bear no relationship to one another. But the test bureau can also accommodate all individual simulations into one large task or a couple of combined tasks. This is more efficient, because there is no need to give more than one background explanation. It may also better approach a real life situation.

In a typical integrated assessment, after reading a detailed background explanation, the candidate begins with a solid task: the in-tray exercise. From here, he or she can deduce that there are different 'dialogues' to perform (think of a bad news discussion with a colleague who has seen a promotion slip through his fingers, or an evaluation talk with another colleague); the marketing plan in the in-tray must be analysed, and missing information must be filled in via fact-finding. Such an assortment of tasks would then be presented in its entirety to a group of investors (assessors). Finally, a meeting would be held on the subject, either internally or externally. The candidate can spend the whole day on such an integrated assessment.

The term 'assessment centre' has a threatening ring to it. That is one of the reasons that the name is sometimes replaced by 'development centre'. That sounds more optimistic. Beware of this term! This is just an ordinary AC, where you will be evaluated. Don't be misled by the friendly comment that they will 'only' be looking at you in order to develop you further or to evaluate which courses you must attend to perform your job better.

> ***TIP*** If you are struck by something during your (latest) interview, then bear in mind that this may be an important dimension in your assessment.

> ***TIP*** An interview forms part of every AC. The behavioural dimensions on which you are judged when carrying out the tasks can also form the basis of the interview!

The ORCE model

This stands for Observation, Registration, Classification and Evaluation.

Observation: Everything that you say or do is being observed. Your written work has been read through, and commented on. Does this mean you must behave like an 'ISO 9004' standardised man or woman? Not at all. But spontaneity can lead to consequences. Even your non-verbal behaviour is being held up to the light. The observer is all fired up, and so are you. But, luckily, they cannot read your thoughts! Perhaps, the next development in occupational psychology will be the 'thought centre'.

Registration: The researchers don't stop at pure observation – ultimately, they are being paid on their ability to gather proof, and that means in print. Your behaviour is therefore defined, on paper. It wouldn't surprise us if this primitive business disappears in the future and it goes straight onto a handheld computer. Then you'll see assessors very busy with their newly acquired toys!

Classification: Your behaviour has already been classified into the behavioural dimensions which were handled earlier in this chapter. It is usually a matter of a limited number of dimensions, between 6 and 10. Case closed?

Evaluation: The last step, for the time being at least, is for each observer to give his or her evaluation, on a five or seven point scale. Let's say we are talking about the 'listening' dimension. If you seem to be an excellent listener (in a role play) and all assessors agree, then you might get the top score, a 5.

 Sometimes, the assessment day is filmed. Can this happen without your express permission? Do you have a choice? What are the consequences of refusing? Perhaps you will have to explain (in your defence) why you are against being filmed. Who owns the film? Do you first want to know the purpose of the film? Who will see it? What will happen to it after use? Do you yourself want a copy? You do have some rights before your 'soul' and face is captured for eternity.

The assessors

The assessors are the cameras and the microphones of the AC. They register and describe your behaviour in terms of certain behavioural dimensions. They spend the whole day looking at your behaviour and then go off to confer. Because they are all sniffing at the same thing!

If a candidate's behaviour is striking either before or after the assessment tasks – e.g. behaving in an arrogant or unfriendly manner – then this will be included in the final report. Because in any type of psychological investigation, anything goes. The client will be tremendously grateful ...

The employer's assessors are often one step higher on the corporate ladder than the candidate. They think it necessary to have a good overview of the job. Research has proven that those at the same corporate level probably make better evaluators, especially with behavioural dimensions which are easy to verify! (Shore et al.)

Time management

Every assessment task has a clear time limit. For a role play, you often have 15 minutes' preparation time for example, then a further 15 minutes for the role play itself. For an in-tray exercise, the selector will ask for an hour of your time. So, you know exactly where you stand – that's always nice.

Admittedly, there are some tasks where every candidate must work against the clock. But, in principle, there should be sufficient time allowed for each task. Nevertheless, candidates still have problems completing the given tasks in time. How does this arise?

1. The candidate thinks that one hour is an 'endless amount of time' for the in-tray exercise, and then notices that the egg-timer is running out faster than expected.
2. He or she gets distracted by all types of irrelevant details – e.g. in the in-tray exercise. In other words, he or she does not distinguish between important and unimportant material. And that's bad news for a manager!
3. The candidate has difficulty concentrating – thoughts wander off into less productive pastures. Perhaps this has something to do with fear of failure.

If you don't finish within the 'agreed' time limit, then (according to the selector) you have a time management problem. Not only during the assessment, but also in real life. And that will come out in your report. We are speaking about a 'quantitative' problem here. If you tackled the most important issues, but unfortunately did not have enough time to tie up the loose ends, then the problem is not so serious, and can be overlooked.

It is more damaging if you have a 'qualitative' time management problem. By this, we mean that you have made no distinction between important/unimportant issues, and you have tackled all the problems together in a higgledy-piggledy fashion. They won't like this at all!

You should not run into any time problems, if you take heart of the following advice:

a. Time passes much more quickly than you think. Not only when you're enjoying yourself, but also in an assessment task. So, use your (stop) watch.

b. Differentiate between major and minor issues. Solve the most important problems first.

c. Don't get distracted in the in-tray or presentation exercises, for example, by the selector and his or her accomplices. Keep an eye on the time!

TIP Despite everything, you may still run into time difficulties, but don't throw in the towel, or tackle things too quickly. Because what is most important to the assessors is to see **how** you have completed the given tasks. Quality rather than quantity.

For various reasons, the selection agency can decide to 'turn up' the time pressure. In this case, the unsuspecting candidate is given a task, which can either not be completed within the allotted time, or only with great difficulty. Or the selector will say that 'there isn't much time left' or 'that the time's nearly up'. Another method (which is not used very often) is making the telephone ring on the candidate's desk.

Who are your opponents?

The real 'flesh and blood' people whom you come across during your assessment day are either role players, assessors or sometimes a co-ordinator. A large team! The number of people can also be much smaller: the role player is also the assessor, and we'll call the leader of this one-man band the co-ordinator, also known as the director, who manages the evaluation. He or she might be the intermediary between the client and the selection agency and will be responsible for a large number of logistic issues and your personal well-being. In some agencies, the co-ordinator introduces him or herself to the candidate; but, in others, his or her identity will not be revealed.

The role players can be psychologists at the agency (who will have nothing more to do with the assessment), professional actors or even well-meaning amateurs, or assessors who perform a 'stage show' for you. The role player's art is to behave as naturally as possible, just as someone from the (imaginary or real) organisation would do. Furthermore, this person has to ensure that the same role play is performed for each candidate, to be able to compare candidates.

Some critical points regarding the AC

Scientifically speaking, some criticism can be levelled at this method, some of which apply equally to psychological tests. The afore-mentioned problems of reliability and validity play a role here, too. (Please refer to chapter 1 for a critique of tests). Moreover, an element of subjectivity creeps into the assessors' judgements, no matter how well-trained they are. And, of course, the predetermined evaluatory criteria may be chosen somewhat randomly. Where do you draw the line, say, in determining the extent of someone's democratic leadership? What happens when several assessors are discussing your behaviour and they disagree: whose opinion has the deciding vote? And why this person in particular?

A journalist remarked that the proponents of this method find it difficult to provide convincing proof of the AC's supposed objectivity. Can you really draw meaningful conclusions about a candidate's future performance in the job from his or her behaviour during an AC? The eminent Dutch psychologist Hofstee has noted: 'discussions about assessment centres are very much governed at present by amateur, ideological and public relations motivation'.

8

Simulating Your Own
Assessment Programme

Each of us carries the seeds of greatness within us. They must only be cultivated. But, all of a sudden, you are thrown back on your own resources, standing naked and alone, before the assessors. After reading this chapter, you will not, because you will have a fairly accurate idea of what to expect. This chapter offers you the means to chart out the assessment day in advance. Admittedly, this is not a perfect map (that is obviously impossible to achieve, because you cannot take the wishes of the employer who is financing the investigation into account); however, you are building up a solid body of knowledge, so that the agency cannot ensnare you in its web!

What to expect?

In chapter 7, you became familiar with all types of assessment tasks – showpiece tasks as well as those which are used less frequently. But here, in the comfort of your armchair, how will you get to know how hard life may be in the AC?

The first thing to do is to find out which qualities and skills are being measured. You may well cry: 'How do I find that out, for heaven's sake?' That shouldn't be too difficult because the trail is already laid ...

1. In in-house assessments, the qualities and skills are known already (to the boss and the personnel manager). If the organisation is an open one, or if you have a good relationship with them, there is a good chance that you will hear the necessary information.

2. If this is not the case, then you might be able to ask a friend, acquaintance, colleague, 'friendly' personnel manager or someone else

which behavioural dimensions have been used in similar cases. Perhaps you can get hold of a relevant assessment report.

3. Some agencies are very free with their information (most are not, however), and let you know in advance at your own request which behavioural dimensions you will be measured on. Go ahead and ask! What have you got to lose?

4. Often, you can winkle out the necessary details from the job description. Use your imagination! Of course, you can flesh out these details with other information, from the job advertisement, for example.

5. And finally – if you have paid attention (and made notes!) during the interview with the employer or the headhunter, you will already have detailed information.

> *TIP* If you already know that an assessment centre forms part of the recruitment process you can ask the 'right' questions at the interview. Questions which can then be 'translated' into qualities and skills required in the job. As a guide, use the list of behavioural dimensions from the previous chapter.

Your own programme in seven easy steps

The following steps will help you on your way to produce your 'own' assessment in the comfort and quiet of your own home:

1. Following the methods described above, determine the qualities and skills on which you will be assessed.

2. Relate these qualities and skills to the list of behavioural dimensions described in the previous chapter, where applicable.

> *TIP* The same behavioural dimensions may be measured by different tasks.

3. If this doesn't work, then study the list of behavioural dimensions from the previous chapter and divide them into three: which dimensions will

definitely be tested for this job: which dimensions will probably be tested, and which will not be tested. Then, after making this first selection, you should go through the 'definites' and 'probables' with a fine tooth comb. You should be left with about 6 to 10 dimensions.

4. Do these dimensions fall roughly into the following five main categories: individual behaviour, interpersonal behaviour, management style (if relevant), cognitive style and motivational behaviour? If not, then make sure that some of those in other categories are included.

5. You are now ready to 'translate' these dimensions into the appropriate measurement methods/tasks (see appendix 1). It will become apparent that some qualities or dimensions are going to be measured by more than one method. And vice versa, most methods measure more than one quality. To spare the reader, the appendix contains only the most important types of task.

6. Next, look at the 'timetable' (Table 1). You will find here estimated minimum and maximum completion times for each task (including pre- and post-discussion time). Remember, in most cases a day's 'assessing' includes an interview, often intelligence tests (category: cognitive behaviour), and personality inventories. Add all these together and you have 6-8 hours. Have you been invited for a whole day's assessment and is the 'task time' much longer? Then, you will have fewer tasks – or be spending the night (not horizontally) at the agency.

7. You've done the basics; now you must fill in the gaps, which means looking at the appendix. There are examples of all the assessment methods in this book. Read them thoroughly and you will know what to expect!

Table 1 – Estimated time allocation per task

Means of measurement/task	Time (min/max) in minutes
In-tray	60-180
Group exercise	30-60
Analysis	30-60
Presentation	30-50
Role play	20-40
Fact-finding	30-110
Intelligence tests	20-60
Personality tests	15-40

Interview (un)structured   30-90

Other tests   15-45

How is your behaviour evaluated?

We went into great detail into the AC fundamentals in the previous chapter, about behavioural dimensions and assessors. You have to have some knowledge of these, because they evaluate (score) your behaviour. Two or more evaluators observe most of your assignments. Whilst you toil, drudge and sweat, they are evaluating your behaviour, armed with the list of dimensions, often on five-point scales. Here is an example:

TEAMWORK

1   2   3   4   5

Through their training the assessors know what to look for when 'teamwork' is being assessed. (You too, if you've read chapter 7.) Totally independently, they each award a mark on the five-point scale. When all crosses are placed in the same box the judgement is unanimous – a good thing. Every agency places its own meaning on these figures. For one agency, the figures might represent the following:

1. far below average
2. below average
3. average
4. above average
5. well above average.

The assessors must not shirk from noting down everything which strikes them about your behaviour. If you're an above average 'nitpicker' who tends to blow your own trumpet, they will probably be writing that down. If you continuously drum your fingers on the desk, then this will not escape the tireless and diligent evaluators. In both cases, they will place both observations under the heading 'non-verbal behaviour'. Wicked selectors may add to this: 'uncertainty' or 'restlessness'.

However, how you express yourself verbally is also noteworthy. Do you talk about yourself in the first person, or address yourself as 'one'? Do you call the interviewer by his or her first name. Do certain catch-phrases (negative and positive) fall from your lips?

Overall assessment rating (OAR)

In many ACs, it is decided in advance the minimum number of points participants must achieve in order to 'pass'. A simple matter of adding up. Assume that ten behavioural dimensions are being measured on five-point scales, whereby 1 is the lowest score and 5 the highest. The employer is not looking for just a good candidate, but an excellent one. The first-rate candidate must achieve an OAR of 10 x 4 = 40 points. This is above all a handy and extremely objective means of selection: just look at the number. But, despite this numerical approach, there are still some problems.

Assessors are merely human. They do not always agree with each other. They don't get out their laser guns and start shooting at each other, but they need time for a frank exchange of views. An important matter is whether the evaluations correspond closely – for example, a 1 and a 2, or a 1 and a 3. If the distance is greater, then the relevant dimension is prematurely and unceremoniously ignored. Because what it means is that it is not clear to some of the assessors whether or not you have displayed the desired behaviour. Or it means that you have done well, according to one assessor, but done badly according to another. No evaluation can be made from such information. In other cases, the assessors (peace-loving people that they are) try to reach a compromise.

Are hard and fast requirements always set down? Or do assessors look for what is striking about someone's behaviour? (This is known professionally as exploration). The latter does occur, too, but it does allow a lot of room for subjectivity.

Assume that an organisation wants to select a top manager on the basis of ten dimensions, which have been determined by the whole selection team. The smart girl or guy they're looking for will have to amass at least 40 points in total, i.e. score a 4 on each dimension. Three candidates are subjected to the assessment tests. The end result shows that candidate A has 38 points, candidate B has exactly 40 and candidate C has 43. In this cold, hard world, only one conclusion is possible! Candidate C's family can put out the flags! Or can they …?

One of the assessors – a manager with the employer – begins to fret. Candidate C is a great guy, and has really performed well, but he is also arrogant, and doesn't really fit in with the sombre, middle of the road and run of the mill company. Candidate C gets the elbow. Competitor B does not have the confidence of the two agency's assessors. There's something fishy about him. Is it his bad breath? Or the fact that he makes little eye contact and looks past you? Or does his work history have some 'bald patches', as it appears from his CV and from the interview?

But you can really have a good laugh with Candidate A! And go for a drink with her! After one day, the four observers have the feeling that they have known A for years. In short, subjectivity has been dragged into the reasonably objective AC. Is this a good thing?

So, what happens if no one candidate reaches the necessary number of points? According to convention, the employer must begin a new recruitment process. The exceptional candidate has apparently stayed at home. In practice, the wine is sometimes watered down, and then a candidate with only 38 points takes home the job. Subjectivity has set in.

And what happens if two candidates both achieve more than 40 points? Is the highest scoring candidate automatically the best? Or do other factors play a large part in the decision making process? Yes – and again subjectivity creeps in.

Suppose that the candidate who has reached the desired number of points is also described as unpleasant (or too hard, too soft, or whatever). Perhaps the manager (assessor) who must shortly work with her doesn't like her. What then? A subjective decision is taken.

From this, you can learn two things:

- the AC is sold on its objectivity, but subjectivity creeps in the back door
- if you are not the number one candidate in terms of points, don't give up – the race isn't yet over!

TIP   Whether or not you actually solve a problem, in a role play, an in-tray exercise or in the fact-finding task, is less important than how you go about finding a solution. Because there are often several possible answers. If the assessors want to know if you take a flexible approach, demonstrate this by offering several solutions.

Disqualifiers

In some ACs, so-called 'disqualifiers' are set up: these are behavioural dimensions where you must definitely achieve an adequate score (e.g. at least a 3 on a five-point scale). Because the employer finds this behavioural feature is so important for performing the job effectively that nothing less will do. Compare this with the core subjects of the national curriculum where you must achieve a minimum standard. An example of a disqualifier is no clear demonstration of persuasiveness, which the employer esteems vitally important in the salesperson he or she is taking on.

As a candidate, can you 'see' these disqualifiers? Yes and no. On the yes side: you might well guess that some behavioural dimensions are essential (such as the afore-mentioned persuasiveness). On the no side: not all assessments make use of disqualifiers and naturally you don't know all the whims and quirks of the employer. Careful reading of the job profile and the advert, an in-depth conversation with the executive searcher, and an interview with the employer can all help you to pick up on disqualifiers.

How do you want to come across?

Blessed are the meek. But that's not how you want to come across, or how you want to be described in the final report. So how do you want to be painted? As an intellectual? A business person? An ageing hippy? Do you want to get a 'competitive' or 'co-operative' stamp on your report? What does the job require? That's what it's all about! As you see, there are a lot of things to be 'sorted out' beforehand.

What you definitely do not want is to come across as a black and white thinker. Being able to see both sides of an argument is a good thing but don't overdo it! Introduce some humour – yes, it is possible within the bounds of an AC. A couple of philosophical remarks always do well (without appearing too airy-fairy). Talk about the environment and nature, if it comes up. You can suggest, for example, that observing people on the shopfloor is a form of anthropology. And enjoying nature also means: sitting outside a cafe in the summer and watching the world go by.

Use a technical term now and again. Kaizen, the Japanese method of continual quality improvement, is a good one. Or refer to a particular management philosophy that you adhere to (now that you have read the book on it!). Never forget that in AC Land you will often be asked more about your underlying motivation or for further explanations. See also chapter 14, under 'language usage'.

Finally, remember that the ideal manager has a warm heart and a cool head.

Making requests

You will notice to your horror that in many assessment tasks that very little information is handed to you on a plate. (Or sometimes: too much!) If you merely ask where the rest of the details are in order to complete the task, you will be met with a blank stare. Or you will get the answer that all candidates get the same task. Nothing more, nothing less. Life is hard and information expensive. That means that you must phrase requests carefully when you find yourself in this situation.

> ***TIP*** If you are dying to go to the toilet outside the times allotted for this, then ask for a 'toilet break' before you start a new task. This won't impact on your net preparation time.

> ***TIP*** 'Just being yourself' or 'playing for a draw' is often not enough. The hunt for excellent candidates is on. Give a great performance on the assessment day. Keep on your toes!

9

Role Plays

One selection agency explains role plays – workplace simulations in ACs – as follows: *'There are several different types: a sales call, a job evaluation, a presentation, a training session, a 'bad news' talk with an underperforming staff member, an advisory session, etc. You will have time beforehand to study the situation and prepare your approach. Then, the role play itself will start. During the role play there will be one or more participants or listeners. There will also be an observer present who will make notes. After the role play itself, your approach will be evaluated for effectiveness according to a number of criteria.'*

In this chapter, we will explain why the role play plays such a large part in the AC. We will point out how to use your imagination and creativity, and how to handle (difficult) role play 'partners'. A useful list of the most popular evaluation questions awaits you, together with their model answers. At the end of this book we offer mini-course 3 , 'a general problem solving model', to be applied in role plays.

Why have role plays?

An AC without a role play is like Wimbledon without tennis. It's hardly surprising, because in reality it is 'unnatural' to be a leader without good communication skills. Moreover, the one-to-one role plays produce instant results. Not only can the recruiter see that the candidate has lovely (but lying) eyes, but his words may give him away.

In a well-designed role play, the candidate can demonstrate a whole range of (managerial) skills. Amongst other things, an assessment can be made of someone's ability to judge, his or her decisiveness, speed of thought, flexibility, sensitivity, listening skill, persuasiveness, and how much one 'sticks to his guns'. A role play can extract a great deal of information from you, under the motto, 'The truth will come out'. It is also a means of looking at your 'social behaviour'. In other words, how do you get on with others? How do you approach them and speak to them? What types of people do you seem to work well with and what types of people are less to your taste? Quiet, modest folk or real show-offs? How do you come across, as a democrat or a dictator? And does this correspond with the demands of the job?

Generally you will be faced with more awkward situations in the AC than in real life. That makes sense, because anyone can cope with offering someone a pay rise or extra time off. The role play would be over in 33.58 seconds, without the assessor being able to assess how the candidate copes with trickier situations, and what characteristic behaviour he or she demonstrates. In a difficult role play, the 'partner' can pile on the pressure and make things very awkward. How you are evaluated will depend upon the type of role play. A bad news role play starts from different behavioural dimensions than an advisory meeting.

How it works

So at last, it's about to begin ... You have been given two sheets of paper – standard instructions for this (and every other) role play and (a generally short) description of the role you are about to play. We will illustrate this point with an example:

> For the next 30 minutes, you will take part in a simulation exercise in the form of a one-to-one role play. A simulation tries to replicate a real-life work situation as closely as possible. The simulation exercise involves a conversation between yourself and one of your staff. You will be asked to do the following:
>
> 1. You will have 15 minutes to get into the role. Read what your role is, together with the background material in the accompanying literature.
> 2. After 15 minutes, you will be shown to a room where you will meet your partner for this exercise. He or she too has a role to play. It will not be possible for you to step outside your role; he or she will pretend not to understand you. The conversation will last for about 15 minutes. You must monitor the time yourself.

The preparation period allows you to think about the problem, make notes, complete an analysis and how to approach it. This period varies from 5 to 30 minutes, but is usually about 15.

Prepare very thoroughly! Don't think you can just jump straight in and that preparation is for wimps. That's just not common sense. In reality, effective people are always prepared.

Be systematic in your role play preparation. Structure your ideas. In order to achieve this before anyone else, you can make use of the model described in mini-course 3. This has three advantages:

1. It gives you somewhere to start. It's like a roadmap to take you to your destination.
2. You are being evaluated on your systematic approach to this type of conversation. You will gain points for planning, organisation and goal-directedness.
3. A logical step-by-step plan works well.

In the preparation period, you should write down for your own use the **aim of the role play**. What do you want to achieve? Which points do you want to get across? What information should your partner have by the end of the talk? What (fundamental) change should occur in his behaviour?

If you have no aim in view, then you will hardly be in a position to structure or lead the conversation. Furthermore, afterwards, you will be evaluated either in writing or verbally. An assessor may ask about your **role play objective**. If you never had one, or it appears so … then the inevitable question will follow: why then did you have this conversation? Definitely not a good sign! Get into your role. Get a mental picture of the company and of the person with whom you will be holding the conversation. Think about your relationship with him. Do you use first names or are you more formal? Is your colleague older or younger and what does this mean in terms of hierarchy and experience, and for your approach? What type of person will be sitting opposite you – enthusiastic, negative, anxious?

Regard the role play as a game of chess. Think in advance how your partner opposite will respond. How will you reply to certain questions? Is it easy to fathom out your tactics? Are you revealing your 'hand' too much? How far ahead are you thinking?

> *TIP* Your plans, ideas and intentions for the role play are all good. But remember that the assessors cannot see your noble thoughts, so they cannot measure them. That's why you should translate them into observable behaviour. Overdo it a bit, just like on your driving test. 'Look in the rear view mirror'.

You have just received details of your role and the next 15 minutes are staring you in the face. So, try to answer the following questions in order to start and finish strongly on this task. The checklist below will be an important aid for you.

Your role
- Do you have sufficient information? (No, never!) What is missing?
- What role are you playing? (manager, salesperson, administrator)
- How high are you in the organisational hierarchy? (MD, Divisional Director, manager, supervisor?)
- Which tasks, responsibilities and powers do you have?
- What do you know about the organisational culture?
- What restrictions are imposed on your role?

Your partner's role
- Do you have sufficient information (No, never!)
- What is missing?
- What is your partner's job? (Is it actually described? If not, then remember this during the role play itself).
- How high is your partner in the organisational hierarchy? (Divisional Director, manager, supervisor, member of staff, temp?)
- Which tasks, responsibilities and powers does s/he have?
- What type of personality is s/he likely to possess? (Start with someone's negative characteristics).

You have to answer all these questions yourself. So, let your imagination go! In order to swing the game in your favour, it is useful to keep the following key phrases in mind:

- **Be encouraging**: try to get and keep the other person talking – as long as he or she is making sense. So, don't interrupt your partner unnecessarily.

- **Ask questions**: don't be satisfied with incomplete or incomprehensible answers. Some examples: 'What do you mean by that?' 'What else can you tell me about this?' 'How did that happen'?

- **Be informative**: provide your partner with clear information.

- **Confirm and summarise**: avoid imprecise or vague statements. Summarise what's been discussed now and again (or at least at the end of your conversation).

Professional actors

It's dirty work, but someone has to do it. Somebody has to be your sparring partner. At the selection agency, you will probably come across one or more psychologists who play a role (so many times ...). One of them may well be responsible for producing the report about you! There are also agencies who work with professional actors. And the AC might take place in your (potential) employer's company itself, so a future colleague may well be prepared to take on the role (of difficult customer!).

'But I just can't act ...'

Some people feel that they just cannot play-act any role at all – and they warn the selector of that in advance. A good sign? No. Because the agency will not be planning to use another method of selection for this one candidate, and dismisses your objections with: 'Acting? No, just be yourself and behave normally. There's nothing special about that, is there?' But, after all, what is 'normal'? And do you know who you are, without going into one of the most profound questions taxing humanity.

Can't you act? Just ask yourself: why not? Out of fear? (Of what? 'What experience led to this fear?') Lack of imagination? Or is it just that you cannot improvise in a role play – in other words, your flexibility leaves a lot to be desired. The solution – practise and train for your role plays. In fact, you probably do play a role at the bank, the baker's and at work, but you call it something else. You're already on the defensive – even before the role play begins.

As a (future) manager, you will have to spend each day acting, to a greater or lesser extent. Whether you like it or not, it is impossible in reality to tell your staff the 'truth' all the time; sometimes, you have to 'dress things up' a little.

Nervous?

Saying that you are (very) nervous before the role play can also lead to your downfall. Indeed, being a little nervous and tense is good and leads to a better performance. And in everyday life, we all have trouble with nerves every now and again. We must assume that you are only human.

Obviously, you will be trying to keep your nerves under control. Among other things, you can achieve this by being thoroughly prepared, so that you aren't faced with unpleasant surprises, or at least that you decrease the likelihood.

Nervousness is often fear. What are you afraid of? Letting the job slip through your fingers because of a 'bad test'? Leave your fears at home, or someone will sense them and taunt you with them!

Remember TIF

We would like to talk about the TIF of any role play: available TIME, given INFORMATION, and the FANTASY which you can bring to it!

Time: A very common division of time in a role play exercise is: 15 minutes' preparation, 15 minutes for the role play itself, and 10 minutes for discussion or evaluation. You really need the preparation time to note down the following:

- The aim of the conversation (What exactly do you want to achieve?).
- How will you achieve your objective? What strategy have you outlined to do this?
- Which problems could stand in your way? (Your partner will try to make your life hell!) What obstacles will they place in your path? (Don't trust anyone!)
- What approach will you adopt for the role play? (Will you follow a general model, such as in mini-course 3?)
- How can you demonstrate your warmth and interest in the other person? (What personal questions can you ask? Or do you want to keep it business-like and get straight down to business?)
- How exactly will you end the conversation? (What firm commitments can you take home?)

Information: For most role plays, you are given insufficient information.

On a side or half a side of A4, you will see a description of what you need. Will this be enough to produce a world class performance? You are getting exactly the same information as other people – you will have to make do! Asking questions because you feel you have nothing to go on won't help you.

Sometimes, a selection agency follows a different path: the candidate gets snowed under an avalanche of details (via appendices). He gasps for breath. How to decide what's important or trivial in just 15 minutes? But, of course, this is a typical management task: cutting out dead wood.

> **TIP**   Overeating leads to indigestion - it's the same for a role play. You really need very little information to produce an effective role play. Identify the key themes, set down your priorities and assume that some details will perhaps act as lightening conductors!

Fantasy: A good role player has plenty of imagination. Because without it, it is often impossible to get into the conversation. You will have to fill in the gaps yourself in the information provided. Don't be shy.

When you use your imagination, introduce ideas into the role play that make things easier for you. For example, give yourself specific knowledge about something, or put accomplished facts before your partner. Like a magician, you can pull not a rabbit but a letter of complaint or a memo from your hat: *'In my memo of 5th April, I already stated that ... Why haven't you conformed to this ruling ...?'*

How far can you go with your fantasies? Quite far indeed. If the assessors think you have crossed the boundary – which means they cannot identify certain behaviour – then you'll be the first to know. Don't protest too loudly, just get on with it. This is how to play the assessors' (secret) game to your advantage!

Keep a 'spare' solution or strategy in reserve!

Play safe. There is no guarantee that the solution you have chosen will definitely bear fruit. So, it is always advisable to have a solution or strategy that you can fall back on. You will be able to 'sell' this 'crisis solution' to the assessors at your evaluation. You will be applauded for your flexibility!

Formal or casual?

How should you address your partner – Miss Jones or Amanda? Which one do you prefer? The following points will help to clarify the choices:

1. Is the organisational culture of your potential employer formal and stiff or informal and easy-going? Try and fit in.
2. How is the task worded? Is it clear that the imaginary company is formal/stiff or informal/easy-going? Are the first names of both players provided in the role play instructions? If so, use them.
3. Do both players know each other? Do they have a history of working together, or is this their first meeting?
4. Still rather unsure? Then ask before the role play begins how you should address the other player. If you get no answer on this, then ask your partner at the beginning of the role play, *'Do you mind if I call you Amanda?'*

Creativity

Creativity is not daydreaming – not only is it the cheapest and most environmentally sound form of travel, but it is also one of the behavioural dimensions described earlier. And what's more, some assessment tasks can only be carried out with a creative approach. We will highlight this using the example below, where the candidate is playing the role of manager:

Case: the IT expert

It's 4.30pm, Friday afternoon. In the factory, the general manager is speaking to the company IT expert about a special task that needs to be carried out for the directors. The MD's secretary had just told him about this special job. The whole thing will take about six hours to complete, which means that the expert will have to work over the weekend (yet again). He is the only person in the factory with the necessary know-how to complete the task. Neither can the job be sub-contracted to someone from outside the organisation. This job is also highly confidential, and will be on the agenda for the Board meeting on Monday morning at 10. How can you convince this member of staff to work overtime?

And just when you think you've got his agreement … he tells you that he is otherwise engaged this weekend. He's got a flight to Paris booked for 7pm tonight (Friday) and won't be back till late Sunday evening. How do you solve this problem? You can find the key to this puzzle at the end of this chapter.

You need two 'types' of creativity for the role play. For starters, look for creative solutions during your preparation (you will get blank paper to write down the problem, your ideas and your strategy. Use it!). Think really hard and don't be pleased with the first (best?) solution you come up with. Don't be too satisfied with yourself too soon. Self-satisfaction leads to mental obesity. Keep looking for better solutions (within the given time).

But even after your first brainwave, it's still far from over. What is for you a flash of inspiration – you are so proud of your ingenuity – means nothing at all to your fellow role player. He or she has probably heard your solution 83 times before – but is not allowed to say so. He will also keep putting you under pressure. So, you want to be quick-thinking and flexible in the actual role play and able to come up with new or modified solutions at a moment's notice.

Hazardous pitfalls and nagging problems

Jobhunters are not actors, even though it helps. No-one expects award-winning drama. Watch out for the following pitfalls in the role play exercise:

1. You overact, grossly exaggerate. Don't do it. Just acting is difficult enough.

2. You poke fun at the situation. Now, humour in the role play is not a bad thing in itself, but don't go from the sublime to the ridiculous. (Remember that your partner is being paid for this and the assessor's time is also money!) Assessment is a serious business!

3. You set the wrong tone. Here is not the time or place for cynicism. What you are really saying is that you think the selector's method is no good. You stand a better chance of winning this particular battle with compliments rather than with negative or unpleasant remarks.

4. Your role playing partner comes up with all types of excuses for his 'failure'. Stupidity, laziness or whatever is explained by an excuse: the dog fell ill, the weather was bad (result: fewer clients visited the company), a colleague picked a fight, the printer delivered the leaflets too late, etc, etc. If you let yourself be sucked into long-winded discussions on these points, you've lost control of the role play and will certainly hit time problems!

5. Your partner can tempt you into talking about all types of nice or not so nice things which have nothing to do with the problem. For example, you offer your fellow role player a coffee (usually an imaginary one, as we're talking role play here!). A nice gesture. Your partner exploits this by talking for 10 minutes about the failure of the Brazilian coffee crop, the imminent departure of the tea lady which will mean lousy coffee and tea in the future, and then moves effortlessly into a diatribe about merger problems in the office. Twenty minutes have already passed before you notice that: I'm not in control any more, he's got me in the palm of his hand ... and then, he says, completely unexpectedly: 'Well, I've got to leave now. I must attend a staff meeting!' He stands up, shakes your hand, and thanks you for the coffee and the chat. You've lost the battle without a fight. Keep to the subject in question.

6. You don't have an objective and so just go with the flow of the conversation. But, if you don't know where you're going, you'll never get there...

7. You are vague. You speak in general terms. Your arguments can be easily demolished. A few examples: You call the other person lazy. He denies it fiercely. You think his reports are 'not so good'. 'They're just great,' he replies quickly. Your final attempt is: 'You don't get on well with your colleagues in the department'. 'I don't understand what you mean. I play cards with them once a week in the canteen', is his clever response. Avoid falling into this trap. The solution? Be specific and clear. Give factual examples of behaviour which the other person cannot deny. Have proof ready. Use 'written documentation' to back up your point. For example, you can say: 'In my memo of 24th April, I explained that you should keep your lunch breaks to 45 minutes, not an hour and a half. I reiterated this again on 15th May and 1st June, because your lunch breaks were still longer than company policy dictates. You have obviously taken no notice of my warnings...'

8. You are insensitive, show no empathy. You outline the problem and the employee looks crestfallen. During your tirade, she mentions that she is experiencing difficulties. You don't hear anything, and keep rattling on. Your partner alludes to marital problems. You don't pick up on this or you answer crossly: 'We're not discussing this here, what we're talking about is your below-average job performance'!

9. You can see by the clock that the minutes are ticking by and you're still miles away from reaching your destination. Bring on the time demon. A regular quiet look at your watch will help (but don't make it too obvious). Basically, make sure that you finish on time.

Using silence

How do you feel about silence? This is useful to know, because your fellow role player may use silence against you. Would this make you nervous? Do you start talking, chattering or gibbering? Or do you also keep your mouth (wisely) shut? Silent pauses can be deliberate (in order to put you to the test) but they can also happen, because your partner 'dries up' at a particular moment. The role play tries to simulate real life. So don't be afraid of silences. Use them, just as your partner does.

Dealing with difficult 'partners'

Most role plays require you to give your all. Expect plenty of opposition – you'll be in need of a stiff drink by the end of the day. You must persuade the other person to do something, as in the IT expert example. Your 'colleague' will give as many reasons as possible for not being able to work overtime. Can you take the wind out of his sails? Or do you just dry up, unable to reason, for a few minutes? Perhaps the only thing you can cry is: 'That's an order!' Or: 'I'm the boss – and when I say you have to work late, that's what you do. All right!' Some companies find this authoritarian approach works. But, in other more democratic organisations, you will soon be collecting your own P45. So, you must try a different tack, come up with some good arguments and perhaps play on the other person's feelings, because 'power' is something you don't really have.

You may be wondering if your partner (who has been instructed to make things as difficult as possible for you) will resist to the bitter end, meaning that you can never win this uneven battle. Yes, that can happen, of course. But, in the vast majority of cases, the other person will start to respond more to your persuasive ideas and go along with you. Success depends on your own skill at guiding the conversation!

If you have to deal with grumpy, intractable opponents, then it is a good idea to bear the following points in mind:

1. Ask open questions. These are questions which begin with 'why', 'what', 'how', etc., and elicit a response. For example: 'Why did you make that remark?' 'What do you expect to achieve by this?'

2. Demonstrate that you have some insight into your partner's way of thinking, let him or her know that you are listening and observing carefully. Some examples: 'I've noticed that you don't seem to be paying attention. Is something wrong?' 'It's struck me that you've been very negative about everything I've said or suggested ... What's going on?'

3. If you want to come across as more assertive, then the following standard phrases are for you: 'What do you wish to achieve by this (words or behaviour)?'; 'What are you trying to achieve by behaving negatively?'; 'Your behaviour is not helping, it's only making the problem worse ...'

4. Your partner will sometimes look for an escape route. For example, He pr she will start complaining about an old problem. Don't be drawn in. End it right there! If necessary, arrange another date to discuss it. Or show your 'colleague' how this problem could be better solved.

5. If he or she starts to complain about someone else in the company, then don't get involved: 'If you have a problem with Mrs Bigfoot, then take it up with her, not me'.

Are you a good listener?
You will have to prove yourself to be a good listener in the assessment centre (and in real life, too, of course!). There's a good chance that you will be evaluated and measured on your listening abilities.

Ten tough evaluation questions

Obviously, you will breathe a sigh of relief when a difficult role play is over. That's a shame, because you still have to answer 'a few' questions. And not just for statistical purposes. The objective here is to find out about your underlying motives and how you solve problems in your everyday working life. Don't be surprised if you are presented with one or more of the following questions:

Q1:   'What did you think about the task/simulation/role play you've just done?'
Q2:   'What did you want to achieve in this task?' (Or: 'What objectives did you start with?')
Q3:   'To what extent did you achieve your goal?'
Q4:   'Were you put under pressure in this task?' ('And how did you feel about that?')
Q5:   'What did you think about your opponent in the role play?' ('What are his or her strong and weak points?')
Q6:   'Could you describe your partner's personality?'
Q7:   'Did anything prevent you from performing at your very best?'
Q8:   'Looking back over what you did, how would you evaluate your own preparation for this role play?' ('Did you miss certain points, for example?')
Q9:   'If you had to do the role play again, what would you do differently?'
Q10:   'Imagine that the role play had been real. What effect would this have had?'

Tricky questions? Certainly! Because you can shoot yourself in the foot. And that can really hurt. But, of course, you are someone who isn't just satisfied with identifying a problem. You want to know how to solve it, too. We will therefore provide answers to each of the above questions.

Question 1 – 'What did you think about the task/simulation/role play you've just done?'

This could be answered in any number of different ways – including the wrong one. The best answer to this question is a further question: *'What exactly do you want to know from me?'* If your first spontaneous answer is, *'It was really difficult'*, then you will be faced with: *'What did you think was difficult about it?'* If you indicate in your answer that you have no experience with this type of task, which contradicts what you said in the interview, then you have a small problem.

Question 2 – 'What did you want to achieve in this task?' (Or: 'What objectives did you start with?')

It is impossible to undertake a focussed role play without having a clear objective in mind. You want to achieve something? That's why you set yourself a goal (write it down!), so that you can focus on it. If you say: *'I had no real goal, I just thought I'd see where it headed or what I could get out of it'*, then you have not attached enough importance to this particular conversation ...

Question 3 – 'To what extent did you achieve your goal?'

This is clearly a follow-up question. You can really hang yourself on this question, if you admit that you did not achieve your goal. *'What went wrong then?' 'Why didn't you change course in time, then?' 'When did you realise that you couldn't achieve what you set out to do?'* are some of the questions you can expect if you've dug yourself into a hole. Do you sense the accusing tone?

Question 4 – 'Were you put under pressure in this task?' ('And how did you feel about that?')

In many cases, some pressure is put on you. Because if the task was too easy, it would be difficult to measure your behaviour. Nowadays, stress-free jobs just don't exist. Therefore, the selectors want to know how stress affects you and how you cope. If you answer that you felt a lot of pressure was put on you, when in fact only an average amount was, then they know how low your stress threshold is. If you were actually put under a lot of pressure, but state that it felt okay, then you have passed the 'stress test' with flying colours!

Question 5 – 'What did you think about your opponent in the role play?' ('What are his or her strong and weak points?')

Take into account the fact that your 'partner' is also part of the 'plot'. Count to three slowly, before you launch into a character assassination. Pick up on some strong points (compliment him or her). Pick those areas where you also seem to have performed well. In this way, you can also pay yourself a compliment.

Question 6 – 'Could you describe your partner's personality?'

Naturally, after a role play, you should be able to provide a brief description of your partner's character, usually lasting 15 minutes or more! You have 'worked' with him, and have learnt to love him or hate him. What struck you about him? Can you elaborate? (For example, if you found your co-player rather indifferent, then refer to his manner of speaking etc).

Question 7 – 'Did anything prevent you from performing at your very best?'

Now, what really prevented you from performing your best? No one excuse works in the candidate's favour – why shouldn't give you your best performance on such an important day for your career? You went right to the edge but couldn't pull it off! (Whatever you do, don't start an academic discussion about what the word 'best' really means).

Question 8 – 'Looking back over what you did, how would you evaluate your own preparation for this role play?' ('Did you miss certain points, for example?')

If you admit that certain items went over your head during the preparation phase of the role play, then you must expect the simple question 'why?' And another obvious question: *'In your real working life, do you miss (essential) things just as easily?'* If the answer is 'No', the next question will be: *'Well, why did it happen here?'* A safe answer is to say that you had enough preparation time and you completed the role play properly. Perhaps, next time, you would emphasise this more than that – only by doing can you really learn. But that's next time ...

Question 9 – 'If you had to do the role play again, what would you do differently?'

It is sometimes a good idea to approach the next role play slightly differently. People are designed to learn. But, if you state that you will approach the same role play radically differently, the question is simple: 'Why?' but the answer is more difficult.

Question 10 – 'Imagine that the role play had been real. What effect would this have had?'

Did you do something because it was only a 'game'? Do you realise what consequences follow from that role play? For example, a subordinate is demotivated, a client doesn't want anything more to do with you, a promotion doesn't go through, there are a whole number of effects arising from your decisions. Have you dwelt on the potentially undesirable long- and short-term effects?

> ***TIP*** These types of evaluation questions are not only asked at the end of the role play. Take into consideration the fact that one or more of these types of questions will be put to you at the end of other tasks.

The bad news talk

This form of conversation can be expected if conveying bad news forms part of your future job, such as personnel manager. Often, a bad news talk involves announcing (impending) redundancies. But other difficult subjects fall into this category, such as a 'request' to work overtime, relocation to another department or office, a failed promotion or salary rise, extra help that was promised but is not forthcoming, a project or subsidy proposal that has been rejected, and so on. In practice, managers often experience difficulties with this type of talk. It is much nicer to congratulate a staff member with a pay rise or a promotion. It's more pleasing to see a smile than tears, rage or a withering look. In earlier times, the bringer of bad news was always put to death. That doesn't often happen in the AC.

Avoidance behaviour

Frequently, bringers of bad news demonstrate avoidance behaviour; they soften the blow by talking about everything else under the sun! Here is an illustration of how it shouldn't go: the manager must make Henry Dickens redundant:

'Hello, Henry, please sit down. Everything okay in your department? ... Yes? Cup of coffee? Yes, since we've got the new coffee machine, we're drinking more and more. Yes, er, no, really nice coffee. Now, Henry, I thought ... we have to have a talk ... haven't done that for a while, have we? Eh, a cigarette ... No, of course, you don't smoke, now where was I... Henry, as you may be aware, things haven't be running too well recently in the company. Profits are down considerably and blah, blah ... Therefore, we may have to ... You know that blah, blah ... Difficulties here, problems there, blah, blah. This obviously has an impact on the amount of work. So, unfortunately, we will have to let some people go. Of course, we are terribly sorry and I find it very difficult to do this. I really don't like people who tell others this type of thing. You have to understand, Henry, that you are one of the people we must make redundant ...'

The manager starts in a positive tone, which does not belong here. He tries to divert attention by talking about other things, digresses and spills the beans wrongly. The listener can feel the weight hanging over him and gets extremely annoyed by all these deviations. And the boss even suggests that he himself is the victim here! (An appeal for pity?)

The 'ideal' method

So how can you do it right? We distinguish three phases in the 'ideal' method and advise you to apply this simple and logical approach.

Phase 1: getting straight down to business

Be honest and direct towards the recipient (of the news) and convey the bad news as quickly as possible. Preface it with a short sentence, such as: 'I am afraid I have some sad news for you'. This shows that you understand the other person's difficult circumstances. It is important that the news is interpreted as irrevocable. Under no circumstances should you ever change your decision. Convey the message quickly and concisely, using simple words which leave no room for doubt: *'Henry, please sit down ... Henry, I'm sorry but I have bad news for you. Owing to reorganisation, some people must leave and you are one of them. I am afraid I must let you go, Henry'.*

The bad news itself should be accompanied by a very short background explanation. If you begin with a full explanation there is a good chance that the recipient starts speaking and the 'crunch' gets later and later. Once the bad news has been told the attention shifts straight away to the recipient.

Phase 2: the emotional impact of the message

The worse the news, the harder it is for the recipient to swallow. You will still have to get to grips with things, and calm the other person down. The best idea is to let the recipient express his or her feelings and listen to them. Confine your responses to reiterating your understanding of his or her feelings and to repeating and summarising the problems, which have led to the bad news. In short, be empathic. For example: *'I can see you're very upset about this.' 'You feel as though you've been badly treated, don't you?' 'You didn't expect this at all, did you?'* or *'Are you worried about finding another job?'*

In reality, a bad news conversation often lasts a while because the recipient keeps going over the same ground. The news takes a long time to penetrate: *'I can't believe it ... No, I didn't expect this ... I really didn't expect it at all.'*

In the AC, you don't have all the time in the world. Or rather: you have very little time! The best strategy is to let the unlucky soul blow off steam and then inform him or her that unfortunately you don't have much time, because you must catch a plane, for example, or take part in an AC as an assessor, etc. (In the evaluation discussion at the end of the role play, you can explain that in reality you would devote much more time to the problem).

Phase 3: finding a solution

At the end of the day, you have to look to the future. What comes next? This can only be broached once the recipient has grasped the news. (In reality, a follow-up meeting would be made for this purpose. In the AC, this is a poor choice, which is better avoided). The manager must now try to encourage the other person to think about his or her possible options. *'What are you going to do now?' 'Where do you think your future possibilities lie?' 'How do you think you'll get over this problem?'* There is room here for some brainstorming or mental table tennis. Perhaps the time has also come to reveal what you have in reserve, any good news. (Earlier we introduced you to the IT expert case, a straightforward and mild type of bad-news talk.)

Conflict

Another method used to see where your 'boundaries' lie is the use of conflict in a role play. Why should they make it easy for you on your assessment day? You will be confronted by a problem in which you would rather not get involved. Two staff members are squabbling and bickering with each other (known as conflict in today's terminology) and it's up to you to sort it out. According to the agency, as a manager, you should be good at offering words of wisdom.

You have been magically transformed into a poor manager with two hotheads in your department. ('Why can't they leave me in peace', is the first thought that comes to you. But life is hard – and then it's over.) So, you are not yourself party to the conflict; you are told to keep your distance, stay neutral and reach a solution with three winners – the two combatants and yourself.

What type of conflicts/problems could you come across? An example:

> You are playing the role of a manager in a research agency, who is leading a team of 15 researchers and 5 administrative workers. One of the researchers, who is exceptionally ambitious and productive, is constantly complaining that her reports are not being processed by admin on time. The admin manager totally disagrees with her on this. He believes that the admin staff work very hard and that she must adopt a different attitude. The problem comes to a head: a report must be processed ASAP (it must be ready within a week) and admin doesn't have enough time ...

How to begin? How do you solve this problem between two intractable opponents? Take a structural approach rather than just 'throwing water at it'. (Because otherwise you will have to solve the same problem 'next week'.) Look for a workable solution: the researcher must keep to the rules and regulations, just as her colleagues do. Furthermore, she must take into account the fact that admin also have work to do for other people and only have limited capacity. She must try to put herself in their shoes. If there are planning problems, there must be some sort of agreement between the two parties. Co-operation is the key word here, in the end everyone is working towards the same common goal. If both parties still cannot agree (for example because they cannot decide on priorities), only then should you interfere.

You should talk to both parties, but first they must make some concessions of their own, based on your advice. (A small word of warning: if you have to do this, then perhaps they are both dissatisfied with the solution.)

The CFS Model

The CFS Model is not only a mainstay for talks involving conflict, but it can also prove useful in other difficult discussions. It is already such a simple means of support, that we cannot make it any simpler!

CFS stands for Cause-Fact-Solution. Before you start the discussion, you should establish exactly what the problem is. In their excitement, some people jump in with both feet. But you can do your 'homework' in the preparatory period that is deliberately put at your disposal. But it is likely that the 10 or 15 minutes you have alone with your thoughts and your pen is not enough. That means that you have to gather facts during the talk itself.

That is, behavioural facts. You want to know who-did-what-to-whom (when and how?). Sentences like, 'Johnson isn't a nice man', 'Phil Roberts has such conservative ideas', or 'John Evans is sabotaging this case' will not get you one step further on the road to uncovering the true problem, let alone finding the solution.

Do you want to jump to the right, presenting a solution to the combatants? Or to the left, trying to trace the causes of the problem? Particularly if you are looking for an end to the matter, it is better first to investigate the causes behind the problem and – where possible – to eliminate them. In other cases, you may take the 'sedative approach' – just like aspirin, valium or alcohol – nice while it lasts, but the problem remains.

Fact-finding: gaining information and making recommendations

The fact-finding exercise doesn't seem so difficult at first glance. As the name suggests, it concerns gathering information and facts. But that is actually only part of the task. From the information you have gathered, you must then formulate a recommendation and present this to the 'customer'.

This exercise (lasting between 30-110 minutes) always concerns a company problem and makes great demands on your powers of thinking, particularly your creativity and your knowledge of 'commercial life'. Other characteristics that also play an important part here are: **desire to know** (wanting to know what's going on), **drive to action** (need to bring matters to a conclusion, to achieve a result) and **social skills** (listening ability; knowing how to influence others; persuasiveness and sensitivity).

An example of a fact-finding problem: a client has lodged a complaint about your company. Before you can help and satisfy the customer, you must first get hold of more specific details. Another example: you must put together a marketing plan, but you have too little information at your disposal. By asking shrewd and intelligent questions, you must gather those details which you need to write a good report.

 Most fact-finding tasks are characterised by a dearth of information. You must really work to get all the details you need. A danger of the opposite kind is too much information. So much is given to you that you can't see the wood for the trees!

Five phases

A large fact-finding exercise consists of five phases or parts, as described below. (There are also smaller variations on the market).

Phase 1: analysis (written)

The problem before you is deliberately rather vague. In other words, you are missing a lot of information, often the most important. So, without this, you cannot solve the problem – which is your task of course. In the first phase, which you get 15 minutes for, you will have to analyse the problem: check what information you have, and particularly, what information you don't have. What 'missing links' do you want to find? What really matters is formulating intelligent questions which give a broad view of the problem. Furthermore, you must do this pretty quickly because you have only limited time (what else is new?) to ask questions.

Phase 2: asking questions (oral)

The questions you have noted down (and others, which have arisen in the course of your conversation) are now fired at your opponent, the 'co-conspirator' from the selection agency. This psychologist, actor or whoever, can be regarded as a sort of 'databank'. You should draw as much information as you can out of him, so that you can get to the heart of the problem ASAP. Assessors will be watching your every move!

 A common error is to form an image of the problem too quickly. Everyone looks at the world from his or her own perspective, and facts can be easily coloured this way. Don't reach premature conclusions!

It is vital to formulate non-judgmental questions. Moreover, you must think of questions that relate to different aspects of the problem. Ask yourself which details you are (still) missing. This demands creativity, inventiveness and a good knowledge of how companies operate. Approach the problem from several different viewpoints, such as logistical, financial, social, commercial etc.

Phase 3: reaching a solution (written)

A short time is permitted for you to develop a solution or to formulate a recommendation on paper. Restrict yourself to jotting down a plan or an outline.

Phase 4: presenting the solution (oral)

You will now get more time to reach a (formal) solution and to explain it. Don't think that the fact-finding exercise is over, because the last stage is yet to come ...

Phase 5: discussion (oral)

If there is a fifth phase (and this is not always the case), then they will wipe the floor with your solution. With nicely put questions and phrases, they will set about your solution, the reasoning behind it and your defence, and demolish them. Perhaps, you too will feel finished off. This has nothing to do with your solution or recommendations – this technique doesn't work that way. So there's no need to think of your presentation as inferior or pitiful. Be positive: you now have a chance to show how resolute you are! The assessors observe your behaviour and see and hear how you argue and discuss. Are you flexible? Can you persuade others? Do you have your own, considered opinion? And, of course, they are equally interested in the quality of your solution.

> *TIP* How you come to this conclusion(s) is just as important as the actual advice that you give!

An effective approach

In order to stand an excellent chance in this task, you should allow adequate time for the 'pre-task stage'.

1. Quickly read through the information provided by the agency.
2. Cast a **critical** eye over the text. Ask yourself some questions and write these in the margin. Write down what you have in the way of information, but also what's missing! Always start with the broad questions and then go into them more deeply.
3. Do you already have some idea what the heart of the problem is, what the key issue is? Write down your ideas.
4. You will undoubtedly have more questions. Note them down.
5. A handy and simple technique is to apply the 'journalist's strategy' – who-did-what-to-whom-how-when-and-why?
6. Next, put together a list of questions for the talk itself. Begin with a few broad questions and then sharpen them up, make them specific.

(The filter technique.) Are they **relevant** questions? (You will be evaluated on this!)

7. And then the talk begins ... You fire questions. In some cases, you'll hit the jackpot but in others you will get no response at all. You will have to revise your questions and **improvise** if you want to build on the answers provided. Until a picture emerges – or you are told that the task is over.

The following in-depth example will enhance your knowledge of the fact-finding task.

> You have been appointed as external advisor to the Personnel Director of a multinational. A management trainee from one of the foreign divisions has been sacked by the Divisional Manager. He is said to be performing badly and must be sent back to the UK. The employee has voiced some objections: he had never received any prior verbal or written warnings. The Personnel Director finds this case rather difficult (particularly so as it concerns a management trainee) but has no time to handle it herself. So you have been handed the task. You must now get the necessary information to complete the task from the Personnel Director. (You cannot ask her for her opinion – you won't get it). You do know that the company subscribes to the 'sink or swim' management philosophy.

You will get 10 minutes for the first phase (written preparation), 15 for phase 2 (verbal questioning) and finally about 10 minutes to present your (thoroughly thought out) recommendations to the Director. NB. You don't know either the organisation or its staff members.

As you can see, there are always more questions than answers. And to help you on your way, here are some questions which you may well come across.

About the member of staff/trainee

- On what grounds has the person been dismissed?
- How long did the person work for the company?
- What were his terms of employment? (Temporary or permanent contract?)
- What exactly were his tasks and responsibilities as trainee?
- What did he do wrong (where and in what way)?
- In what areas were there problems? (professionally, dealing with

colleagues, dealing with customers, etc.) How serious were these problems?

- Had he received any warning (verbal or written)?
- Did he ask for help and was it given?
- Are there records of job evaluations?

About the Divisional Manager

- How long has s/he been with the company?
- What is his or her reputation like?
- How does s/he get on with fellow staff members?
- Has s/he often sacked people? On what grounds?
- How does s/he manage (co-operative or autocratic)?

About the organisation

- What procedures exist for management trainees?
- Are management trainees often dismissed after a short period? And for what reasons?

Suggested answer to the IT expert case (see page 146)

Divide the working time of 6 hours into smaller parts, such as three 2-hour segments, or other smaller time periods. Perhaps the first two hours can still be covered on the Friday afternoon, and perhaps another two hours can be found during the weekend trip. And, if the worker can start a bit earlier (8 o'clock, say) on Monday, and the item concerned can be moved further down the agenda, then the time problem is solved!

10

The In-tray

The in-tray exercise makes a guest appearance at almost every AC. In fact, in-tray exercises and ACs are practically synonymous. The in-tray task simulates a piece of management reality: dealing with incoming mail. In your in-tray, you will find a large amount of written information – mainly letters and memos but there might also be reports, accounts, telephone messages, notes, financial data and order forms. Depending on the amount of time you have, there will be between 10 and 35 items in your in-tray. This task doesn't just tap into your administrative ability but also into how you structure your work, how you bring order into chaos, put plans into actions and much more besides. Don't get snowed under with the mountain of letters and bits of papers . Read this chapter through thoroughly, so that you don't falter in the 'out-tray'.

What is being measured? How are you evaluated?

The in-tray task is assumed to be picking up on an exceptionally large number of managerial skills and qualities. Amongst others, we can identify: **commercial insight, decision-making ability, supervisory capacity, creativity, ability to delegate, to take the initiative, empathy, management control, customer orientation, planning and organisation, problem analysis and problem solving, written communication skills, ability to form judgements** (and the qualities of those decisions)**, ability to set priorities, resoluteness, exactitude, independence.** It is also interesting to know how you cope with unstructured information and incomplete data under time constraints – the list is very long. This diversity affords the in-tray task a central place in the AC.

> *TIP* Something important is going on in many in-tray tasks. For example, a merger is about to happen or mass redundancy; you may have a badly performing sales department; someone who 'sits on' important information; perhaps a departmental budget to be halved in the next 12 months or some other financial problem; an impending reorganisation, or plans to buy up a major competitor, etc. Amid the muddle of details, look out for **items that go together**, or that relate to each other, for the thread running through. (Sometimes this is the key to the whole thing!) And report back on this later on in the discussion.

Sometimes, you can get away with a short-term solution: a tablet to take the headache away. In other cases, it is better to assume that a full cure is possible. You will score better if you focus eyes and ears on the long term, when you indicate, for example, that there is something fundamentally awry in the organisation or in 'your' department.

In some in-tray exercises, you are evaluated to a greater or lesser extent in a casual way. However, in other cases, your written solutions will be compared with the 'expert solution'. Thus, you will score more highly if your actions correspond to the solutions previously formulated by expert managers.

Outline of situation and task

In-tray exercises can take place in rather diverse situations. A university institute, a bank, an hotel, an oil exploration company, a technical organisation, a retail chain, a transport company. In principle, the in-tray exercise can be found in any organisation which receives mail (and where a 'memo culture' prevails). Besides, in most cases it is not your knowledge of a particular field that is being tested in the in-tray exercise, but rather how you manage.

In order to make the assessment situation as real as possible, usually something like the following picture is outlined:

Today is Saturday, 27th November 2004. You are Mr/Ms Lee Hood, co-director of Beaute Ltd, a cosmetics manufacturer. You will be spending the next two hours in the office of Mr Casper de la Maniere, director of Farmacia, a pharmaceutical enterprise, located in Hinklewater, and Beaute's sister company.

During their holiday in Peru two weeks earlier, Mr de la Maniere and his wife were kidnapped. Since their ransom demand, nothing more has been heard from the kidnappers. The directors of the company fear that negotiations could last some time. (No publicity has been allowed for this case). Meanwhile, the work continues to pile up. You have been asked to sort things out today and to 'empty out' the director's office. Unfortunately, later today, you have to go to Hong Kong and Bejing for two weeks on your own company business. The taxi to Heathrow is already ordered ...

Mrs Amelia Hamilton, the director's helpful secretary, offered to give up part of her weekend to give you a hand. But, alas, you have just received a phone call from her husband to say that de la Maniere's right hand woman has been laid low by an awful migraine. She is in bed and cannot be contacted. You will have to spend two hours on Saturday alone in the gleaming glass building.

You must imagine that you are actually performing the job function described. Now, you are responsible for tackling the in-tray within the allotted time as effectively and efficiently as possible. Usually, for each item, you must specify what you are going to do with it and why. So, account for your actions, and jot down why you did this or that. All your actions must be in writing – your staff will have to proceed according to your instructions.

What letters and memos can you expect to find on the ill-fated tourist's stately oak desk? Ten diverse indications, for you to feast upon:

1.   A letter from Moot's Chemists, stating that the product, Digestamonide-4 causes skin rashes. Four patients have complained of this.

2.   Prof. Carti will be pleased to accept the job of company advisor next year. But due to the extensive foreign travelling he does, he hopes that Farmacia will understand if he finds it difficult sometimes to attend all scheduled meetings.

3.   A scrawled note from company lawyer, Jenkins, whereby she lets him know that the (packaging) contract with Konia Design Studios has not yet been signed. There are still some details not settled.

4.   Johnny Harmon, the son of one of de la Maniere's relatives and a pharmacy student, is looking for work experience. His father has persuaded him to contact de la Maniere... Is there anything going?

5. An anonymous internal memo, stating that two storeroom workers have recently been stealing pills. He or she doesn't know how many or which ones, but thinks it advisable to let the director know about it ...

6. The East Anglian Pharmaceutical Society invites Farmacia's director to come and give a talk in two months' time on the following subject: 'The great future of the pharmaceutical industry in a great country'.

7. A telephone message from Amelia: Lord Justin of Hinklewater has invited de la Maniere to a reception in 10 days' time to celebrate 25 years' service to the Hinklewater community.

8. Dr Julia Peters, QA manager, has handed in her notice after 2 years' service. She will be leaving on 31st December (her notice is one month). She has been unhappy for some time with the way in which her recommendations and suggestions have been received. She also notifies the director that she has accepted a similar position with Farmacia's greatest competitor.

9. A telephone message from Amelia: she spoke to the editor of the 'Post' yesterday, Mr Joe Stone. He is currently writing an article on the overinflated price of medicines in the UK and is asking for background information from all the major market players. He wants to make an appointment with de la Maniere sometime next week for a 1-2 hour interview. Please call!

10. Internal memo from Phil Warmer, Head of Finance & Administration. As expected, the figures for the third quarter were worse than ever. To date, the figures for the last quarter look disappointing. Please could you organise an urgent management meeting to discuss how to improve the results next year? (Don't forget that the company will be slowly grinding to a halt from 15th December onwards due to 'early' holidays!)

Of course, you might also come up against some heavy artillery in the in-tray exercise. Suppose that you are the Assistant General Manager of the South African branch of a multinational company. Your boss, the General Manager, has been away longer than originally intended and you must handle his mail effectively, and act upon these types of correspondence:

- an abusive letter from a revolutionary nationalist movement which is threatening to drive all multinationals out of the country very soon
- the president would very much like to visit the company's head office in the UK
- the mother of one of the French workers has died unexpectedly
- your largest local customer is threatening to go over to your chief competitor.

Other activities which you may also be asked to participate in, and as you can see, there is a wide choice of tasks on offer:

- convening or rescheduling a meeting (externally or internally, and informing all those concerned)
- calling, faxing or emailing someone (which also means, specifying the reason for and aim of your call/fax)
- drawing up a plan (or planning how to do it)
- asking for clarification on something that is (in your opinion) unclear or unusual
- placing an order
- inviting a client or someone else from 'outside' to attend something
- requesting a member of staff to attend something (e.g a performance review)
- undertaking any other activity which you believe will improve the situation – the choice is yours!

Three types of in-tray activities

Exactly what you have to do with all the 'bits and pieces' depends on the in-tray that you have to 'empty'. Broadly speaking, there are three types of responses, which can sometimes be combined:

1. Indicate briefly in bullet points (orally, written using 'post-its' on the letters, or listing key points on a separate sheet) what you are going to do with each letter, which action will be undertaken, and why.

2. Write some 'real' memos and letters of your own, which will also be evaluated for their structure and tone (use of language, customer orientation etc). Assume that a memo is 'a means of informing the recipient, and not an instrument of advancing the sender', as Levitt, the management expert, once cynically remarked.

3. You may be asked to keep a diary handy (sometimes it may be already partly filled in), so that you can note down new appointments and deadlines. It looks very professional if, a few days before a certain meeting, you write in a date and time to check if, for example, Joe Bloggs will really be ready with his report by the appointed time. Efficient use of the diary demonstrates your planning skills!

 Avoid double bookings! In many in-tray exercises, you are almost forced to do this ...

Three hours of sweat and toil?

In-tray tasks come in all shapes and sizes. A quick in-tray exercise must be done within one hour. The most comprehensive version of this simulated office task has the candidate sweating and toiling for three hours. Generally speaking, the higher the position one is selected for, the longer the in-tray task. (And of course, the more complicated the problems to be solved).

To clarify – in the (short) time you have available to you, you do not have to bend over backwards to complete everything. What really matters is that you 'demonstrate' how you do things in 'your' organisation – and let them see this, for example by keeping your diary up to date.

> ***TIP*** In some in-tray tasks, the only instrument at your disposal is your own fountain pen (you didn't take in a cheap plastic Bic, did you?!). In others, a fair assortment of tools is available: black and coloured pens, pencils, different markers, post-it stickers (of different sizes), rough paper, a small calculator. In some cases, you may even have use of a computer. Are you the worrying type? Then put a black and a red pen in your bag, together with a calculator and some post-it notes (handy as reminders). Just in case!

Time pressure and time management

Regardless of the time available, a lot of people come up against time difficulties. So, work quickly, keep your mind on what you're reading and concentrate. Note down things that you mustn't forget. In some in-trays, you are allowed to write on the memos and letters themselves. So, do it! Underline important passages, use a marker for crucial data, names and dates. Some people work too quickly and certain essential information goes over their heads.

It is probable that, during a (long) in-tray exercise, your activities will be interrupted by an interview. Your flexibility is not being tested here (except if you refuse to stop working on your task) – the selection agency are only doing it for logistic reasons.

In some in-tray exercises, you are not expected to finish within the appointed time. Little effective time management is needed. In other in-tray exercises, you will score badly on the dimension 'planning and organisation' if you don't finish. In yet other in-tray exercises, the 'inquisition' investigates the quality of what you produce: did you deal with the most important letters and memos and did you leave the unimportant ones? This is damage limitation.

Keep to the 80-20 rule: devote 80% of your time to the most important things, but keep some time in reserve to handle other items that need attention.

Any more questions?

After time up is called in this exercise, you will have to face a short (sometimes an hour long!) discussion where you will have to account for your actions and defend them. This is also a chance to see how you react to disappointment and criticism, if you are defensive, flexible, have your own opinions and stick to them. This discussion may be held directly after the in-tray exercise, or at the end of the day. Make sure that your written 'output' matches up with what you say in your defence, many hours later! You will be faced with questions such as:

- How did you approach the in-tray task? And what made you decide to approach it in this way, what reasoning lay behind this decision?
- How did you decide on priorities?

- What opinion did you form about the organisation, which you have got to know via the in-tray?

- You have been playing Mr Johnson for the last 90 minutes. What type of person is he?

Perhaps you feel like shouting: *'He seems a bit of a weirdo to me!'* Or: *'Can't you leave me in peace?'* You know that this is not very sensible, and instead you come up with a carefully worded answer, and report back in sugary terms over the 'person' whose shoes you have just been filling.

Why do they ask you these questions? Firstly, to find out if you can 'go beyond' the practical task. Did you think about what you did? Did you reflect? Could you identify with the role? Did you have some understanding of the difficulties facing 'him' and the solutions he chose? Remember that your answer can be a good selling point: if you claim that the manager you played is energetic, intelligent, a good problem solver and so on, then you're describing yourself!

Another question which comes up a lot is: *'What did you think of the in-tray exercise?'* Even here, you can give a positive response. Compliment the assessment specialist, praise him to the skies: *'It was very interesting and true to life. An excellent way of finding out about one's management qualities. This task is very relevant to my future job.'* (If you choose to give a negative answer, then expect the next question to be: *'What don't you like then about this exercise?'* Would you like to explain that one? You are forced onto the defensive. A bad position.

'If you had to do the same in-tray assignment again, what would you do differently?' An assertive answer is as follows: *'Nothing! Because I completed this task very well!'* If you sound doubtful, or admit that you would have done something differently with certain items, then you can expect the next question to be: *'Why didn't you make the right decision in one go?'* In short, you have the ammunition for an excellent defence at your disposal.

 Sometimes the discussion comes hours later. (A memory test, or a logistical problem at the selection agency?) You must then fully explain why you have carried out certain actions. They will ask about all sorts of details. Can you remember these 3 or 4 hours later? Probably not … make a mental note of your actions and any special details.

Standard versus specific

An in-tray exercise can be specially developed for the selection agency's client. Therefore, comparable (incoming and outgoing) post is used to that of the customer. There are two major advantages to this.

1. The situation is less artificial. The candidate who has already had to immerse him or herself in his or her future employer's organisation recognises a number of things and perhaps a couple of names.
2. The employer knows what 'good' responses are. He sets these against what happens in reality, or against company policy. In this way, he is able to evaluate if someone does or does not fit into the **company culture**.

The major disadvantage of this type of evaluation is its price tag. However, by far, most in-tray exercises are standard, and the disadvantage to you is that you are a logistics manager, who has to play the role of an employment agency manager.

TIP Find out in advance if you have to tackle a specialised in-tray. If so, prepare for it by immersing yourself in the company's problems. Generally, multi-nationals use specific in-tray exercises, but just once or twice you can expect one at a small selection agency.

In-tray advice

At first glance, the pile of paper that is called the in-tray looks chaotic. You have to bring structure to this chaos and get a picture of the organisation and the things going on in it. We advise the following approach:

1. Read the background information and instructions very thoroughly and critically. Without this knowledge, you will lose your way. Perhaps you will have already done one or more things, even before you get to the first item! *Systematic* and *ordered* are key words for the in-tray. Work neatly, or otherwise the 'MAMM Law' soon applies – otherwise known as 'muddle attracts more muddle' – and before you know it, you'll be lost in the paper jungle.

2. What is your name and function, what type of organisation is it (service, production, profit or non-profit), what is the starting point? What is the date? Be aware of superfluous details. (You will probably make no use whatsoever of a nicely laid out historical description of the firm, for example).

Confusion can be a deliberate part of the in-tray instructions. For example, a change of name (a secretary marries and adopts the name of her new spouse) or there are lots of sub-divisions, which are similar to each other but yet all very different.

3. If, in the instructions, you discover that you 'yourself' are not contactable for a week or so, that doesn't mean that you can't call, e-mail or fax anyone! Or that you yourself cannot be called. Even climbers in the Himalayas call their homes in Maidenhead via a satellite link to ask whether little Johnny passed his test or not.

4. Scan the memos, letters and other postal items and sort them out into areas of importance (projects etc). Look at names and dates! The most important letters and memos are not necessarily going to be at the top of the heap next to each other! Try to work out the context to the items. Put these items together in chronological order. You'll find that sometimes one problem is therefore already solved! Form a picture of the most important and most urgent problems, and prioritise. Make the connections!

 Reading in-tray items demands staying alert. Some mistakes may be deliberately included, so that they can scrutinise your eye for detail. Letters may have the wrong date; 'your name' is spelt wrongly; appointments have been made for impossible dates (30th February); order forms may contain errors (e.g, some are missing an essential signature); an internal memo which goes against the spirit of the company. Note these errors down on a **separate** piece of paper! This shows you are paying attention and have an eye for detail.

5. Think about the consequences of your actions.
   Example 1: if you give one of your staff a job to do (by memo) – you delegate a task – then you must give him or her a deadline and also note down somewhere (in your diary) when you will contact him or her, if you won't see him or her beforehand.
   Example 2: If you start an (internal or external) project, appreciate that this has **consequences** for yourself (in terms of time) as well as for others. Note that you can't possibly be in two places at once.

6. Show them your **empathic** side. Don't throw all your tact and social

skills overboard due to time pressure. If you come across as overly task-oriented, then you will be disqualified (from most selection procedures).

7. If you want to or have to write letters and memos yourself, then keep them short. But be customer-oriented if you're handling a commercial letter!

8. If you are not provided with an organisational chart, then make one yourself with the key players. You will see that putting together a staff chart is time well spent! It saves on reading time, reduces the chance of confusion and you can see reasonably well what responsibilities the figures on the chart have and where they stand in the organisational hierarchy.

9. In an in-tray, nothing is obvious. You must be able to offer **proof** for all your actions. In certain respects, this task is like a driving test (if you can remember that far back!). Every driving instructor advises the potential 'boy racer' to exaggerate looking in the rear view mirror (do it often and intensively). This is the only way that the examiner can see that the candidate is actually looking at the traffic behind him or her. Just saying, 'It's logical to watch the traffic behind you' is no proof. Don't assume that your actions are clear to everyone without further explanation, because even you always do it that way, the assessors don't know that!

10 If you are running out of time (we have already explained how this may occur), then think about bluffing: tell them that you're used to working at weekends, in hotels and other places and that you always carry a notebook computer with built-in e-communication facilities. (Unless the instructions state explicitly this is not the case).

11. What about enclosures? Some in-trays are full of these! Attached to letters and memos, you will find for example: planning notes, maps, annual reports, excerpts from brochures, other letters and memos, budgetary proposals, organisational charts, company history, marketing plan(s).

   If you go through all these enclosed documents in great depth over your coffee, then you're soon going to hit time problems. So, you will have to give them a 'superficial' glance. Just a thought – in most cases, the 'enclosed information' is wholly unimportant or of very little importance. These red herrings are added to test if you can keep focused on the big picture (as befits an effective manager). So, be warned!

12. How does 'your desk' look, while you're working and after the battle? Complete chaos? Will you ever find anything again? If *you* cannot decipher what you have written from your own scrawl, then don't be upset when you are asked curtly if this is typical of your everyday working behaviour. What can you say? Any answer is the wrong one.

Try to keep a few minutes in reserve at the end of the exercise. Tidy up everything neatly and leave a well-organised task behind you.

Towards excellence

You would rather score an 8 than a 5 on a nine-point scale! You want to be noticed, to dazzle and shine, and you can. Always ask yourself the following questions at every in-tray exercise:

1. Is this the best (most creative) solution I can come up with?
2. Is my response very obvious? (Will nine out of ten of the candidates come up with this solution?)
3. What else can I do with this letter? (For example, someone who sounds as though he will be off sick for a long time must be replaced. But also remember that visiting a sick colleague or sending flowers will make you go up in the assessor's estimation).
4. Am I thinking enough about 'my people' (also see point 3). Am I a 'people manager' or more of a 'paper pusher'?

11

Group Play

The lone wolf may be a genius or a fool, but most of us live by other rules. We must perform in the 'rat race'. (Okay, so generally wolves also hunt in packs.) And employers too want to know if and how you work as part of a team and/or if you are a 'natural' team leader. Group exercises also reveal how you influence others and how you contribute to the group. It is a useful simulation, because there are relatively few jobs where teamwork doesn't feature.

We will start this chapter with an explanation of the role which you may be allocated during the group exercise. Then, we will discuss the group discussion – an exercise that takes place quite often. You will read about different variations on the group theme and topics for discussion, such as 'Is man a true thinker?'

Next, we will look at the so-called 'building task', followed by the more formal meeting, which is applied less frequently in ACs. The mini-course at the end of this book will also teach you how to lead group discussions more effectively.

Your role

Group exercises measure various behavioural characteristics: amongst other things, decisiveness, creativity, flexibility, group-oriented leadership, initiative, negotiating skills, analytical reasoning, interpersonal skills, verbal communication, sensitivity and teamwork.

There are three variations in group exercises:

1. the candidates are left completely to their own devices
2. every participant gets his or her own 'script'
3. the candidates are left to themselves, but are not allowed to allocate any roles at all, such as chair or secretary.

Group exercises, such as a group discussion, are usually held with four to six candidates. Before the participants can form themselves into a group, they are given certain information.

1. **Type of task**: What exactly is the task about? What is the aim behind it, or rather, what are the assessors looking for in me? What must be achieved? What is the background to the task? Is it a situation familiar to me, or am I skating on thin ice? Try to establish very quickly what it's not about. Even better – think of a few possible answers, so that you are not caught out in the discussion.

2. **Building a picture**: From all the documentation you have before you, build a picture of what is required or desired. Put some priority listing on these wishes and needs.

3. **Reaching a judgement**: What are the possibilities? Compare these with the list of wishes and needs. Can you see a balance?

4. **Making a decision**: Make your choice and try to stick to it during the discussion, because you have really thought things out. But you will soon see that your fellow team-players (with the greatest respect) have reached totally different views!

In most group exercises, after preparation and the actual play, your part is over. The assessors then start work. But, of course, there are always exceptions. So there are exercises, where you must note down on a special form your views and preferred solution, which you have reached in the preparatory phase. You may not discuss these with your fellow team members.

How long does the group exercise last?

Group exercises come in all shapes and sizes, and that applies to their duration as well. Most last between 30 and 60 minutes, and there are a few which stretch to 75. And sometimes, the preparatory time varies from 15 – 60 minutes. A long task, all things considered, which may last about two and a quarter hours in total!

> *TIP* Use your preparation time **efficiently**, because often you will be given far too much information. All types of figures and tables from which you must elicit the main points. There may be details which you want to bring into your discussion. (The 12 pages outlining the company's history generally don't fall into this category.)

The group discussion

The group discussion is often aimed at revealing **management potential**. Therefore, you must try to become the group's (formal or informal) leader. In any case, you must **demonstrate** your ability to influence.

Group discussions are particularly appropriate for recent graduates. As one of the chosen few, you may well have to race against a large number of direct competitors, for several vacancies. For more senior posts, only a few candidates reach the AC stage, which makes it more difficult to hold a group discussion. Because anonymity now evaporates like water, this method is regarded as unethical. Apparently, this isn't a factor that applies to young graduates. But coming up against the competition has one advantage – you can look them right in the eye! You know how good they are and can respond accordingly. One example:

All participants get 15 minutes to prepare themselves for a 45 minute discussion. In this time-frame, a budget must be allocated to a particular activity, which will foster team spirit and loyalty within the company. The players all know their roles beforehand. Some will want to blow the whole lot on a gargantuan company party, with food, drinks and dancing elephants. Others prefer a training programme or a company outing. Yet others will be looking for a balanced distribution of funds.

If it is a question of allocating money to a good cause, then the players may be subjected to the following 'old chestnuts'. Candidate 1 wants to sponsor a lecture theatre or a university chair. What greater goal is there?! Candidate no. 2 proposes helping the poor in Africa. He would like to finance new wells. The third candidate thinks that the money should be invested in agricultural training and education. The fourth person wants to do something closer to home: the local football club needs sponsorship, because the MD's son plays football there.

Here are some other examples of problems looking for a solution: financial cutbacks; devising a marketing plan, from different viewpoints; implementing a new company vision or mission (and every participant has his or her own views...); setting up a new subsidiary – but where?; organising an agenda for a company visit – where all your 'colleagues' have something to say about it!

The discussions are set up in such a way that they necessitate a mixture of co-operation and struggle. The group must reach a joint decision – that requires co-operation. But each player must also look after his or her own interests. If there are £300,000 to be shared amongst 5 participants, and you only get £10,000, then you've performed badly! The reverse is equally true: the candidate who gets away with £200,000 by tough negotiating and not putting himself in other people's shoes, also ends up disqualifying himself.

Variations

Broadly speaking, group discussions in an AC fall into one of two categories. In the first type, only one hard and fast rule is laid down: that no-one should be appointed as chair, because the selectors want to keep the procedure as open as possible. (The chair would automatically have an advantage). For example: 'If the country is under threat, then the government should be free to gag the press'. The key feature of this type of set-up is that there are as many arguments for as against and fairly general progress must be made to achieve a good outcome.

> *TIP* It is advisable to practise beforehand with these types of broad problems. Think of a couple of examples, or get them from the paper. ('UN: should they go to war to preserve peace?') Then write down arguments for and against. It doesn't really matter what your views are - the aim is to learn how to play the game!

The second type of discussion occurs more frequently: finding the solution to a concrete problem that the candidates have already been allowed to study beforehand – for example, investing in a new factory.

Other exercises include: appointing a new senior Civil Servant, whereby each participant puts his or her 'man' forward and defends him to the death. The group must put together a brochure, again taking into consideration all the different interests represented by each participant. It will become clear that the interests you are promoting in such an exercise are often different, sometimes diametrically opposed, to those of your colleagues. It is very rare for a quick agreement to be reached. Because, if that is the case, then your behavioural profile cannot be compiled.

In the leader-less group discussion, one of the oldest assessment tasks, you are being observed to see who emerges as the 'natural' leader. One of the main criticisms against this task is that it does not predict someone's effectiveness as leader. It only shows what someone does in order to be seen as a leader.

 Each assessor is closely observing one or two participants. You can't afford to rely on a couple of sharp remarks or actions to get you through. Your competencies are examined continuously.

Positive comments

PCs are positive comments – and you should aim to make plenty of these during the group discussion. That sounds easier than it is, because negative comments spring to mind more than positive ones.

If you want to influence the group, you must make yourself heard. That doesn't mean that you should just mouth off – that won't achieve anything. No, you must say just the right thing to strike a chord with your fellow team members. The following PCs will help you along your way:

- 'That's a very good criticism. But it is perhaps more sensible now to stick to coming up with ideas.'
- 'Let's go round the table: what do you all think of the (3) proposals before us?'
- 'Let's just have a look at what we all do agree on.' (Differences can be handled at a later stage).

The building task

In a building exercise, you are asked to construct something with your group. Sometimes, this could be a enjoyable game or a challenging puzzle.

You have one clear objective: in the limited time available – you're not here for fun! – you must assemble a machine, for example. Often, the task is so large that the work must be carried out by the whole group (maximum 6 people). If the team cannot agree on objectives, implementation, division of labour, etc. then the job cannot be completed within the allotted time. And apparently there is a co-operation problem. Not a good sign according to the observers, who are paying close attention to how 'their' candidates work together. Because, for many jobs, this is very important. Other behavioural characteristics measured by this type of building task include: flexibility, supportive behaviour and all types of interpersonal skills.

The meeting task

Although many managers spend a lot of time in meetings – it forms an important part of their daily working life – this simulation (chairing or participating in a meeting) is infrequently used. 'Meeting techniques' may be the cornerstone in some selection procedures. We are not offering you a complete course on how to behave in meetings here, but just some key points to watch out for in general.

> *TIP* If you know very little about the 'rules of engagement' and formalities, and have little experience, then study the practical manuals on this subject and try to sit in on real meetings to capture their flavour. Even better, take part!

Although people who hate meetings tell another story, meetings are useful, because, in a relatively short space of time (or long, as opponents would say!), there can be an exchange of knowledge, information, opinion, observations, ideas, requirements and desires. In this more or less formal, businesslike group discussion, roles are often allocated to each participant: one is the chairperson, one is the secretary and others are ordinary members – from whom a contribution is nevertheless still expected.

Usually, there is an agenda and minutes are taken. But meetings can also have a much more informal feel to them, such as ordinary workplace meetings, where practical everyday problems are discussed.

> ***TIP*** Make sure that you do have an objective in 'your' meeting. And is it clear, or can it be interpreted in many different ways? You can improve your scores by voicing this criticism. But beware! If you go over the top, then you might be seen to be too busy with formalities, and regarded as an academic who cannot achieve practical results in reality.

Types of meetings

You will probably be involved in two types of meetings; each with their own goal: problem solving, or decision making. Take note of what type of meeting you are taking part in, because you will have to alter your behaviour correspondingly!

Problem solving

The group is seeking solutions based on information available. The structure of such a meeting may be as follows:

1. formulate the problem, linking issues together (is there really a problem?)
2. analyse the problem, establish causes and consequences
3. set criteria/guidelines (these must be measurable)
4. think of solutions
5. outline pros and cons for each solution.

Decision making

This is more interesting! You must now make a choice between two or more solutions. Which criteria will you use to reach these solutions? These are discussed and you reach a decision.

Chairperson's tasks

The tasks of the chairperson can be divided into 3 phases: before, during and after the meeting.

Tasks before the meeting

- **Orientation**: the chairperson must know who will attend the meeting, and what their function will be. In this way, you can also prepare yourself for their behaviour during the meeting. This is

especially good if there are certain interests playing a role (which is usually the case...)
- Deciding on the agenda.
- Outlining the goals for the meeting.
- Designing the layout of the meeting.
- Making notes for the introduction.
- Making notes on various matters to be raised (e.g. who will get the final say on each subject?).
- Estimating the time needed for different parts of the agenda (time management!).

Tasks during the meeting
As chair, you have a number of formal tasks to perform, such as opening the meeting, leading the voting, deciding how to proceed with a certain decision (acceptance, or rejection), and closing the meeting.

Tasks after the meeting
This involves checking the minutes, sending them out and making sure that any agreements are indeed being adhered to. You will not be faced with this during the AC.

It may well be that, as the chairperson or as one of the attendees, you will be expected to give a (formal) presentation. This means that you may have to explain something to the rest of the group, probably without a flipchart. See chapter 12.

12

Analysis and Presentation

It is estimated that about 40% of ACs make use of a combined analysis/presentation task. As the name suggests, this task contains two parts: analysing a problem (mostly with a great deal of data) followed by presenting the conclusion to 'management'. The analysis results do not necessarily need to be presented in an extensive form. They can also be disclosed in other ways, such as in a role play or in written form.

What is being measured?

Analytical and planning tasks tap into the following behavioural dimensions: **ability to adapt easily; ambition; commercial insight; scope of interest; creativity; flexibility; ability to take the initiative; adherence to management policy; attention to detail; planning ability, problem analysis and solution.** What is measured in a candidate's presentation? **Assertiveness, creativity, risk-taking ability, flexibility, ability to improvise, innovative behaviour, independent stance** and **persuasiveness.** If your employer is particularly interested in your future job performance as a versatile presenter, then additional items may be noted down.

Types of analytical tasks

In the small room where you are hidden away, you will find a pile of papers. You read that you will be playing the role of advisor and will have to report to the management on a problem. Your basic material is in writing – a few pages of printed text. If they really want to probe your analytical abilities, then you will find in this pile for example annual reports, company turnover, letters, reports and memos. You will certainly need more than 30 minutes to read them through properly. You must therefore look out for information which helps you to solve the problem.

TIP Make your advice positive, but don't lose sight of reality.

Analytical exercises often contain either too little or just too much information. You must fill in a lot of details, or ruthlessly separate the main items from the superfluous ones in order to perform well. Don't be distracted by the large volume of information with which you will probably be faced. Many reports, memos and figures seem to be unnecessary frills, but which can still do you some personal injury. The problems often concern specific but wide-ranging organisational issues. Think about a decision on IT, investment in a project, choosing the site for opening or closing a branch. Your task is: to get to the root of the problem and present the 'right' solution.

TIP You will see that there is often more than one logical solution to the problem or more than one piece of advice you can give. Still, you have to choose... So, take into consideration that it is more important how you arrive at a solution (advice) than which side you come down on.

One example of a 'limited' exercise is to find a solution to an important global problem. You can get your teeth into 'reducing third-world debt'. What do you think about solving an environmental problem such as 'dumping chemical waste'?

Such exercises require you to be locked away alone, to give you time to explore the problem and to consider a plan of action. If a presentation is also involved, then you have five minutes on how to save the world. (Not a lot of time really for a comprehensive solution.) Don't forget to explain at the last minute in your notes that the available time is really far too little to deal fully with such an enormous problem. And then all hell breaks loose ... because you'll spend the next 10 minutes (or more!) defending your arguments against a barrage of questions from the assessors. What they want to judge amongst other things is: do you stand firm? Do you stick to your position, come what may? Or, do you blow with the wind?

The next task is even broader:

'You are George Baker, who works in the Head office of a bank. The Board of Directors have requested you to advise them on an efficiency operation. You have 45 minutes to study all the relevant material, before you have to present your reasoned judgement before several members of the Board. You must outline why one out of two branches in a region must close. Both offices are still making money, although profits are falling. Furthermore, the idea has been put forward that the overlap between clients and services is so large that two offices, so close to one another, are not really producing much extra.'

Note – With other similar problems, you are asked to recommend which of three hospitals, three hotels or three factories should stay open, with the other two closing down.

Plough through all the material (financial and economic details) and come to a decision.

The total time allotted for such an exercise is usually between 30 – 60 minutes, excluding the presentation itself, the question and answer session and the post-presentation discussion.

Suppose you have to give advice on the purchase of a new computer system. First you make an analysis of the problems and opportunities of the organisation in general. Then, you turn your attention towards the computing needs of the company. Your first thought is that it is not a bad idea to buy the cheapest system in difficult times like these. But, wait, experience has taught us that users always need more capacity than they think at first. And, added to that, companies want to (and have to) expand – and they often do. Your advice as an optimist: buy the system with the greatest capacity – the most expensive possibility. But then you consider the other realistic option: the middle category as regards cost and capacity. **You can defend all three decisions equally well!**

> *TIP* Cast a critical eye over the numerical information provided. Do the essentials make sense, or do you spot some illogical or incorrect information? Rely on your own logic and experience!

Different perspectives and systematic approaches

Always look at the problem to be analysed from different viewpoints. If possible, turn the problem on its head. You have been asked (not implored or begged) to shed light on one aspect, whilst there are (as always) more sides to the same story. The world is a complicated place. Watch out for the hidden agenda!

It is even better to apply a systematic approach. Thus, for example with an organisational problem, you can tick off one by one which problems and solutions can be found in the following areas: logistics, finance, social (personnel), commercial, IT, legal.

Such a systematic approach will score highly, because a skilled manager will be expected to check on each of these issues. With a computerisation problem, for example, ask yourself what the financial and personnel-related consequences are of introducing a new system. (This could be general resistance to change; compulsory computer training; changes in the internal communications system).

For marketing problems, it is better to choose the five 'P's of the marketing mix: Product, Price, Promotion & advertising, Personnel and Place (of sales and distribution).

If you have to increase a product's market share, for example, then don't just harp on about price cuts. Also think about motivating your salesforce (with a suitable and justifiable bonus scheme), a striking advertising campaign or product quality improvements.

Another approach to problems is the SWOT analysis. SWOT stands for:

- **Strengths** – what are the strong points of the company or product? What unique characteristics does it have?
- **Weaknesses** – what weak and vulnerable points are there?
- **Opportunities** – which unique opportunities does the company or product have? For example, due to its cast-iron distribution network?
- **Threats** – what threats exist or can be expected? For example, parallel imports.

The strength of this approach lies in giving you a true picture of a plan or an organisation, because the systematic four-pronged attack forces you to look to the future.

How to approach the analysis task

1. Set a firm objective and a vision as 'problem solver'/advisor. What exactly do you want to achieve? (Is it crystal clear what is expected from you?)

2. Glance over the material quickly at first. This will help you to determine the relative importance of the different parts, which may be presented in a rather jumbled and haphazard fashion.

3. Look before you leap: ask yourself which details you absolutely must have in order to solve the problem and which details make some contribution to the final solution.

4. Look for the essential details. Note these down as a point of discussion or interest for the presentation to follow.

5. Have you missed crucial information? Possibly. So, formulate some logical assumptions. Use your experience where applicable. It is sensible to make it clear (during the presentation) which standpoint you started from.

6. Combine details and make an interpretation. Distinguish between key and side issues, and structure them.

7. Is it quality information? Are all the details and facts equally reliable?

8. It is sometimes handy to make a distinction between facts, opinions and interpretations. You are more likely to be attacked on opinions and interpretations than on plain facts.

9. An efficient method is to transfer the information to a matrix, so that in one glance you have an overview – and detect possible gaps.

10. If you have to compare two or three different scenarios (banking subsidiaries, hospitals, factories), then write down all the relevant issues and requirements for each outcome. For example, the issue of a hospital's accessibility – only a factor for patients? Now the accompanying requirement: accessible in less than 10 minutes? Or 30? And to broaden this out: think about public or private transport, and the car parks which go with it (at what cost?)

11. Take into consideration other possible visions and solutions. (In the ensuing discussion, you can beat them round the head with these.)

12. Those questioning you (the assessors) will not usually be in agreement with your vision, plans and approach. They fire difficult, critical questions at you and you will notice that they know the material better than you yourself! Logical, as they probably wrote it themselves! If this isn't the case, then they have certainly done this already with many other candidates. So, write down any tricky questions you are expecting and focus on these!

Presentations

Presentations form the 'centrepiece' of many ACs. Obviously, that it is not unusual if you consider that, for more senior (managerial and staff) functions, ideas, plans and campaigns must be presented to larger groups. This can take the form of special presentations, but also meetings, sales demonstrations, and conferences. Even if you expect to give few presentations in your new job, you may still be faced with this situational test.

Experts can discover a lot from your presentation: can you organise facts? Do you listen to and have respect for your audience? Do you pick up their non-verbal signals? Do you explain (even complex) problems plainly and clearly? Do you come over as relaxed and self-assured even during tense moments? Do you radiate enthusiasm? Can you get your message across? Do you get your audience involved? We could go on ...

Your name is Mark Mott, management consultant with Affia UK Ltd. You have been invited by Pyramid Growth Investments Ltd, who have branches in the UK, the Netherlands, Gibraltar, and the Channel Islands, to give a short presentation to their Board of Directors. One of the company's founders, Mr Bernard Cornfield, extended the invitation. He will be present, as will his fellow directors, Max Wells and Fiona Smith. Your task is to give them advice on purchasing a new computer network.

You have been working for the company for some time, and know that 'something's going on'. The three directors do not always see 'eye to eye' (very rarely in fact!) and staff turnover is huge. Company profits are growing annually between 30 and 40%; the number of personnel is steadily increasing (internationally) and two new branches are being planned: Germany and Spain.You have also noticed that the office costs are rising fast, averaging at least 30% per year. Purchasing a new computer network (quicker, more flexible, more possibilities) should bring down costs. You have received bids from three manufacturers. Pear's system costs £100,000 and has a fairly limited (but adequate) capacity. Bear Ltd is offering a system at £150,000 and Lear is offering a fantastic system for £250,000. All the proposed agreements meet the minimum required specifications. But some questions remain: what is the lifetime of the Pear system before it becomes too small? And is the Lear system too expensive at the present time? The costs of changing systems are substantial (at least £60,000), if you are moving from one brand to another. Running costs also vary between systems. Moreover, if you withdraw early from a hire agreement, you incur a hefty penalty (at least £50,000). (In an AC you would get a longer task with more information and even more complications).

Another example – a fictitious head office wants to relocate. But where to? There are two alternatives, each with advantages and disadvantages. Which place do you choose – and why? It may be obvious that it is mainly your decisiveness that is being measured here and how you convey your decision to a hungry audience ...

> ***TIP*** Inject some creativity into your presentation here and there! Your speech doesn't have to be scintillating, but certainly thorough and sparkling.

Preparation: who, what, where, when and how?

The preparatory work for the presentation is done in the analysis phase, beginning with the setting of goals. You must ask yourself what you want to make clear, where you are going. How do you want to come across? What response do you want to evoke in your audience? Next, you must do one of the most important things for a lecture: give it a structure. A logical structure gets your message across more easily to your listeners and your analytical skills will be valued more highly. You won't have time to write out (parts of) your presentation, so you must work with key words.

Look at which 'architecture' best suits your subject matter, including the central theme and key questions. (There are often several possible structures available). One such model is outlined below:

'How useful are psychological tests?'

- what are psychological tests? – define them
- why is selection necessary?
- arguments for
- arguments against
- what else must be taken into account, marginal issues
- are there alternatives?
- recommendations.

Know your audience

In the preparatory phase, ask yourself the following questions:

- What are the audience's interests and how do they relate to the subject? (For example, buyers, directors)
- How does the audience see you? Are you an expert, an outsider, or one of them?
- What do they expect from you? Advice? A decision? Impartial information? A recommendation to buy? A warning?

Humour

Humour is always a good thing in any speech, as long as silly Friday afternoon pranks are left to one side. Ration your humour. Not so witty? Then, don't force it during your presentation. You will do more harm than good.

Handouts

In many 'real' presentations, it is customary to give handouts to the audience before (or sometimes during or immediately after) the presentation, often in the form of one or more A4 sheets.

You can score highly on professionalism! How? Take a few blank sheets of paper (your rough paper) and give these out as handouts to each assessor (with plenty of eye contact!). You can explain it so: 'This handout outlines the key points in my argument. You can use this sheet to make notes, or for reference during the presentation'.

The 'delivery'

After your incisive analysis of the problem, it is now time to present your findings to the management. You can normally deliver your monologue in relative quiet; in principle, you are not to be interrupted. But, after the presentation, the assessors start asking awkward questions and casting doubt on your arguments. It is important to react appropriately to this. (Sometimes the assessors are senior managers who have earned their spurs). Happily, by the end of the discussion, they are much less strident. (Probably to avert the dangerous possibility that after the presentation, you could make their lives a misery!)

Try to involve the listeners now and again in your story. Ask some questions: *'What do you think about that? What personal experience do you have of this?'* It will liven up your performance noticeably. Make the assessors warm to your subject! For non-verbal behaviour see chapter 14.

Premature questioning

Advise your audience that your presentation will provide enough material for questions. You will answer these questions gladly, but would ask your audience to save up their questions until the end of your presentation (because this will involve less disruption and some questions may prove to be superfluous).

Don't exclude the possibility that the assessors want to test your assertiveness by asking questions during your presentation – and even by talking over you! If they succeed in this, then your presentation is destroyed before you know it. Take firm action: intervene and say loudly and clearly that you will be pleased to discuss your views with them shortly, but that you would firstly like to round off your arguments.

Answering questions

At the end of your presentation, you can expect some tricky questions. These questions will be directed mainly at the content of your argument, and to a lesser extent at your approach. You must decide for yourself if you are going to stand by your points in the discussion, or if you will (partially) go along with the views of one or more of your listeners. That's a choice between flexibility, opportunism and resoluteness! Answering effectively is an absolute requirement for achieving a good result.

Before you can answer a question, you have to understand it. If you have misunderstood the question – there's no shame in that – then ask for clarification. It looks really bad spending five minutes answering a question that was never asked. A good way to respond (to longer questions) is to check first if you've correctly understood the question and then start your answer.

It is very polite to thank the person asking for his or her question. You can do this by saying things like: *'I'm glad you asked me that,'* or: *'Your question brings me nicely to ...'*, *'this is an important point'*, or: *'This question allows me to look more closely at ...'*

Never let one person dominate the whole group. Give others a chance to speak. If you are answering someone, then make eye contact with him or her. But don't forget to also look at the others in your audience. Give them the feeling of belonging too.

Handling criticism

You will have to deal with a large dose of criticism! That's why it is important to be clear about your own opinions. Say what you stand for. Nothing is truly black or white. Perhaps you can (partly) agree with what your critics say.

Positive criticism is specific, clear, manageable and relates to issues that can be changed. Focus only on clear criticisms, not on vague remarks such as: *'I don't think this is clear'*. To handle this type of remark, you should ask for clarification or respond with a further question: *'What exactly are you unclear about in my presentation? Which aspects do you feel I've not covered thoroughly enough?'*

Audiovisual aids

Sometimes during an AC, you will have a flipchart, overhead projector or white board at your disposal. If this isn't the case, then ask for them. In any case, your request shows that you are familiar with these materials. And you can't fail on the assertiveness scale! Audiovisual aids can be a source of support in your presentation. Certain information is easier to grasp in the form of diagrams and charts than in words.

Just one more point: only use audiovisual aids if they add something or help you to emphasise a point.

Control your nerves!

Some characteristics of a nervous presenter are:

- hurried and fast speaking, resulting in the assessors being less able to follow what's being said (amateurs always speak far too fast!)
- poor articulation
- incessant playing with objects (pen, marker, ruler)
- walking to and fro
- fiddling and picking at face or clothing
- continually looking at the cribsheet, without reading it – because the speaker doesn't allow him- or herself time for it.

How is nervousness revealed in your case? Can you cover it up, or are you an open book? Remember that some tension, fear or nerves is good – it makes your performance even better. (Jargon: positive fear of failure). And, anyway, you are allowed to be a little nervous in these special circumstances. But showing it too much suggests that you're not used to making presentations, dislike doing it, are over-concerned with yourself, rather than with your audience. Conclusion: presenting is not your strongest suit – a shame, as it forms an essential part of the job.

13

Producing Written Pieces of Work

If, in your view, the goal of an AC is to learn more about your behaviour, then you are on the right lines. But your 'written behaviour' also falls into this category. You will have to show your skills with a pen in one or more of the tasks: a memo in the in-tray exercise, answering a letter of complaint (outside the in-tray task), interpreting commercial stats, writing notes, etc.

Are written tasks difficult? That depends on who is asking the question – and answering it. Compare the question with this one: 'How much grass do you have in your garden?' The answer depends largely on who does the mowing.

In this chapter, we will present examples of written material, including commercial information, letters of complaint and policy directives. But other written work which you may have to produce or which you may have to deal with will also be investigated. You will be informed of how you got on in your written work by way of ticks or phrases in your final report. If you enjoy seeing your name in print, you'll be disappointed – your assessed masterpiece won't be around for eternity! For further information, we refer to mini-course 2, 'Ten rules to make your script more readable'.

What is being measured?

Written tasks are obviously measuring your ability to communicate and express yourself in writing. A rather broad behavioural dimension. More specifically, are you able to construct a letter or an important commercial plan? And in passing, attention is also paid to your style, grammar, spelling and reader or client-orientation. Other dimensions which can be investigated here include **adherence to management directives, ability to form judgements, persuasiveness, planning ability, problem analysis skills, tenacity** and **self-confidence**.

A general case

> You must describe a situation which affected you deeply – use a work situation if possible. If you have never worked, then use an example from school or college. If you cannot answer this question, then you should provide a description of a company, organisation or department you know well.

As far as time is concerned, you are normally allowed 30 minutes to complete this task, but you may find you need longer. This is permitted. So, what is this apparently simple exercise actually about?

The instructions are deliberately vague. This is true for the task itself and for the time allowed. They are interested in the following aspects:

- Which event has made an impression on you, and why?
- Have you something useful to say?
- How do you tell your story? (In an adult fashion? Are you able to express yourself well? Do you separate the key themes from the side issues? Do you make things clear?)
- Do you use good English (spelling, style, grammar)?
- Are you creative? Perceptive? (Do you pick up on the unusual, original aspects of the event?)
- Which role do you yourself play in the story? (Central figure, objective bystander, or interested party?)
- How do you describe yourself: as a leader (either formal or informal), as a 'player' or as a bystander?
- How do you use the time available? Do you keep an eye on the time? In other words: what's your time management like?

If you find yourself faced with this type of task, then you need to watch the following points – unless you want to fall into their trap.

- **Subject**: keep it business-like and work-related. Tailor it towards the particular job or organisation you are applying for.
- **Your role**: stress the leading role you played in the story. If you find this difficult, then emphasise how creative you were in the event. Don't play yourself down. Don't portray yourself as an objective bystander.
- **Style**: write clearly, concisely and in a business-like way. Don't overdo it on the 'I's.

- **Spelling/grammar**: watch your English. Take the exercise seriously and read through your work very carefully.
- **Vocabulary**: write clearly, but vary your vocabulary. Use synonyms – throw the odd 'difficult' word in now and again.
- **Time**: finish within 30 minutes. If possible, try and work faster, but don't let the quality of your story suffer.

TIP Remember that during the interview, your responses to this exercise may well be discussed. (Questions about the whole story or only certain specific points.)

Management cases

What do you think about the following (generation gap?) problem, which you must now solve as a manager? You have 25 minutes to put down in writing your strategy and to develop an action plan.

> A while ago, Mr Charles Johnson took up a position with the Finance & Admin department. It is his first job since gaining qualifications in this field. He seems energetic and keen to learn, and he gets on very well with his colleagues. But as time went on, the relationship cooled between Charles and his fellow workers, who were all about twice his age. They reproached him for handling too much work, giving advice and plans to management without being asked, and busily introducing a whole new system of administration. Why can't he stick to the job he's employed to do!?

Another problem:

> You are in charge of a department and receive a letter from an ex-colleague who left the company a year ago. You didn't think much of him, his work left a lot to be desired. And on top of that, he barely got along with his fellow workers. The ex-colleague is asking you for a reference in connection with a new job. Your words of recommendation will determine whether or not the dream job is his!

How do you respond? Do you meet his request or refuse? What is your underlying rationale? You **must** respond in writing!

Commercial writing: some case studies

Are you going for a commercial job? Commercially minded folk are well known for their preference (and penchant) for speaking rather than writing. Yet, there is still the possibility that you'll have to put pen to paper (or electronic devices for that matter). Some examples of what you may get are presented below:

> **Building a client base.** You are employed by Retail Training Services Ltd, a training bureau specialising in retailing, particularly for small retail chains. Without the prospect's knowledge, you have been calling on some shops belonging to Mr Adrian Does' 'DO IT' chain, DIY stores in small towns. It has struck you that staff in these stores avoid contact with customers rather than seeking it out, that they offer little personal service and do not sell very convincingly. The company gives a rather old-fashioned, amateurish impression. After visiting the shops, you decide to write a letter to Mr Does to inform him of your findings. Your aim: to be invited to see the owner, so that you can present a training package for improving the sales effectiveness of his sales staff and to offer better customer service. The task: write a letter with your findings, aiming for an invitation. (You will not have to present your proposal).

Too little information? You will have to make do! And after 25 minutes, the whistle will blow for the end of the assignment. Make sure to ration your work, to avoid time difficulties.

> *TIP*   Write neatly, be logical in your letter and pay attention to your grammar and spelling. However, the most important thing is: your persuasiveness. Will you manage to get the contract?

> **Letter of complaint.** We are stepping forward in time. Your company was allowed to provide the sales training for the 'DO IT' firm. About thirty salespeople (both full and part-time) have attended the two-day training course. As far as you know, from the written and verbal evaluations at the end of the course, the sales staff were all reasonably pleased. But Mr Does takes an alternative view, witnessed by you find this letter on your desk ...

Dear Mr Flame

We entrusted you with training a large number of our sales staff. As a man of few words, I have only this to say: it seems this trust was misplaced!

I have received a number of complaints about you and your agency. And I too am less than satisfied with what you have delivered.

1. The training sessions began 30 minutes too late on both days. 'Traffic' was the trainer's excuse, according to our participants. However, we were still charged for this time.

2. Some of our female staff went home very upset after a couple of hours. They found the trainer's remarks about 'treating people with kid gloves never helped anyone' very distressing. That also cost us money.

3. The comprehensive training handbooks from your presentation had changed into flimsy 20 page pamphlets.

4. I received many calls, including one from one of my oldest and most loyal managers, who said that you had apparently never worked in a (DIY) shop. We came to you to improve our sales techniques not to listen to theories. But nothing was said on this.

5. In our previous discussions, you made great play of a 6-10% increase in turnover which would definitely be achieved. Since your training sessions, turnover has fallen!

6. How your office deals with phone calls is very poor and you never seem to be available. In any case, you have never responded to any of my calls.

You will understand quite clearly that we will not be allowing you to train the rest of our sales staff, contract or not. As for your suggestion that you can offer our people service training, we will not be going ahead. Furthermore, we have notified our lawyers of our intention to pursue damages against you. You will be hearing from us again shortly.

Yours sincerely

A. Does

Managing Director

Your task:

1. Write a written response to this letter.
2. What lies behind the writing of this letter? (What motives have provoked it?). Note these down on a separate sheet of paper.
3. Are there other things you want to do?

There is no time limit on this task.

Marketing plan

The commercial AC comprises many types of marketing case studies, some very brief, some very comprehensive. You may well overdose on information (reports, recommendations with appendices, financial summaries etc.) In some commercial case studies, you will be helped (?) by an avalanche of statistics. Purchasing costs, sales costs, financial forecasts and predicted profits. A huge mish-mash of figures. Don't let yourself get confused. Think about what is expected of you:

1. to be able to distinguish between key and side issues
2. to advise in your capacity as a key commercial employee on how the organisation can 'dish out' its money
3. to save money for the organisation in your role as financial manager.

Also, approach the problem from a people perspective, aside from all the numbers. Don't write money off but do keep your eyes open to potential conflicts, say, between departments or colleagues.

The following task relates to giving advice:

An American manufacturer of synthetic products is very successful in its home market at selling artificial grass. This product is used for sports grounds, balconies and smaller gardens, amongst other applications. US consumers find it has a good price/value relationship. The manufacturer has drawn up a plan to export this product to Europe (with a view to manufacturing locally at a later date). The UK seems an ideal testing market. The manufacturer has no European experience. It is common knowledge that an American competitor who wanted to sell artificial grass in Germany has not gone ahead. It is unclear as to the precise reasons why.

Your task: write a concise marketing plan for the exporting manufacturer, in one hour.

This task assumes that you are familiar with the 5 'P's of the marketing mix. This structure provides a handy framework, as the following questions demonstrate:

1. **Product**: What exactly is the product? Strong and weak points? What varieties are there? Is it suited to the UK market? Or the European market in general? Why did the competitor's product flop in the German market? Do we know what the consumer (buyer/end user) and the

purchaser (sports ground) wants or requires? How much maintenance does the product demand? What competing products are already on the market? How do they differ from 'our' product?

2. **Place (of sale)**: Where and how will the product be sold? Locally? Or only in certain regions? In what type of shops? Is mail order a possibility?

3. **Price**: What should the ultimate price be (per m2)? Who should set it, and how? What profit margin does the American company wish to achieve? How many years before a 'break-even point' is reached? Is there price differentiation between the different varieties? What about 'introductory' discounts?

4. **Promotion/Advertising**: How much will the promotion and advertising budget amount to? (How big was the budget for the failed German product?) How much do your competitors spend on promotion and advertising? What image should the advertising foster? Is there an appropriate advertising agency for 'our' product? Should we make a distinction between advertising for professionals (e.g. sport and recreational facilities departments in councils) and consumers?

5. **Personnel**: Which salespeople will be selling the product (age, experience, selling style, etc)? Which requirements need to be placed upon them? What training will they need?

As you can see, many questions (you can probably think of even more!) but no answers. You can answer some questions (advice or recommendation) but not others (your competitor's advertising budget). You can (almost always) recommend a market research survey by your own company or via an agency to find out what your competitors' advertising budgets are for their products and other essential details.

Whatever else, the key to solving this type of marketing problem is to structure it.

If time permits, it is good to write down three scenarios: an optimistic one, a pessimistic one and a realistic one (the one in the middle).

> ***TIP*** Take a pocket calculator with you from home. Perhaps you'll need it for some calculations. (Some agencies lend out calculators for the duration of the task but don't count on it.) If you are definitely not allowed to use calculators, you'll be the first to know. Don't forget that vision is just as important (and sometimes even more important) than being able to put figures in the right order!

Policy information

When recruiting for Civil Service jobs, often a candidate is tested for his or her knowledge and ability to draw up and rewrite **policy documents**. Policy making is initiated when a problem or (potentially) undesirable situation is diagnosed (by a person, an institution, through scientific research). The precise problem is then analysed: this is the job of the policy planners, researchers, advisors and the secretariat. Afterwards, a framework must be established, alternatives reviewed and the potential consequences of various decisions investigated. Finally a decision is reached. Policy is to do with the future – which is always difficult to predict. That's why policy-making and uncertainty go hand in hand.

We must distinguish between **planning documents, action plans** and **evaluation reports.**

Planning documents, which lay down new policy, fulfil three important functions:

1. The documents must exist – it's traditional. (Not a strong argument)
2. They help to structure ideas. (That can be done better on paper).
3. They make a speedy decision possible. (Although...)

What matters here is correctness, relevance and clarity. Therefore, using correct terminology is very important. Issues that must always come up for discussion are:

- What is/will be the problem? (Why is it a problem – why will it become a problem? For whom is it/will it be a problem?)
- Can we distinguish different aspects of the problem?
- What solutions present themselves?
- What frames of reference must be taken into account?

- What possible decisions are there? How feasible are they? (What positive side effects are there?)
- What negative effects can be expected?
- What problems are we likely to be confronted with during implementation? (Time, cost, legal battles, lack of clarity, etc.)
- To whom will the policy plan be presented and how?

Action plans are written for those who are involved with implementing the plan. Consequently, the language used needs to be simpler and the information more concrete, because the readers must know:

- what is going to happen or change
- why this is the case
- exactly how the policy must be carried out.

After a policy has been implemented, it must be assessed to see if the desired results have indeed been achieved. This brings us to **evaluation reports**. These documents need to address the following questions.

- What result were you aiming for?
- What priorities did you set?
- Were the policy goals achieved?
- What policy instruments were available?
- Did the implementation go according to plan?
- Did problems arise when carrying out the policy? What exactly?
- In what way does the policy need to be adjusted?

In such a task, you must take into consideration the fact that you are being evaluated on the following points, amongst others:

- written communication (as you'd logically expect ...)
- speed of reviewing complex policy documentation
- appraisal of opposing views
- problem analysis
- insight into a variety of situations.

> *TIP* Don't be a waffler. Don't try and hide behind a smoke screen of empty words. Use concrete words for concrete people.

Rewriting a policy document

Until now, we have assumed that you would be writing a document from scratch. Another test of your knowledge is to ask you to evaluate an existing document. What do you think of the 'quality' – and what is your view based on? What changes do you propose? And sometimes, rewrite this (usually shorter) document!

Before you can respond to a question of 'quality', you must first establish exactly how quality improves the written text. Never launch into a question like this without prior preparation.

Structuring

A few simple tips to help you structure your report:

- Begin at the beginning – write a short introduction. Briefly summarise the problem and the aim of your report, and note down how you think you can come up with a solution.

- End with a summary, stating your conclusions.

- And in the body of the report, describe the kernel of the problem and potential solutions. If you can, set out the key points in the form of a list. Do the same for any solutions and actions to be undertaken. Sometimes solutions can have negative side effects. Which ones do you foresee in your plan?

- Set out a timetable. Your ultimate deadline is the overall tally of all the interim deadlines. Take 'overrun' into account and keep some extra time into reserve.

TIP Always read the test through fully before doing anything else. You then have some idea what it's about. Afterwards, read the text through one more time, but now keep an eye on the (important?) details. Next, go through the exercise a third time, underline key issues, and make some notes. Do you understand it fully?

Then, study your questions. You should note how much time you have available and use your watch. One thing to bear in mind: you will not be given any additional information, apart from what is on paper. You must rely on your own resources.

> *TIP*   You have just familiarised yourself with some rather diverse case studies. Why not work on them at home, at your own leisure? Keep an eye on the time! And be critical of your own work.

14

The Interview

In nearly every AC you will come across an interview. 'Why?' you may ask. 'I've already been subjected to this several times before'. The answer is amazingly simple: the selection agency wants to get to know you even better and there is always time enough left over in an entire day to have a 'good chat'. (After all, your potential employer is paying plenty of loot to avoid any 'reasonable' risk).

We will remind you to be on your toes in your interview with the psychologist and sell yourself constantly. We will show you how to pay attention to your non-verbal communication: your own body language may betray you. We will also look at a typical interview, the extent of your desire for the job, moral dilemmas designed to test your ethical code and use of language during the interview.

The more experienced and professional the selector, the more you have to raise your performance during the interview. We will cover various aspects of this, including difficult questions and examine the 'behavioural criteria and Q & As'; the latter being a preview of the sorts of questions you can expect in the interview. You can prepare thoroughly for this: if you are being questioned on 'ambition' (one of the behavioural criteria), then you shouldn't answer that you are quite happy to ride round in an old jalopy for the rest of your life. Don't be too modest, and avoid mentioning the fact that you like to do 'moonlighting' (jobs on the side). This chapter is also good to use if you have to deal with any type of interviewer be they a headhunter, Head of Personnel, Divisional Director or recruitment consultant.

A typical interview

Sometime during the day (either first thing, after lunch or quite often at the end), a professional 'bloodhound' will subject you to an interview. Don't be too flippant about it! The selectors do not only get an impression of you from the tests, but also from this interview. Subjective? Yes, of course. But no less important for that.

Perhaps you have been 'unlucky' with the tests you have done, or you had no experience of any of the exercises. Happily, there is still one saving grace: your 'gift of the gab'. You can still salvage something from the interview.

The interview may be rather dull. (Don't bank on a sparkling glass of vino and a cream crackers with Stilton!). You will probably have to make conversation for around 30 minutes to an hour. Subjects which are often on the list are: your personal, educational and professional background, based on what you have said on your CV. So be very careful that you have no inconsistencies! (Watch out for the well-known 'CV Law': the poorer the candidate, the longer the CV).

What do they want to know from you? In summary:

- What type of person you are: do you 'fit' in with the employer?
- What your motivation is in applying for this job.
- How stable you are and how well you cope with stress (whatever that is).
- How well you get on with others/colleagues.
- How intelligent you are.
- Why you are looking for a new job.
- How you deal with your staff, and with your bosses.
- Your leadership style (if relevant).
- How well you know yourself, what you can say about your knowledge and abilities, what drives you, occupies you.

The answers you give to the above questions will lead the psychologist to form a picture of your aptitudes, skills and personality.

Your reactions to the assessment tasks are also a popular topic of conversation, covering areas that have not already been discussed immediately after the tasks themselves. Your real-life experience is also important. Do you keep both feet on the ground? Or are you a daydreamer? Keep your daydreams realistic.

Test-related questions

The psychologist may pose you a number of questions relating to the tests you have done. We give you some examples below. The rationale behind these questions is explained and we suggest one or two 'ready-made' responses as well.

Question: 'Have you ever done a psychometric test before?' ('What was the outcome?')

Aim:
The psychologist may be asking this question for various reasons:

1. Is the candidate 'test-wise'? The more often you are tested, the better the test results may become. This is due to experience: you are learning. The psychologist will want to take this into account.
2. If the candidate has already been tested and failed, then the question 'why?' becomes paramount. The psychologist can then easily see that someone has discovered something in this candidate that he did not notice.
3. Maybe he can catch the candidate out, if he is fibbing. Maybe the psychologist knows that this candidate, who works for XYZ Bank, must have been tested to get his present job, as tests form part of their standard procedure. (Covering it up may be a risky strategy.)

Your answer: If applicable, answer 'no'. Very assertively, so that there is no need for any further questions. (The psychologist cannot ask, *'Why haven't you been tested yet?'* This question is on a par with, *'Why haven't you murdered your neighbour yet?'*) Let sleeping dogs lie!

But beware! Sometimes a positive answer is required. If you have to say 'yes', then ask yourself if they can check whether you are answering truthfully or not. (It is generally difficult to check out.) Then provide a weak – and non-psychological – reason for your poor performance. For example: *'I received a positive report, but the person who got the job had more experience in this field'*.

Question: 'Did you recognise yourself in that report?' ('Why not?')

Aim:
● Perhaps they want to use this question to find out how well you know

yourself. (That's good.) Or they want to draw you out more. This question is a good vehicle to do this. Once again, you feel anger over the unjustified rejection you suffered. You may want to get it off your chest! (This is bad.)

- A totally different reason is pure curiosity from the agency on how a competitor handles things ...

Your answer: A negative response will certainly be followed by a *'Why not?'* or more accurately, *'In which areas didn't you recognise yourself?'* It's a sure bet that the areas you're talking of are less than flattering. If your response is, for example, that *'they assessed that I was poor at thinking abstractly. I don't understand it at all – could you explain?'* Then you might as well give up the ghost!

Are you a declared opponent of psychometric tests? If you want to voice your opinion, then you may start an interesting discussion. But what are you trying to achieve? The agency knows that people who score well never complain about tests.

Question: 'The questionnaire results reveal that you are very extrovert. But talking to you now, I find the opposite: you seem rather withdrawn. How can you explain this difference?'

Aim:
You probably know that to get the job (really this applies to most jobs) you have to come across as extrovert. Because this means you enjoy getting along with others. You gave the 'right' answers in the questionnaire. But your behaviour during the interview tells a different story. The psychologist is suspicious – and rightly so!

Your answer: The greatest mistake that you can make is to say honestly what the problem is. Or make all kinds of excuses. The best response is: *'You're the expert, I cannot explain it'*. End of story.

Question: 'You scored badly on the test for commercial comprehension. Particularly low considering your present sales job.'

Aim:
You are working in sales (or you are hoping to do so), and the test has apparently revealed your lack of commercial insight. If you state that you

have been very successful in this field, then the interviewer may well start to have some doubts.

Your answer: First thing to remember, you haven't actually been asked anything yet. So you don't have to answer. This may be the strategy you wish to adopt but remember that sales people are rather extrovert and grab every opportunity to have a 'good chat'. So, keeping quiet is not a good idea. Why don't you ask a question: *'What exactly would you like to know?'* The more accurately you word your question, the more accurate the answer will be. You then know which aspect your answer should emphasise. Even better is to ask what exactly 'commercial comprehension' means. Everyone has a different understanding of this concept. You would like to answer the charge, but first want to know if we are talking the same language: what's his definition?

If you can agree on a definition, then you should also ask what the relationship is between commercial insight and sales behaviour. Are the two actually synonymous? Depending on the job you are seeking, you could argue that insight is important for a salesman but that behaviour is even more crucial. That is what the customer sees. Insight is not visible to the purchaser. Another response can be used by the marketer: a creative marketing specialist may well be unable to sell his four year old's bike, but he can think up imaginative sales promotions.

Question: 'Your IQ is too low.'

Aim:
This may be a sincere observation: you are scoring lower than the employer would like for this particular job. The psychologist may want you to know that the 'cat's out of the bag'. Or he may be interested in the way you deal with disappointment. Another reason is provocation. Who likes to hear that he's 'stupid', because that's what he has said in so many words. How do you react?

Your answer: Firstly, remember that the word 'low' means nothing. *'In what respect too low?'* might be your first response. And after the answer, your second question should be: *'What does this mean for the job I'm applying for?'* Then you can start an (intelligent!) discussion about the relationship between IQ scores and actual behaviour. (The correlation is generally rather poor. IQ scores are a poor predictor of 'success' in a job).

The 'stress interview'

In this type of interview, the candidate is placed under a lot of pressure. The psychologist tries to uncover your emotions. This can occur in a number of ways:

- The interviewer begins in a very friendly, relaxed manner, but suddenly and without warning, starts to become hostile. He is confusing you and forcing you onto the defensive. After this 'interlude' the selector returns to his friendly manner for the rest of the interview. How quickly can the candidate recover from this sudden change?

- Another technique is to belittle the candidate's achievements, to be critical of his motives in changing jobs, and about his personal attributes.

Motivation

One of the problems with an AC is that it rarely explores the reasoning behind behaviour. Therefore, after the tasks have been completed, there are often questions asked about the underlying 'motivation'. In so doing, it will be discovered what drives the candidate (the manager). Why work so hard, why give up all that free time, why take unpopular measures, why work under pressure, day in, day out? What is he or she doing it for? (Why do you do it?)

There are many different motives for working. The best one is **intrinsic motivation**, because this comes from the heart. Why does someone work hard and put his or her heart into it? Because the work itself is interesting and gratifying. Another good motive is setting oneself high standards, and seeking to achieve them. This is the type of person who constantly wants (and has) to prove him or herself. Yet another good motive is the satisfaction that comes from co-operation and working with others. This is the 'social' type. The last type of person that we'd like to present to you is motivated by power (who would rather talk about influencing people, because that sounds better). We can safely say that these people hope to use their expertise to guide their teams in the right direction for the good of the company.

Motivation is closely related to ambition. A company such as Unilever, which offers career (rather than job) opportunities, will use the following four questions to determine how ambitious the candidate is:

- 'Where are you now?'
- 'Where are you going?'
- 'How will you get there?'
- 'Why do you want it?'

Don't imagine that these are simple questions, with simple answers. The selectors have a whole battery of questions at the ready, and really want to have acceptable verbal 'evidence'.

> ***TIP*** The CV is a good means to 'philosophise' over your motivation and ambitions. Read through your 'brochure' before you make the journey to the selection agency!

Hobby horses

Every selector likes to flog his or her own hobby horse or philosophy. Don't be surprised then, if you are questioned, either directly or indirectly, on examples like:

- 'What is your view of the world of commerce, in general?' (As if you could actually answer a question like this!)
- 'Have you ever heard of George Price, the management guru? Broadly speaking, do you agree or disagree with his views? And why?'
- 'Have you, by any chance, read a book called New Management Heights, by John Peterson, the American professor? What did you think of it?'

General background

Don't be surprised if the selector also asks you some general background questions. How much do you know about current events and trends, politics (at home and abroad), what do you read to keep up-to-date? Below are some examples to give you an idea of the types of questions to expect:

- 'What radio programmes do you listen to?' 'What TV programmes do you watch?'

- 'Which daily papers do you read?'
- 'Are you a member of any clubs? Which ones'?
- 'What type of holiday do you enjoy?'
- 'How do you spend your weekends?'
- 'Do you attend any evening classes?'
- 'What is your opinion of the unions?'

TIP Leave your extreme personal opinions, idiosyncrasies and judgements at home. If you state that spendthrifts are made, not born, they may well accept this. But their eyes may roll if you state that all architects who build skyscrapers are sadistic megalomaniacs, because their buildings make people feel insignificant.

Difficult questions

There are questions that are annoying for you, and are not actually aimed at eliciting factual information. Why would they ask you this type of difficult question? Four possible reasons why:

1. If you were to be offered the job in question, you would have to deal with difficult questions in your work, from customers, for example. The selector is testing how you deal with this type of questions. You are being subjected to a 'difficult question test', as it were!
2. The interviewer is new, inexperienced, poorly trained and doesn't know which questions to ask, or he might just be a bad interviewer.
3. The interviewer is tired – so many interviews – disinterested, aggressive, wants to be rid of you quickly etc.
4. This is just the interviewer's personal style. He is only trying to liven the applicants up in his own way.

Below you will find a number of questions, which most candidates find difficult to answer:

- You are 55 years old – and you want a new job. Aren't you a bit old to change jobs? Or: shouldn't you take it a bit easier now?
- Why aren't you on a higher salary (at the moment), bearing in mind your age/experience/achievements?

- Why were you unemployed for 3 years?
- Don't you think this job is beneath (too much) for you?
- You took a long time to graduate. Why was that?
- Does your career to date show continuous upward development?
- What are your long-term plans?
- Where do you see yourself in five years' time?
- What have you achieved in your career?
- What is the most difficult thing you've ever had to do at work?

Remember that these and other similar questions can always be followed up by so-called 'follow-up' questions. Questions which mainly begin with 'why'. You need to explore your answers more deeply, to think about reasons why you acted as you did. It can be very difficult to 'get out' of these questions once you start!

Moral dilemmas and ethics

The interview offers selectors a prime opportunity to explore your principles and values. Some employers find it important to recruit workers who are incorruptible and honourable. (In reality, we know every man has his price ...) Often, 'imaginary' questions – *'Imagine if ...'* – are asked as well as direct questions. Sometimes the employer wants to know if you eat with a knife and fork or with a shovel and spade. But respectable generally means are you ethical or not? (Perhaps the employer has had a bad experience with your predecessors.) Or possibly the organisation has a very honourable image, or it must be beyond reproach. Also, sometimes, specific professional ethical standards are demanded. Below we outline as an example a problem which demands appropriate answers.

Problem: As Director of a training company, you are faced with a difficult problem. Two weeks earlier, one of your male trainers presented a three-day training course to your best client-organisation. Initial feedback reports suggested that every participant was extremely satisfied with him – as you had expected from your no 1 trainer! But, a week later, you received a letter from one of the female attendees who was less happy. She stated that the trainer tended to have 'wandering hands' and constantly flirted with her. She wanted nothing to do with him. But, at every meal, he insisted on sitting next to her. And, in the evening, he sidled up to her at the bar. She ended her letter by requesting his dismissal; if this didn't take place, then her company would no longer use your training agency's services.You have already shown the letter to the trainer, who has been with your company for five years. He couldn't believe his eyes. He remembered this lady, who, as he put it, wouldn't leave him alone the whole week. She was the flirt and he was the one pushing her away!

How would you respond to this problem, as director of this training agency?

If your ethical stance is being investigated, it can be done by a number of interview questions. The role play is also an appropriate device to lay bare your moral principles; for example, using the 'temptation tactic'. You play the buyer and your fellow player plays the seller. The latter offers you a 10% discount on the selling price no questions asked (or a free weekend or whatever). Do you accept the offer? Or do you turn it down without hesitation and show the salesperson the door?

Some interview questions:

- What do you do if you are asked to do something that you don't agree with?
- Imagine that by chance you hear two of your colleagues discussing how they are about to sell sensitive company information to a competitor. How would you react?
- Suppose that you heard that your company had a secret division selling poison gas to Third World countries. What would you do with this information?
- Are you always honest, even in situations where a 'little white lie' could help you out?
- Have you ever refused to do something at work? Why?

How should you react when your ethics are called into question?

1. Do you have or have you ever had a conscience? Well, listen to it!
2. Remember that honesty is always the best policy. (Well, at least, it helps you to get a good night's sleep!)
3. Find out (but of course you've already done this long ago) which type of cultural identity the organisation has, and what attitudes your future colleagues hold. This is obviously not always easy to do.

Some banks present themselves as extremely upstanding, even writing their

PR in the same ink they use to launder illegal money. Adapt your behaviour to suit the employer (if you wish to), but show off your cleanest, whitest side.

One more thing – you should never fear the lie detector, whereby you are attached to a piece of electronic apparatus with electrodes. These machines are not used (yet!) in selection, only in Hollywood spy films.

Justifying your answers

After a role play (and also after other exercises), questions are asked in order to find out why you chose certain solutions, what reasoning lay behind your judgements etc. These questions, and others similar in tone, may find their way to the interview as well. Be prepared for the following:

- 'What is your overall impression of today?'
- 'What have you enjoyed most – and why?'
- 'What did you least enjoy – and why?'
- 'What have you learnt from this assessment centre?' 'If you had to take part in another one, what would you do differently? (Why didn't you do it this time round?)'
- 'Have you had the chance today to show us what you are really worth? (If not, why not?)'

Behavioural criteria and 'question database'

Chapter 7 already introduced you to behavioural dimensions or criteria, whereby you – or rather, your behaviour – is determined. A number of these behavioural dimensions, including the less well used ones, are revisited in the interview.

Below, you will find some of them, together with the 'relevant' questions. In other words: if your future employer is interested in your adaptability, for example – perhaps because in his eyes, it's a big step going from working for the Sleepytown council to a tough but glamourous life as a sales manager – then he will be able to watch you thoroughly during your role play. Afterwards, during your interview, he can then ask the following: *'Give me an example of a work situation when you had to adapt to a sudden change in circumstances. How did you manage?'* Naturally, there must be some relationship between your answer to this question and the way you behaved in the role play designed to measure your adaptive behaviour.

The selector can map out your answers in many different ways. For example, he can divide your answers into 'good', 'acceptable', or 'unacceptable', or he can be more exacting, and use a five-point scale. He can also make use of one or more disqualifiers, which are categories so crucial to success in the job that you must achieve an acceptable score, at the very least.

TIP The interviewer will not be content with a simple answer, but will ask for examples and explanations! Don't show off and boast about your achievements too much, though. The smart and experienced interviewer will find it easy to 'burst your bubble'. He or she will ask you for facts, names, actual events, concrete examples to back up your 'successes'. Can you provide this?

Please refer to chapter 7 for definitions of the following behavioural dimensions.

Adaptability

- Generally, how well do you adapt to changing circumstances? (How do you demonstrate this?)
- Give an example of how you have adapted to changes at work.
- Give an example of how you adapted to changes at school/university.
- Please give an example of a work situation when you had to adapt to sudden changes in circumstances. How did you do this?

Involvement

- Are you a member of your present company's staff association? Why? Or why not?
- What motivates you about your present organisation?
- Have you ever done anything for your present (or a previous) employer which was exceptionally good? If so, what?
- How would you describe the atmosphere at work?
- What are you looking for in an organisation?

Creativity/inventiveness/innovation

- Would you describe yourself as creative? What makes you think so?
- Are you someone who is always innovating? Where does this come from?
- Do you like to try new ways of doing things? How would you sell new ideas to me?
- What is the best example you can think of to demonstrate your inventiveness?
- What important changes have you made in your work?
- What crazy ideas and plans have you had in the past two years at work? (And at home?)

Emotional stability

- What is the most stressful situation you have ever found yourself in?
- Can you withstand stress? (Why do you think so?)
- Do you enjoy working under time pressures, or do you find it annoying?
- What frustrates you about your job?
- Which events have influenced your career (dramatically)?
- What has been the most difficult decision in your life? (or greatest disappointment?)
- What conflicts have you had in your work?
- Why have you changed jobs so often in the past x year(s)?
- What has made you angry recently at work? (What problem was it?)

Drive for power/influence

- Why do you want a supervisory/management position? (What is so attractive about it?)
- Describe someone who is a good leader/ a bad leader.
- What does 'power' mean for you?
- How do you see your own career progressing?
- Are you competitive by nature? (What makes you think so?)

Independence

- How do you respond to leadership?
- What makes you think you go your own way as much as possible?
- On what types of issues do you find it hard to agree with your boss?
- If you don't agree with your boss, then do you say so?
- Which role do you usually choose for yourself in meetings?
- Do you think of yourself as an enterprising type?

People-oriented sensitivity

- How do you break bad news to someone working for you?
- What do your colleagues think of you? (How do they see you?)
- What type of people do you enjoy being with the most?
- How do you respond when a colleague comes late to work several times a week and you don't believe his excuses?

Sociability

- What type of activities give you the greatest satisfaction?
- How do you behave in group situations?
- What type of people do you dislike? (And why?)
- What type of people do you like to be around?
- Do you have a lot of acquaintances, or a few good friends?
- Can you cope with only a few people around you?

TIP Modesty can (sometimes) be a virtue. But, in the test procedure, you must sell yourself - and that doesn't always fit in with a modest attitude. If you don't praise your achievements (but don't overdo it!), then who else will? The interviewer can't assess your actions if you don't tell him or her about them.

Language usage

It is worth knowing that there are some golden rules surrounding the type of language you should use in the interview. They are as follows:

1. Use adjectives to clarify things and to add colour to your story. Try to give longer answers – don't make the interviewer have to drag every word out of you. So, instead of saying, *'I was Assistant Manager in Stocks and Shares with Lloyd's,'* you should say, *'I was partially responsible for running the department. We were dealing in stocks and shares, at a time of great change, and we did it successfully.'*

2. Don't witter on and on, and tell shaggy dog stories. Be business-like and to the point.

3. Avoid officious and vague language, and an indirect style of speaking.

So, instead of *'it was customary for the directors to fully consider the pros and cons of each decision ...,'* say something like, *'the directors always weighted up each decision carefully.'*

4. Avoid technical words and jargon as much as possible. It's a cheap shot, which will probably not impress the interviewer. It's more likely to work against you. The interviewer will think that you have something to hide, that you are imitating your betters, that you are trying to look important, and so on.

5. Be specific when talking about your achievements and experiences. If you are vague, then the interviewer will ask for clarification, explanation and concrete samples. So don't say, *'I spent some time visiting shopkeepers in different areas,'* but, *'I spent one year selling window displays to retailers in the North of England. My turnover was 40% higher than that of my predecessors.'*

6. Never exaggerate: you will come across as 'too good to be true'.

7. Use positive words and terms which indicate dynamism and action.

We have drawn up a list of positive words which interviewers like to hear. There are nouns, verbs and adjectives, divided into a few useful categories. These are only examples, of course. You can easily extend the list yourself. In any case, select words from the relevant categories, which make you sound good, before your interview. We haven't attempted to classify them in simplistic personality traits; what matters is the 'feel' for these characteristics. Therefore, some words will appear in more than one category:

Social contact:	Helpful, good sense of humour, polite, personable, open, pleasant, sociable, sympathetic, friendly.
Insightfulness:	Analytical, thoughtful, contemplative, patient, intellectual, philosophical, logical, independent, thinker, self-reliant, conceptual.
Loyalty:	Committed, reliable, proper, honest, loyal, upstanding, faithful.
Controlled:	Balanced, decisive, calm, unruffled, grown-up.
Decisiveness:	Constructive, diplomatic, task-oriented, methodical, combative, forceful, free-thinking, tactful
Demonstrating:	Showing, achieving, advertising, PR, cuttings, visible,

	verifying, written, published.
Leadership:	Active, alert, democratic, task-oriented, energetic, enthusiastic, sense of humour, enterprising, inspiring, reasonable, progressive, self-reliant, leading, initiating, showing the way, starting up, eliminating, dismissing (workers), reorganising, managing, supervising.
Courage/ambition:	Ambitious, creative, daring, flexible, innovative, combative, promotion.
Style of working:	Consistent, task-oriented, economical, efficient, methodical, perfectionist, practical, realistic, systematic, service-oriented, customer-focused, initiating.
Creativity:	Artistic, imaginative, flexible, innovative, enterprising, inventive, open to ideas, design, introducing, discovered, promoting, research, solving
Success:	Performance, completion, achieved, objectives met, approval, created/built, consolidated, brought under control, saved, developed, doubled, earned, effectiveness, founded, extended, implementation, improved, launched, produced, sold, strengthened, won.
Organisation:	Implementing, negotiating, operationalisation, asserting, planning, delegating, purchasing, reducing, reorganising, manning, streamlining, training/teaching, transforming, fusing.

 Remember that many questions can be followed up by so-called 'follow up' questions, which mainly begin with 'why'.

Personal subjects

The psychologist may be interested in your youth, parents and upbringing. His aim may be:

1. To know how far you've come since childhood; he hopes to pick up data about your intelligence, your willpower and ambition. He may find it significantly important if you've had to overcome a difficult childhood to climb to your present level.

2. To find out how easy or difficult it is for you to talk about this period of your life. (Trauma?) How do you come across when you talk about your attitude to authority and discipline: your relationship with your siblings? If your present behaviour strongly suggests something from your past, then it is customary for them to ask where exactly it emanates from.

- 'Did you have a happy childhood?'
- 'What do you remember most clearly?'
- 'What type of work did your father (mother) do?'
- 'Who do you most closely resemble as far as personality is concerned, your father or mother?'
- 'What do your brothers and sisters do?'

Upbringing

- 'Tell me about your upbringing.'
- 'What were your best subjects at school?'
- 'Which subjects did you find the most interesting? And which ones the least?'
- 'Which subjects did you find the most difficult?'
- 'What did you study? Why? Why that university/college?'
- 'How did you find the life of a student, in general?'
- 'What did you do in your free time?'
- 'How does your degree/qualification fit in with your chosen profession?'

Personality and personal philosophy

Sketch a positive picture of yourself and link your strong points to the job you are applying for.

Give the information that the selector needs to reach the desired conclusion. This also applies to your 'weak points': if you say you have none, this sounds unbelievable. (You don't know yourself well enough.) So, mention some weak points, those qualities which either can be interpreted positively, or are completely irrelevant for the job in question. Usually you will not be asked outright about your political or religious views, but they may try to wheedle them out of you indirectly. These views are not that interesting in themselves; the underlying question is if you are sufficiently tolerant of other people's beliefs.

- 'Describe your personality.'

- 'What do you think about the forthcoming elections?'
- 'What changes do you think should be made to the employment laws?'
- 'What is our greatest national problem at the present time? And the greatest international problem?'
- 'Can you tell us about a difficult decision you had to make within the last year?'

Always bear in mind that one or more of the questions above has some relevance to the job you are applying for. If they ask you directly about your political views, or they want to know your opinion about the political situation in Iraq or another country, then it is reasonable to take your time answering. Try to determine what exactly the underlying rationale is behind the question and then throw the question back at them: 'I do have an opinion, of course, but could you tell me first what relevance my opinions have for the job I am applying for?' If you receive a vague or unsatisfactory answer, then you can always say that you don't feel you can answer this type of question. Respond in a friendly and self-confident manner.

Family life

A peaceful, stable family life is generally of paramount importance. You cannot fight a war on two fronts. So, don't be surprised if you get asked questions about your domestic situation. But, where is the line between your private life and those details that the selector finds important? One 'joke' that many selectors play is: *'How come that you haven't mentioned your wife/husband/partner? Isn't s/he very important in your life?'*

- 'How long have you been married? Is this your first marriage?'
- 'Tell me about your partner.' (Background, family, education, work, qualities, interests, activities, ambitions?)
- 'Tell me about your children.' 'Have you enough time for your children?'
- ' Would you describe your marriage as 'happy'?' ('What makes you say that?')

Avoiding problem areas

One golden rule is never to give away information that you think could be used against you. Why bother to mention that you have been divorced twice?

The wrong conclusion may be drawn that you are rather unstable. Roughly between the ages of 35 and 45, many people, particularly men, go through a period of depression which has to do with important physical and emotional changes. ('The end of youth'). Psychologists and other selectors are aware of this and aren't pleased if you start showing signs of mid-life crisis. If you are having trouble with your age, then don't show it. Don't talk about your problems, just your successes. Nothing succeeds like success.

If the interviewer becomes difficult, then you can always say: *'Mr Jones, can't we continue this conversation in a more pleasant way?'* Let's be clear on this point, though: most selectors do not employ these tricks, but conduct their interviews in an agreeable manner.

In some organisations, the selector asks the receptionist or secretary for their opinions on candidates. They have the chance to evaluate you in secret. 'Big Brother or Sister may be watching you!'

Non-verbal behaviour during the interview

The psychologist is watching what your body is telling him or her – and your body can betray you. Many people believe that psychologists can 'see through you', that you can't hide anything from them. That's a myth, of course. Some psychologists are good people-readers (some aren't) – but you don't need to go to university for that. What psychologists have learnt is how to make use of non-verbal communication, a useful aid for the observation and evaluation of people. We would like to begin with different non-verbal signals, tell you what they mean to psychologists and inform you of the 'medicine' to take.

Shaking hands: in our culture, it is customary to shake hands at the beginning and at the end of the interview. If the interviewer doesn't offer you his hand, then extend yours first. At least, you have conformed to all the social niceties.

Men are expected to have a firm handshake. Why? Because a weak handshake suggests femininity, gentleness and uncertainty. We won't bother to ask whether this assumption is correct or not. You are rather at the mercy of the interviewer's own judgements. Women can get away with a weaker handshake, but a firm one won't do any harm, either!

Sweaty, clammy handshakes are beyond the pale. They reveal how tense you are feeling, but also suggest that you are a nervous person. So, it's always a good idea to rinse your hands before your interview (if possible). Or you can wipe them with a handkerchief, or, if absolutely necessary, on your clothes. But do it surreptitiously!

Eye contact: research has shown time and time again that, when people have to evaluate each other on their honesty, reliability and trustworthiness, they rely mainly on eye contact to make the evaluation. These are qualities that you want the interviewer to notice in you. So, you must maintain eye contact. No cynical glance, look of irritation, or a silly, false grin, but an open and honest look.

Body and position: sit comfortably in your seat, with your back against the back of the chair. Your arms should hang down at your sides. You can also put your hands in your lap, if you prefer. That's a neutral spot. If you are sitting close to the interviewer's desk, then you can also rest your hands on the desk. But make sure you keep your hands 'still'. Avoid drumming your fingers. Do you know what that communicates to the interviewer? That you are impatient, bored, irritated, uninterested, and want to be on your way. Is that how you want to come across?

You want to radiate an image of enthusiasm, someone who listens well, concentrates and so on. If you are sitting at the interviewer's desk and listening to him, then put your hand under your chin. Turn your head a little in his direction. But, when it is your turn to speak, you should lean your head and your body back a little.

Gestures: it is always good to use your hands to 'speak', to gesticulate, giving an enthusiastic and dynamic impression. Exaggerate this when you are talking about things that you want the other person to believe are very important to you. These could be the organisation that you are hoping to work for, your present job, your hobby etc. (Make sure you don't spend too much time talking about your hobbies!)

There are a few gestures that you should never make, like playing with your hair, fiddling in your ear, putting your finger in your mouth and scratching your body. All these gestures show uncertainty.

Never ball your fists: that signifies aggression.

Nodding: nodding your head shows that you agree with the other person's point of view. Shaking your head suggests disagreement. If you notice the interviewer often nodding, then you know that you are on the right track – or that he is deliberately seeking to mislead you.

Facial expression: avoid surprised or shocked expressions and looking disbelieving.

Emotional undertone: by this we mean how you say things. Do you speak in a monotone (avoid this!) or in a lively manner? Do you want to suggest that you believe in yourself, or that you doubt yourself? Remember that if you don't believe in yourself, no-one else will. It is particularly important to put some emotion into your voice, when you are trying to convince someone.

Attention

You should check several times during the interview if you have the others person's full attention.

Verbal signals: The type of remarks and questions that the other person asks can reveal if he is paying attention.

Non-verbal signals: If the interviewer is staring out of the window, seems to be obsessed with his new digital watch, or is making a detailed inspection of his fingernails, then you know you've lost him! Also when he is absolutely silent, doesn't smile, nods his head or asks questions, you can tell that you haven't captured his attention. This may well be a ruse to see how you cope with this situation. So, ask him a question, which he is forced to answer.

15

The Report and Your Rights

Some people follow the adage: 'I spend therefore I am'. And others find evidence of their existence in their test report. Reports can come in different shapes and sizes. The heart of this chapter consists of an example of a report, where the emphasis is strongly on demonstrable behaviour. This chapter also discusses your rights as a candidate and the legal status of reports and potential further uses.

Example of an AC report

Despite the fact that candidates have to work long and hard during an AC, the report itself is rather limited. Generally speaking, only those dimensions that are important to the employer are mentioned. Quite rightly so perhaps, but maybe there are other aspects of your work behaviour that you would be interested in. Why not ask for a more elaborate explanation (free of charge) which may cover those points that are of personal interest but not relevant for this particular job? This is your opportunity to hear from an expert how you come across.

This is how one agency reassures anxious candidates waiting for the arrival of that important final assessment:

'Within two weeks, you will receive your report. This will show all the evaluative criteria that the assessors have used to reach their final decision. You will see that for each practical exercise you have been assessed on certain criteria, and for each criterion you will see a numerical score and text. This gives you an impression of how you performed on each task and for each criterion. It is very rare for candidates to score consistently badly or consistently well on every task and for each criterion. What generally happens is that candidates have a variable pattern of scoring, have strong and weak points'.

A 'full' report describes observed behaviour for each behavioural dimension, preceded by a brief description of each dimension . Next there is a short overview of the (often five-point) scale used for each dimension. And last but not least, comes the conclusion and recommendations.

Report on Mrs Young

Aim of the assessment

The aim of the assessment was to evaluate the candidate's strengths and weaknesses, with a view to the appointment as Commercial Director with the 'Thinktank Bank'. This report will also cover the candidate's personal profile.

This report has been generated from the results of an assessment centre. A strong/weak point analysis has been made on the basis of the candidate's behavioural characteristics. Her behaviour has been observed in practical simulations and interviews. The choice of tasks was specifically tailored to this job function. Therefore, the results are only applicable to this job.

Leadership

Mrs Young has a clear, direct leadership style. She gives feedback to her team on their strong and weak points. Generally, she is task-oriented, stating what she expects from someone, but not making it clear how this will be achieved. She delegates very rarely, seen particularly in the in-tray exercise – as she says, she doesn't often handle this in her present job. Her staff may regard her as distant because of her harsh and unfriendly manner. In the role play, she was very aware of her position, which she abused to some extent. She used this to motivate the employee, with whom she showed little patience. In conclusion: her ability to motivate is rather poor.

Persuasiveness

Principally, Mrs Young uses her position of authority to persuade others. *As regards the member of staff:* from her position higher up the hierarchy, she sometimes stated something without explaining it or motivating the worker. *Towards the client:* she acted as an authoritative advisor and expert. Her sentences often begin with, 'You must ...' She does not check to see if the customer agrees with her. She uses words carefully: her vocabulary is at university standard. She makes far too little eye contact.

Sensitivity

Mrs Young finds it easy to make contact with others. She demonstrates varying degrees of understanding for others' feelings. She is also aware of their worries and tries to reassure them. Towards the 'employee', she was less sensitive. She said, 'I understand', but did little more than that. She created distance by her use of 'Mr'.

Planning and organisation

The candidate scored well here. In the in-tray exercise, she picked up on problems with appointments; she supervised and planned her time well. In her conversations, too, she stated clearly what her objective was, set priorities, monitored the course of the conversation and set up specific follow-up meetings.

Problem analysis

She has a moderate level of analytical ability. She did not pick up on a number of problem points in the in-tray exercise. In the role play (particularly in her role as advisor), she did not demonstrate sufficient insight into the problem. She did not see the links between issues well, but solved individual problems. Her verbal reasoning capacity is lower than the undergraduate norm. She asked few questions and rarely used the other person in a conversation as a means of gaining information.

Business acumen

In the advice task, Mrs Young demonstrated relatively little insight into the customer's market position. She was very focused on her own 'chances of scoring'. Her in-tray performance suggests that she has a good eye for costs and efficiency.

Judgement

Mrs Young performed very inconsistently on this dimension: the more familiar the problem is for her, the more realistic her judgement is. She evaluates people in her workplace on the basis of her own experience: stepping back a little would do her no harm. Due to time pressures, she missed the broad picture a couple of times and she tended to change her mind at times. This made her come across as rather inconsistent.

Customer orientation

Very patchy. On the one hand, Mrs Young saw the customer as the most important person in the world at a given moment, and therefore tried her best to keep the customer happy. On the other hand, she was not involved enough in her customer's requirements. She made too many assumptions and failed to check them out.

Overview

Behavioural dimension	1	2	3	4	5
Leadership			X		
Persuasiveness		X			
Sensitivity		X			
Planning & organising					X
Problem analysis			X		
Business acumen			X		
Judgement			X		
Customer orientation			X		

Interpretation of the scores

Scores	Description
5	Good. A strong point. Very well developed. No need for further development.
4	Reasonably well developed. No need for further development.
3	Moderate. Recommend further development here, via feedback, training, courses and/or coaching.
2	Weak. Further development is definitely essential, via feedback, training, courses and/or coaching.
1	Inadequate. Urgent development, via feedback, training, courses and/or coaching, is essential.

Conclusions and recommendations

Based on behavioural observations during the simulations and the interview, we have formed the following impression: we believe that Mrs Young is not suitable for the position of Commercial Director with 'Thinktank Bank', in view of her strong and weak points described above. The points below influenced our decision.

'Thinktank' Bank's latest marketing approach requires its staff to change their behaviour. This won't come about on its own; management must start the process and supervise its progress. Given the leadership style of this candidate, her sensitivity and methods of persuasion, she will find it difficult to supervise and encourage her staff through this period of change, particularly senior staff. Furthermore, it seems to us that Mrs Young's capabilities in the field of marketing approach and strategy are inadequate.

We would recommend Mrs Young to try to develop her strongest points more fully: namely, her knowledge and experience of the bank's products and services, and her talents vis-a-vis customers.

Testing and the law

There are laws which the test user must not transgress, particularly the Equal Opportunities Act. Therefore, test results or tests themselves should not discriminate against anyone on grounds of race, gender, sexual persuasion or religious beliefs. For data on candidates' test results that are stored on a computer, the Data Protection Act ensures that these are kept and stored confidentially, and can only be seen by a third party with the candidate's express permission. Finally, there are copyright laws which protect the test publishers, ensuring that companies do not plagiarise from normed and validated tests, thus rendering the value of their own 'homegrown' tests useless.

In the UK, the governing body responsible for managing test usage is the British Psychological Society (BPS). As non-psychologists are allowed to administer tests in the UK and give feedback on results, the BPS set up a national 'competency scheme' in 1991 to ensure that test users were knowledgeable about the tests they were selecting and were equipped to convey feedback to candidates. Test users undergo a training scheme to attain either Level A competency (which allows them to use ability tests) or the more advanced level, Level B (personality tests). The only people allowed to train for these levels are Chartered Occupational Psychologists, who must be on the BPS register. (For filing a complaint, refer to appendix 2.)

Test users who are members of the Chartered Institute of Personnel & Development (CIPD) should abide by the organisation's Code of Conduct, which is not legally binding, however. If they are not a member, then really they have 'carte blanche'.

However, no legal framework exists (yet) in the UK to deal with candidates' complaints regarding psychological tests. Candidates have little direct redress if psychological testing goes wrong.

Legal right to the report

Even though your name is on the report, that doesn't mean you own it. The potential employer and/or the selection agency are the legal owners. Is this right? That remains to be seen, because without your information, there wouldn't be a report at all!

You should always request (demand) a copy of your report. Company policy in many selection agencies states that you will automatically receive a copy. It is generally accepted that every candidate should inspect his or her report and receive some feedback. (This doesn't necessarily mean that you will get a copy to take home).

In some ACs, the candidate is videoed. Can you take the video, CD or DVD home, to proudly show your fans? No. You have already given your permission to be filmed (perhaps without considering the consequences).

The post-assessment discussion

You may have the right to a free post-assessment discussion – use it. You will find out:

- how you came over generally, in the eyes of the professional assessors. *You don't have to agree with their verdict. Perhaps you don't recognise yourself at all in the picture they paint. But something must have led them to this conclusion. What?*
- what relationships (between dimensions?) have been found, and on what are they based.
- areas that need improving. *Which characteristics should you change?*
- your possible job profile. *Which jobs and professions suit you, and which do not?*
- what you must watch out for at your next 'test'. *Did you really believe this one is your last? Don't bet on it …*

Recycled reports?

Suppose the selection agency gives you a really fantastic report. A glowing, gleaming recommendation. You think the job's in the bag. But it doesn't go through, perhaps because there is a job freeze due to cutbacks. You have invested your time and effort (a day's pay perhaps) and now all you have are a few pieces of paper. And then it hits you ... a great idea. Why not use your report as a 'guarantee' for all your future interviews. Not only does your potential employer know what he's letting himself in for, but he's also saving himself the costs of a new examination!

Employers will not fall for your scheme. Why not? Firstly, they do not know how many times you have been assessed (perhaps at your own cost) to achieve this truly fabulous report. Secondly, it is highly unlikely that your old report will be for the same job and the same sort of company with the same requirements. So, the report cannot contribute anything to the new procedure. And were this the case, then the selection agency would certainly find the old report inadequate: who can trust a second hand report?

Bibliography

Anastasi, A. & Urbina, S. Psychological testing (7th ed.), Prentice-Hall, Upper Saddle River, 1998

Bader, W., Burt, D. S. & Steinberg, E. P. Miller Analogies Test, Prentice-Hall, New York, 1993.

Barnette, W.L. Readings in psychological tests and measurements, Dorsey, Homewood, 1964

Born, M. Ph., Algera, J.A. & Hoolwerf, G. Dilemma's bij het meten van management kwaliteiten; Gedrag en organisatie; 1988, 1,1, 30-46.

Briggs Myers, I., Introduction to type. Cosulting Psychologists Press, Palo Alto, 1987.

Camilli, G. & Shephard, L.A. Methods for identifying biased test items; Sage, Thousand Oaks, 1994

The College Board, 10 SATs. College Entrance Examination Board, New York, Annual edition.

Constable, A., *Bridging the gap; linking assessment to development;* International Journal of Career Management, 1993, 5, 5, 1-11.

Cooper, D. & Robertson, I.T. The psychology of personnel selection; Routledge, London/New York, 1995

Crawley, B., R. Pinder & P. P. Herriott, Assessment center dimensions, personality and attitudes; Journal of Occupational Psychology, 1990, 63, 211-216.

Cronbach, L.J. Essentials of psychological testing; (2nd ed.) Harper & Brothers, New York, 1960

Dam, K. van, W.M.M. Altink & Kok, B. De praktijk van de assessment center-methode: een inventarisatie van knelpunten; De Psycholoog, 1992, 27, 509-514.

De Raad, B. & Perugini, M. Big Five assessment; Hogrefe & Huber; Göttingen, 2002

Drenth, P.J.D. Testtheorie; Bohn Stafleu van Loghum; Houten, 1999

Eysenck, H.J. Know your own IQ; Pengui, Harmondsworth, 1983

Fissini, H-J. & Fennekels, G.P. Das Assessment Center; eine Einfuhring fur Praktiker; Verlag fur Angewandte Psychologie; Göttingen, 1995

Fletcher, C. & Kerslake,C. Candidate anxiety level and assessment centre performance; Journal of Managerial Psychology, 1993, 8, 5, 19-23.

Flier, H. van der, P.G.W. Jansen, and J.N. Zaal, J.N. (eds.), Selectieresearch in de praktijk; Swets & Zeitlinger; Amsterdam/Lisse, 1991.

Flynn, J.R. Masssive IQ gains in 14 nations: what IQ tests really measure; Psychological Bulletin, 1987, 2, 171-191

Gould, S.J. The mismeasure of man; Norton, New York, 1981

Guion, R.M. Assessment, measurement, and prediction for personnel decisions; Lawrence Erlbaum, Mahwah 1998

Guerrier, Y. & M. Riley, Management assessment centres as a focus for change; Personnel Review, 1992, 21, 7, 24-31.

Grensing, L., Employee selection, Self-Counsel Series, Vancouver, 1987.

Hakel, M. D., Employment interviewing; in Rowland, K. M. and Ferris, G. R. (eds) Personnel Management, Allyn & Bacon, Boston, 1982.

Hawkins, K. L and Turia, P. A. Test your entrepreneurial IQ, Berkley, New York, 1986.

Hernnstein, R.J. & Murray, C. The Bell curve: intelligence and class structure in American life; The Free Press, New York, 1994

Hogan, R., Curphey, G. J. & Hogan, J. What we know about leadership: effectiveness and personality; American Psychologist, June 1994, 493-504.

Holzhauer, F.F.O. & van Minden, J.J.R. Psychologie, theorie en praktijk (4de dr.) Stenfert Kroese; Leiden, 1993

Iles, P., Centres of excellence? Assessment and development centres, managerial competence and human resources strategies; British Journal of Management, 1992, 3,2, 79-90.

Jaffe, E. D. and Hilbert, S. How to prepare for the GMAT. Barron's Educational Series, Hauppauge, 1991.

Jansen, P. G. W. & de Jongh, F. Assessment Centers, een open boek, Het Spectrum/Marka, De Meern, 1993.

Joyce, L.W., S. B. Pond & P. W. Thayer, P.W. Managerial functions: an alternative to traditional assessment center dimensions? Personnel psychology, Spring 1994, 47, 1, 109-122.

Kaufman, A.S. & Lichtenberger, E.O. Essentials of WAIS-III Assessment, Wiley, New York, 1999

Kesselmann-Turkel, J. & Peterson, F. Test-taking strategies, Contemporary Books, Chicago, 1981.

Kirksey, J. & Zawacki, R.A. Assessment center helps find team-oriented candidates, Personnel Journal, May 1994, 73, 5, 92.

Koontz, H., O'Donnell, C. & Weihrich, H., Management, McGraw-Hill, New York, 1984.

Lievens, S., Steverlinck, H., Tjoa, A. & Verhoeven, C. Vragenlijst voor commercieel inzicht. Swets & Zeitlinger, Lisse, 1985.

Lowry, P.E. Selection methods: comparison of assessment centers with personnel records evaluations; Public Personnel Management, 1994, 23, 3, 383-395

Martinson, T.H. & Ellis, D., GMAT. Prentice-Hall, New York, 1991.

Meeren, W. vander & Gerrichhauzen, J. (eds). Selectie en Assessment, theorie en praktijk. Lemma, Utrecht, Open Universiteit, Heerlen, 1993.

Miller, K.M. Psychological testing in personnel assessment; Gower, Westmead, 1980.

Miller, W.J., Haller, M.A., Freedman, G.P & Morse-Cluley, E., SAT Verbal Workbook, Prentice-Hall, New York, 1992.

Millman, J & Pauk, W., How to take tests. McGraw-Hill, New York, 1969.

Meeren, W. vander & J. Gerrichhauzen (eds), Selectie en assessment, theorie en praktijk; Lemma BV, Utrecht, Open Universiteit Heerlen, 1993.

Van der Molen, H. te Nijenhuis, J. & Keen, G. Effecten van Test-Training: voorbereiding op het psychologisch onderzoek bij personeelsselectie; De Psycholoog, jan, 1994, 3-7

Van Naarsen, L. & Meijer, F. (red.) Klinische diagnostiek: casuistiek; Swets & Zeitlinger, Lisse, 1996

O'Neill, B.; The manager as an assessor; The Industrial Society, London, 1990.

Rarick, C.A. & Baxter, G., Behaviourally anchored rating scales (BARS): an effective performance appraisal approach; SAM Advanced Management Journal, 51, 1, 1986, 36-39.

Roberts, G. Recruitment and selection; a competency approach; Chartered Institute of Personnel and Development; London, 2000.

Robinson, A. & Katzman, J. Cracking the new SAT; Villard Books; New York, 1994

Roe, R.A., Grondslagen der personeelselectie, Van Gorcum, Assen, 1983.

Serrano, P. et al. Municipal police evaluation: psychometric versus behavioural assessment; Police selection and training, NATO ASI Series, Martinus Nijhoff, Dordrecht, 1986.

Shore, T.H., L.M. Shore and G.C. Thornton, Construct validity of self- and peer evaluations of performance dimensions in an assessment center; Journal of Applied Psychology, 1992, 1, 42-54.

Spence, M. Miller Analogies Test Preparation Guide, Cliffs, 1995.

Super, D.E. (ed.) Measuring vocational maturity for counseling and evaluation; American Personnel and Guidance Association; Washington, 1974

Testpsychologie en selectie en beweging. Conference Reader, Psycom, Amsterdam, 18th March 1988.

Tiffin, J & McCormick, E.J. Industrial Psychology, George Allen & Unwin, London, 1968.

Toplis, J., Dulewicz, V. & Fletcher, C. Psychological testing; a manager's guide. (3rd ed.) Institute of Personnel and Development, London, 1997

Whetton, D.A. & Cameron, K.S., Developing management skills, Scott, Forestman, Glenview, 1984.

Woodruffe, C. Development and assessment centres; (3rd ed.) Institute of Personnel and Development; London, 2000

Zeeuw, J. de., Algemene psychodiagnostiek. Deel 1. Testmethoden, Swets & Zeitlinger, Lisse, 1981.

Mini-course 1

How to Lead a Group Discussion

Selectors are often interested in who emerges as the ('natural') leader in open discussions. We will familiarise you with some aspects of how to lead a group discussion, so that you can increase your chances of the much-coveted leadership. If you don't succeed in becoming the main (wo)man, don't worry too much. Even as a non-leader, you can still get great results from this task!

Phase 1: Orientation

We can distinguish three phases in the group discussion. In each phase, the interim goal is different and it naturally follows that the 'leader' must also bear these differences in mind. Opt for a goal too quickly and you may damage your chances of the leadership.

Phase 1 – Orientation
In the first phase, there is a need for sussing each other out, testing the ground, trying to find out what everyone's expectations are. Because you are in a competitive situation, there is a good chance of being wrong in your observation of others. This may lead to a false impression of the group, which could wreck the final group outcome. The good group leader ensures that there is sufficient time in reserve for familiarisation. Let everyone have a chance to have their say. (But keep an eye on the time, which marches inexorably forward!)

Implication: ensure that everyone can get used to one another and be familiar with each other's views. Take the initiative here.

Phase 2 – Building relationships
Based on mutual sympathies or interests, subgroups or alliances can sometimes emerge. This leads to divisions which may not only be damaging for the final outcome but can also intensify! At most, you can shine as leader of one of these camps. But you want to lead the whole group.

Implication: ensure that everyone speaks his or her mind individually, and look for common ground; differences do not contribute to your final result. State what you find good about others' arguments, and follow this by outlining your own views. Don't push your own point, but seek consensus as much as possible.

Phase 3 – Acceptance

This is the decision-making phase. Opinions and viewpoints have all been expressed and now some agreement must be thrashed out. If you haven't done so already, you will now see in this phase whether you have been accepted as leader by the group (and how). Try to find as much common ground as possible between team members and take the initiative to reach an acceptable solution. Summarising and reiterating points already agreed on can be helpful here.

Implication: try to establish who your supporters or opponents are. The latter must be 'diffused'. Address them in particular and try to win them over. Always keep your eye on the group objective and if necessary reiterate the group standpoint.

Balance

Often, groups can take quite a while to find a true balance. (How long this takes is difficult to say, but it will always take longer than the duration of the group exercise). This means that the hard-earned leadership can be easily lost. So, you must keep your mind on the group dynamics. If others look as though they are gaining an important edge, then stay calm. Don't be tempted to oppose them. Don't be pig-headed. By stressing the positive in others' viewpoints and fostering understanding and sympathy for your own, you can demonstrate that you are someone who gets things done. Don't keep on defending your own interests. Don't get drawn into other people's weak arguments, but try to turn the discussion back to the essentials. It is better to accept part of someone's contribution than to reject it!

A leader is someone who ensures that the work is done, preferably with full support and contribution from all. The biggest mouth, who always wants to force his opinions down other people's throats, will certainly not achieve this.

Task and people-oriented behaviour

There is a difference between task- and people-oriented behaviour. An effective leader demonstrates both.

Task-oriented leaders focus particularly on the main group objective, often without any distractions. Here are some features of this approach:

- asking people to be more specific
- summarising what contributors have said
- clearly voicing their own opinions
- reaching a speedy solution.

People-oriented leaders pay more attention to the views, thoughts and feelings of their group colleagues, whom they clearly respect.

It is a good idea to try to achieve an equilibrium between the two approaches.

Dysfunctional behaviour

Another way to gain influence is to deal effectively with other group members' dysfunctional behaviour. You should intervene when someone digresses, holds a monologue, starts a misplaced discussion on ethics, tells stupid jokes or makes silly remarks. Do this tactfully and don't belittle the person involved. If someone is digressing, don't question the content of what they are saying, but the meaning. If someone is rabbiting on, then try to cut him or her short. The best way to do this is by summarising what's been said.

Don't get stressed about wasting time. Try to turn the discussion round to the essentials as much as possible and always focus on the positive aspects of someone's contribution.

Mini-course 2

Ten Rules to Make Your Script More Readable

Follow these ten rules to improve your written performance:

a. Put yourself in the reader's shoes.
b. Explain your aims.
c. Stay concise and business-like.
d. Write clearly.
e. Keep it short.
f. Try to be 'complete'.
g. Organise your ideas.
h. Write proper English.
i. Make your script look attractive.
j. Write legibly.

a. Put yourself in the reader's shoes
The best start for any script is to ask yourself, what would I want to read, as a reader?

b. Explain your aims
If you write something down, then do it with an objective in mind. Make this goal clear! Is your aim to inform? To persuade? Or something else? (Many in-tray exercises do not require you to write anything down. Whether you write anything or not, you must account for your actions in the discussion that follows. Therefore, it is strongly recommended to know in advance which goal you had in mind.)

c. Stay concise and business-like
It's difficult to keep it short! But just remember that your memo or report, though important, is not the only document that the recipients (in real life) have to read.

d. Write clearly
Clarity means: write in such a way that the image that you have as a writer is also conveyed to the reader. There is no room for misunderstandings or

misinterpretations. The fuzzier the expressions ('to a large extent' is vaguer than 'three quarters') and the longer the sentences, the greater the chance of lack of clarity. (Some people have to be deliberately vague in their daily work. Avoid this in the AC.)

Perhaps your handwriting is terribly difficult to read. (Think about the assessors with their red-rimmed eyes). Their trouble deciphering your hieroglyphics will certainly not go in your favour.

e. Keep it short

Try to get your message across using as few words as possible. This doesn't mean writing in 'telegram style' but does mean avoiding words which don't add value, 'fillers' etc. Bear this thought in mind: writing = skimming. People often think that complex sentences demonstrate great learning. Nothing is further from the truth. A great scholar can explain difficult things often very simply (and without using jargon).

NB. Short and compact are not one and the same. Short means one page, for example. Compact means efficient use of words.

f. Try to be 'complete'

Perhaps after reading the rules above, you are writing in too short and compact a style. The intention is not to leave out important information. So, always ask yourself: does the reader have enough information to ... (perform the desired action, for example).

g. Organise your ideas

Make things as easy as possible for the reader (your 'client!'). Ensure that your letter, memo, document etc. is an accessible 'travel guide'. Use paragraphs and sub-paragraphs to divide up your work. Start with a system. For example, try to divide a memo in the following way:

1. problem
2. aim
3. solution
4. action.

Other divisions are also possible of course, as long as the memo is clear and the reader can understand it.

h. Write proper English

'Well, obviously', I hear you say, 'that's easy'. But do you have any idea how many letters, reports and brochures with all types of spelling and grammatical errors land on our doormats every day? (Loads!)

Linguistic mistakes may well result in the following responses.

1. If someone is careless with his or her written work, he or she is likely to be careless in other ways.
2. The writer has poor English (which may be bad for the company's image).
3. The writer has little regard for the reader, who is apparently not important enough.

i. Make your script look attractive

Make use of:

- space between paragraphs/margins
- underlining
- highlighting
- summary points.

j. Write legibly

1. Use short sentences. It is advisable to use no more than 12 words per sentence. (Sentence too long? Then, divide it into 2 or 3 parts.)
2. Use simple words wherever possible (e.g. replace 'converse' with 'talk').
3. Make good use of punctuation. Texts read better with 'rest stops', such as commas, full stops, question marks, etc.

Key points and side issues

Always try to limit your texts to one single key theme and preferably one other side issue. If you produce a script with three main themes and three side issues, you will already be covering nine subjects! This can be very confusing. Once more, keep it short to come across well! Keep asking yourself the critical question: what is the key theme in this piece and what are my side issues? Distinguish them from each other by numbering them or by using a certain typography.

Who-what-where-how-when-and-why?

A journalist once stated that his job was very easy. All he had to do was to answer the 'who-what-where-how-when-and-why' question for every article. In your case, of course, it will look very different. But, mostly, you can still get by very well with this simple set of questions.

For reporters, it often goes as follows:

- last night (when)
- someone (who)
- started a fire (what)
- in Trafalgar Square (where)
- with a Molotov cocktail (how)
- because he was over the edge (why).

Mini-course 3

A General Problem-solving Model

The following model can be applied to almost every role play situation (except the bad-news one – where you must just 'give it to 'em straight'). It is evident that the emphasis will vary according to the situation, but we will leave that up to your own judgement and creativity! The full model has three phases; each one is broken down into a number of stages:

Phase 1: the beginning
    Step 1:   Welcome the other person
    Step 2:   Set out the aim of the conversation
    Step 3:   Explain what will happen

Phase 2: the middle
    Step 4:   Identify the problem
    Step 5:   Let the other person respond
    Step 6:   Look for solutions
    Step 7:   Set deadlines

Phase 3: the end
    Step 8:   Summarise the conversation
    Step 9:   Set up a follow-up meeting
    Step 10:   Close and farewell

Phase 1: the beginning

Step 1
Welcome the other person, offer coffee or tea, and put him at ease. How? Make 'small talk' – either private (*'Did you have a nice weekend?' 'How are the children?'*) or business (*'Are you really busy in your department all of a sudden?' 'Don't you think the packaging on the latest product is fantastic?'*)

But remember: keep this part short. You shouldn't overdo the chit-chat – after all you have some hard nuts to crack! So, you may be wondering, why bother with the chit-chat at all? It's simple. The other person might smell a rat. He or she is not sure what to expect and may be rather uptight.

Your 'opponent' may put you to the test, perhaps talking endlessly about his great weekend in Brussels or the latest exploits of his children. Let him have his say, but then take control of the conversation again (nicely); grasp the initiative. Step 2 is coming up …

Step 2

Set out the aim of the conversation. If there is one clear reason why you have invited this staff member for a talk, then say it. For example: *'So this is the second time this year that we are sitting down formally to talk about how the department is running'*. Of course, your aim may be different: *'You've probably read that we are facing great changes which will also have an impact on our department. That's why I asked you here today to discuss these further'*.

Step 3

Explain the procedure and outline the different points of discussion. Let's assume that there is a personnel evaluation policy in this organisation. You can explain this briefly: *'… you will receive a copy of this form for yourself, one goes to Personnel and I keep one. I will just ask you to sign the three copies as seen, so that no misunderstandings occur'*.

Phase 2: the middle

In this section, you have to outline the problem and try to reach a solution which both parties agree to. If there are several different problems under discussion, then take one at a time. For each problem, start again from step 4.

Step 4

Identify the problem. Describe the problem as accurately as possible, so that 'evasion' is not an option. Say what you've seen or noticed. Do this in a neutral, non-judgemental voice, using precise terms.

Step 5

Let the other person respond. For every problem that arises, you should ask if he or she agrees that there is a problem. If he or she recognises the problem, then carry on to step 6. If not, convince your opponent that there really is a problem. You can explain the situation once more, introduce new arguments or try to find out more about your opponent's objections by asking questions. *'Why do you think this isn't a problem?' 'What do you think happened?' 'Can you tell me how you see the problem?'* You should carry on until your opponent is convinced that a problem exists or until he or she comes around to your ideas. As long as the individual cannot 'see' the problem, then he or she will not be ready to work towards a solution.

Use the word 'understand' regularly: *'I understand'*, or *'I understand that you feel unhappy when you hear ...'*

Step 6

Look for solutions. Ask your 'colleague' to come up with his or her own solution (for each problem), because this will be easier to accept and carry out. Appeal to his or her creativity or ingenuity. Don't put forward your own solutions too quickly but try to get the other person thinking. Be positive. If the other person comes up with a suggestion that you like, the problem is solved and you'll have gained a new ally. If you are not able to reach an agreement, then you'll need to go for heavier ammunition. Inform the other person that it really would be better for him or her to come up with a solution as yours will probably be much less pleasant.

As a last resort, and permissible in very clear-cut cases (e.g. manning a security post, getting a report in by a certain deadline), then use the following solution. Make reference to the organisation's rules, regulations and customs, and then to the fact that YOU are responsible for the department. Put forward your solution and order the other person to obey. If it gets this far in a role play, then don't be surprised if you get a negative evaluation.

Step 7

Set objectives. Briefly reiterate what has been discussed and agree on concrete, quantifiable and achievable objectives. Check they have been understood and accepted as fair. If you hear no word of understanding and/or agreement, you must carry on until you get this.

Phase 3: the end

Step 8

Summarise the conversation. If several subjects have been under discussion, then give a brief summary, to avoid misunderstandings. (If they already exist, get them out of the way now). It is always advisable to write down what has been agreed. The human brain can be very frail. So: *'I will get this in writing to you by tomorrow morning'*.

Step 9

Set up a follow-up discussion. Do this straight away, thus clearly demonstrating that you will keep an eye on this matter. But, let him or her know that your door is always open for problems, and advice, before this date.

Step 10

Closing. Voice your pleasure over the fact that you have reached agreement and wish the other person luck. Don't emphasise any doubts you may have about how it will turn out, and end the conversation on a positive note. At the end of the day, the other person needs to be motivated as he gets back to work. Stand up and extend your hand, to formally seal the agreement. Don't be surprised if the other person still has things to discuss; perhaps something is still not clear.

A final piece of advice

As the guest of a selection agency, you will probably be observed by psychologists or other '-logists'. They would like to discover something 'human' in you – some warmth, sensitivity, empathy, or whatever you'd like to call it. So, don't be too task-oriented. Think about the other person's feelings as well.

Practice Test 1 – Numerical Series

	Series	Alternatives
1	1/3 2/3 ? 5/3 8/3 13/3 7	4/3 3 2/3 1 1/3 1
2	64 8 9 3 4 ?	5 16 2 1 -3
3	? 26/8 20/9 40/10 34/11 68/12	14/7 16/3 8/26 13/7 20/7
4	4/3 6/8 16/12 24/32 64/48 ?	82/68 96/128 32/24 8/6 86/68
5	4/3 14/11 16/13 6/5 20/17 22/19 ?	8/7 24/23 26/21 10/9 9/8
6	7 49 39 23 529 519 ?	503 493 256 483 305
7	3 2 3 8 13 24 ?	25 21 45 43 37
8	? 3 6 18 108 1944	0 -2 1 2 3
9	3 5 9 15 ? 33 45	17 23 19 27 21
10	75 39 14 -2 -11 -15 ?	9 -5 -16 0 -12
11	121 100 81 64 49 36 ?	24 21 25 16 33
12	1 3 16 6 1 49 ?	7 9 82 5 39
13	5 25 4 16 2 4 3 ?	-9 0 16 12 8
14	½ 2/4 8/6 48/8 384/10 ?	480/12 3840/12 834/14 3072/12
15	18 3 9 1½ 4 ½ ¾ 2¼ ?	3/8 5/6 4 1 1/8 7/16
16	2 12 3 18 4½ 27 ?	6½ 6 45 6¾ 11¾
17	-7 -4 2 11 23 38 ?	45 56 62 -2 53
18	4 27 16 125 36 ?	343 245 223 49 155
19	90 20 75 4 72 1 71 -¼ 1/3 ?	70 71 69 70 1/3 851/12
20	81 27 9 3 1 ?	½ 1 1/3 1/6 3

Correct Answers

1. 1 **2.** 2 **3.** 13/7 **4.** 96/128 **5.** 8/7 **6.** 503 **7.** 45 **8.** 2
9. 23 **10.** -16 **11.** 25 **12.** 39 **13.** 9 **14.** 3840/12 **15.** 3/8
16. 6¾ **17.** 56 **18.** 343 **19.** 71 **20.** 1/3

247

Practice Test 2 – Syllogisms

Each item on this test consists of two statements. You must draw the only logical conclusion that follows from both statements. There is only one right answer, so circle either A, B, C or D.

You will find the correct answers at the end of this exercise.

1. **All pilots are brave**
   Some pilots are women, so:
   - A. Some brave people are not pilots
   - B. Some men are pilots
   - C. Some women are brave
   - D. Some women are not brave.

2. **No salesman is shy**
   All traders are salesmen, so:
   - A. Some salesmen are not traders
   - B. No trader is shy
   - C. All traders are brash
   - D. Some shy people are salesmen

3. **No scholars are prophets**
   Some pianists are scholars, so:
   - A. No pianists are prophets
   - B. Some pianists are not scholars
   - C. No prophet is a scholar
   - D. Some pianists are not prophets.

4. **All small girls are funny**
   Some small girls are fat, so:
   - A. Some small girls aren't fat.
   - B. Some funny people aren't small girls
   - C. No fat small girl is funny
   - D. Some fat girls are funny

5. **Some posters aren't successful**
   All posters advertise, so:
   - A. Some posters are successful
   - B. Some advertisements aren't posters
   - C. Some advertisements aren't successful
   - D. Some successful things are not posters.

6. **No teacher is stubborn**
   All tutors are teachers, so:
   - A. No tutor is stubborn
   - B. Some teachers are tutors
   - C. All tutors are reasonable people
   - D. Some stubborn individuals are teachers.

7. **No healthy person is sick**
   Some directors are healthy, so:
   - A. Some healthy people aren't directors
   - B. Some sick people are healthy
   - C. Some sick people are directors
   - D. Some directors aren't sick.

8. **Some novels are classics**
   All classics are worth reading, so:
   - A. All novels are worth reading
   - B. Some items worth reading are novels
   - C. Some classics aren't novels
   - D. Some items worth reading aren't classics

9. **Some women are mothers**
   All women are beautiful, so:
   - A. All mothers are female
   - B. All beautiful beings are female
   - C. Some beautiful beings are mothers
   - D. Some women aren't mothers.

10. All apples are red
No car is red, so:
      A. No apple is a red car

      B. Some red things aren't apples

      C. All cars are black

      D. No cars are apples

11. Some songs are hits
All hits are moneyspinners, so:
      A. Some songs aren't hits

      B. Some moneyspinners re songs

      C. Some hits aren't songs

      D. Some songs aren't moneyspinners

12. All divers are swimmers
Some divers are sailors, so:
      A. Some sailors are swimmers

      B. Some swimmers aren't divers

      C. All sailors are swimmers

      D. Some divers aren't sailors

Correct Answers 1. C 2. B 3. D 4. D 5. C 6. A 7. D 8. B 9. C 10. D 11. B 12. A

Practice Test 3 – Numerical Reasoning

For many jobs it is important to have some level of numerical ability. It is one thing to be able to solve simple sums or recognise patterns of numbers; being able to interpret numerical data, though, is another matter entirely. This test is primarily used for selecting managers working in the financial and banking sectors. Below you will see some questions to get your teeth into.

TABLE 1 – TOURISTS INTO THE UK

Country of Origin	Number of visitors – 1995 (000s)	Total expenditure during stay (1995) £ million	Average length of stay (days) 1995	Total expenditure during stay (1994) £ million	GDP per head of country of origin (£ 000)
Germany	103	78.9	5	70.5	38.04
Australia	138	55.6	32	57.4	14.5
Spain	86	28.5	4	34.2	25.84
USA	134	123.8	11	117.5	45.27
Netherlands	65	13.9	3	11.6	22.9
Japan	53	56.3	7	49.6	39.75

1a. Which country visits the UK in greatest numbers?
1b. Who spent the most per visitor on holiday in the UK in 1995?
1c. Which country spends the most per head, as a proportion of GDP?
1d. Which nation has most increased its gross expenditure on last year in percentage terms?
1e. Who spent the most per day on holiday in 1995?

TABLE 2 – MEMORY CHIP PRODUCTION

	1989	1990	1991	1992
Cost price per unit	£2.80	£2.40	£1.50	£0.90
Factory A production (000s of units)	120	200	240	360
Factory B production (000s of units)	140	200	220	310
Industry Average (000s of units)	145	172	216	332
Sale price per unit (Factory A)	£2.50	£2.30	£1.80	£1.20
Sale price per unit (Factory B)	£2.90	£2.60	£2.00	£1.60

2a.   What operating profit did Factory A make in 1989?
2b.   As a percentage of turnover, which factory improved the most between 1990 and 1992 and by how much?
2c.   By what percentage did Factory B's production differ from the industry average between 1990 and 1992?
2d.   What price should Factory A sell chips at in 1992 to become as profitable as Factory B in relation to turnover?

TABLE 3 – EMPLOYMENT ACCORDING TO SECTOR

Sector	1988 (000s)	1989 (000s)	1990 (000s)	1991 (000s)
Education	1452.3	1256.7	1105.8	1218.8
Manufacturing	1789.5	1452.3	1393.6	1255.9
Banking	1205.6	1189.3	1095.8	1247.6
Civil Service	978.5	990.6	857.9	888.6
Retail	992.7	1085.9	1128.4	1152.9

3a.   What sector saw the greatest changes in employment levels during the period 1988-1991?
3b.   What percentage of people was employed in the banking sector in 1990?
3c.   How many fewer people were employed in total in 1991 compared with 1989?
3d.   What percentage of people was employed in non-manufacturing in 1991?
3e.   What was the average growth rate of employment in the retail sector between 1988-1991?

Correct answers: **1a.** Australia **1b.** Japan **1c.** Australia **1d.** Netherlands **1e.** Germany **2a.** £36,000 loss **2b.** Factory B by 36.3% **2c.** 11.2% **2d.** £1.60 **3a.** Manufacturing **3b.** 19.6% **3c.** 211,000 **3d.** 78.2% **3e.** 5.16%

252

Practice Test 4 – Antonyms (opposites)

You must denote the answer (a, b, c, d or e) which is opposite, or nearly opposite, in meaning to the first word (printed in bold). Only give one answer. The correct answers are at the bottom of the page.

1. Good: a. reasonable b. bad c. sour d. common e. ugly

2. Premature: a. timely b. powerful c. old d. common e. overdue.

3. Recollect: a. disapprove b. dispense c. forget d. pardon e. defer

4. Spiritual: a. effervescent b. significant c. adaptable d. felicitous
e. worldly

5. Juvenile: a. broken b. full-grown c. eclectic d. friendly e. intransigent

6. Suppress: a. air b. accuse c. initiate d. perplex e. astound

7. Distant: a. cordial b. graceful c. scholarly d. diligent e. sizable

8. Cowardice: a. heroism b. aggression c. boldness d. courage e. anger

9. Coddle: a. summon b. clarify c. abuse d. separate e. confess

10. Death: a. tedium b. maliciousness c. information d. antagonism
e. bounty

11. Neologism: a. nameless article b. foreign object c. exaggerated
movement d. impoverished condition e. obsolete expression

12. Sorrow: a. isolation b. indecision c. pleasure d. perplexity
e. preference

13. Depreciate: a. prove b. attack c. dawdle d. establish e. raise

14. Indefatigable: a. durable b. temperate c. anonymous d. independent
e. listless

15. Objective: a. uneven b. pure c. controllable d. modest e. personal

16. Egoism: a. friendliness b. nostalgia c. goodness d. altruism
e. gentleness

17. Labile: a. characteristic b. self-conscious c. assertive d. controlled
e. stable

18. Shame: a. honour b. praise c. pride d. compliment e. sorrow

19. Avarice: a. wealth b. waste c. poverty d. condescension e. greed

20. Evolution: a. revolution b. regression c. restriction d. recession
e. repression

Correct answers: 1b 2e 3c 4e 5b 6a 7a 8d 9c 10e 11e 12c
13e 14e 15e 16d 17e 18a 19b 20b

Appendix 1

Behavioural Dimensions and Tasks

Behavioural dimension	In tray	Group exercise	Written task	Analysis & Planning	Presentation	Fact finding	Role play
Ability to adapt		☒		☒	☒	☒	☒
Ability to cope under stress	☒	☒		☒	☒	☒	☒
Ability to delegate	☒	☒		☒		☒	
Ability to influence	☒	☒	☒	☒	☒	☒	☒
Ambition		☒		☒	☒		☒
Analytical skills	☒	☒	☒	☒		☒	☒
Assertiveness	☒	☒	☒		☒	☒	☒
Attention to detail				☒		☒	
Attitude		☒		☒	☒	☒	☒
Commercial sense	☒	☒	☒	☒	☒	☒	☒
Conformity	☒	☒	☒				☒
Creativity	☒	☒	☒	☒	☒	☒	☒
Customer orientation	☒		☒	☒	☒	☒	
Decision making ability	☒	☒	☒		☒	☒	☒
Determination	☒	☒				☒	
Discipline	☒	☒	☒		☒	☒	☒
Drive for power/influence	☒	☒		☒	☒	☒	☒
Energy	☒	☒		☒	☒	☒	☒
Ethical behaviour	☒		☒		☒	☒	☒
Flexibility	☒	☒	☒	☒	☒	☒	☒
Group-oriented leadership		☒		☒	☒		
Independence	☒	☒			☒	☒	☒
Individual oriented leadership	☒						☒
Initiative	☒	☒	☒	☒	☒	☒	☒
Integrity/Honesty	☒		☒			☒	
Judgement	☒		☒	☒		☒	☒
Listening skills		☒			☒	☒	☒
Loyalty to management policy and direction	☒	☒	☒	☒	☒	☒	☒
Motivation	☒	☒				☒	
Oral communication skills		☒			☒	☒	☒

Behavioural dimension	Task						
	In tray	Group exercise	Written task	Analysis & Planning	Presentation	Fact finding	Role play
Organisational sensitivity	☒						☒
Perfectionism	☒	☒			☒		
Persuasiveness	☒	☒	☒		☒		☒
Planning & organisation	☒	☒		☒	☒		☒
Presentation skills					☒		
Risk-taking ability	☒	☒	☒	☒	☒	☒	☒
Scope of interest			☒		☒		
Self-confidence	☒	☒	☒		☒	☒	☒
Self discipline				☒			
Self-reliance	☒		☒		☒	☒	☒
Sense of responsibility	☒	☒	☒				☒
Sensitivity		☒			☒		☒
Social skills		☒			☒	☒	☒
Supervisory abilities	☒						☒
Teamwork	☒	☒		☒			☒
Tenacity	☒	☒			☒	☒	☒
Tolerance							☒
Working tempo/pace	☒	☒	☒		☒	☒	
Written communication skills	☒		☒	☒			

Appendix 2

How to File a Complaint

This is how you file a complaint with the BPS. According to this association:

We are committed to giving an equal service to anyone who complains to us. This means we will not treat you any differently from someone else because of your race, colour, nationality, ethnic, regional or national origin, age, sex, marital status, sexuality, class, political or religious belief, or because you have a disability.

Can we investigate your complaint?
We can investigate your complaint if:

it is about a Chartered Psychologist or any other member of the Society, and it is about a professional conduct issue. We cannot investigate complaints about a psychologist who is not a member of the society or any matter which is the subject of court proceedings.

What is professional misconduct?
We publish a Code of Conduct which sets out certain standards of professional conduct with which our members are expected to comply. The Code is supplemented by other guidelines and statements of good practice to which our members are expected to aim.

Professional misconduct will occur if members act outside the Code or they are:

- failing to recognise the boundaries of their own competence or practising any form of psychology for which they are not qualified
- failing to maintain the confidentiality of information acquired through their professional practice
- exploiting any relationship of trust or influence with a recipient of their services
- conducting themselves in a way that damages the interests of recipients of their services
- failing to obtain the consent of participants before undertaking investigations or interventions.

How do you make a complaint?

All complaints must be in writing. If writing is difficult for you, seek help from a CAB or other advice agency or advocacy group. Or you can get someone to write on your behalf. If English is not your first language, we can arrange translation facilities. If you have any documents or other evidence which support your complaint, please send them to us. We will return them to you if you want them back.

Who deals with complaints?

Initially all complaints are considered by our Investigatory Committee. There are six members of this Committee who must also be Fellows or Associate Fellows of the Society. The Committee includes the President and president Elect.

What happens next?

When the Committee receives a complaint, it will write to the subject of the complaint to seek their comments on the allegations which have been made. Once it has received a response, the Committee will consider all the evidence to hand. It may recommend:

- that further investigation is not required because there is no evidence of professional misconduct.
- that an Investigatory Panel should be appointed to undertake further enquiries into the allegations on its behalf. The Panel will be made up of between two and five members who must also be Fellows or Associate Fellows of the Society. Some of the Panel members will have expertise in the areas at issue.
- that it should write to the subject of the complaint to advise them that it has concerns about their professional conduct. The letter will set out the concerns and will remain as a permanent record on the Society's membership records.
- that a Disciplinary Committee should be appointed for a full hearing of the allegations of professional misconduct.

The Investigatory Committee's recommendations (unless it is one to set up an Investigatory Panel) are referred to one of the non-psychologist representatives of our Disciplinary Board for consideration. The representative may accept or reject the recommendations.

What happens at Disciplinary Committee Hearings?

Our Disciplinary Board has power to take disciplinary action against any of our members. The majority of the people who sit on the Board are not psychologists and are not members of the Society. These 'lay' representatives are invited nominees from other professional bodies such as the Law Society and the Royal College of Nursing, who have experience of the disciplinary processes within their own profession. The psychologist members of the Board all are past Presidents of the Society.

If a Disciplinary Committee is appointed, it is the Society, rather than you which acts as the complainant. We may ask you to attend the hearing as a witness, however. Hearings usually last one day and are held at our London Office.

We appoint three members of our Disciplinary Board to sit on a Disciplinary Committee, two of which will be non-psychologist representatives. The third psychologist member will be a past President of the Society. We appoint one of the non-psychologists as Chair. A barrister will present our case to the Committee. The subject of the complaint may present his or her own case or be represented by a person of their choice or by a barrister.

The Disciplinary Committee will decide whether the member is guilty of professional misconduct. If so, it may invoke various sanctions ranging from reprimanding the member, seeking undertakings relating to the practice of the member, expelling the member from the Society or removing them from the Register of Chartered Psychologists. Although we publish the Committee's decision, we do not reveal your identity in any of the publicity. The subject of the complaint has a right of appeal against any decision of the Disciplinary Committee.

Further information

If you are unsure what to do next, please contact our Regulatory Affairs team (St Andrews House, 48 Princess Road East, Leicester, LE1 7DR, Tel: 01162 549568, E-mail: mail@bps.org.uk). They can advise you (or the subject of your complaint) about the complaints procedure at all stages of the process. They cannot advise on the particular merits of any complaint or potential complaints, however. The Team also ensures that the process is administered according to our statutes and rules and provides administrative services to the Investigatory Committee and its Investigatory Panels and to the Disciplinary Board and its Disciplinary Committees.

Steering Committee for Test Standards 2002

People who use psychological tests for assessment are expected by The British Psychological Society to:

Responsibility for Competence

1. Take steps to ensure that they are able to meet all the standards of competence defined by the Society for the relevant Certificate(s) of Competence in Psychological Testing, and to endeavour, where possible, to develop and enhance their competence as test users.
2. Monitor the limits of their competence in psychometric testing and not to offer services which lie outside their competence nor encourage or cause others to do so.

Procedures and Techniques

3. Only use tests in conjunction with other assessment methods and only when their use can be supported by the available technical information.
4. Administer, score and interpret tests in accordance with the instructions provided by the test distributor and to the standards defined by the Society.
5. Store test materials securely and to ensure that no unqualified person has access to them.
6. Keep test results securely, in a form suitable for developing norms, validation, and monitoring for bias.

Client Welfare

7. Obtain the informed consent of potential test takers, or, where appropriate their legitimate representatives, making sure that they understand why the tests will be used, what will be done with their results and who will be provided with access to them.
8. Ensure that all test takers are well informed and well prepared for the test session, and that all have had access to practice or familiarisation materials where appropriate.
9. Give due consideration to factors such as gender, ethnicity, age, disability and special needs, educational background and level of ability in using and interpreting the results of tests.
10. Provide the test taker and other authorised persons with feedback about the results in a form which makes clear the implications of the results, is clear and in a style appropriate to their level of understanding.

11. Ensure that confidentiality is respected and that test results are stored securely, are not accessible to unauthorised or unqualified persons and are not used for any purposes other than those agreed with the test taker.

ITC Guidelines for developing contracts between parties involved in the testing process

(See also: www.psychtesting.org.uk , the Psychological Testing Centre of the British Psychological Society (BPS)).

Contracts between the test user and test takers should be consistent with good practice, legislation and the test user's policy on testing. The following is provided as an example of the sort of matters such a contract might cover. The details will vary as a function of the assessment context (e.g. occupational, educational, clinical, forensic) and local or national regulations and laws. Contracts between test user, test takers and other parties are often implicit and unspoken (at least in part). Making clear the expectations, roles and responsibilities of all parties can help to avoid misunderstanding, harm, and litigation. For their part, the test user will endeavour to:

- b.1 inform test takers of their rights regarding how their test scores will be used and their rights of access to them;
- b.2 give adequate prior warning of any financial charges that may be entailed by the testing process, who will be responsible for their payment, and when payment will be due;
- b.3 treat test takers with courtesy, respect and impartiality regardless of race, gender, age, disability, etc.;
- b.4 use tests of proven quality, appropriate for the test takers, and appropriate for the assessment purpose;
- b.5 inform test takers prior to testing about the purpose of the assessment, the nature of the test, to whom test results will be reported and the planned use of the results;
- b.6 give advance notice of when the test will be administered, and when results will be available, and whether or not test takers or others may obtain copies of the test, their completed answer sheets, or their scores ;
- b.7 have a trained person administer the test and have the results interpreted by a qualified person;
- b.8 ensure test takers know if a test is optional and, when it is, the consequences of taking or not taking the test;

- b.9 ensure test takers understand the conditions, if any, under which they may re-take tests, have tests re-scored, or have their scores cancelled;
- b.10 ensure test takers know that they will have their results explained to them as soon as possible after taking the test in easily understood terms;
- b.11 ensure test takers understand that their results are confidential to the extent allowed by law and best practice;
- b.12 inform test takers who will have access to their results, and the conditions which scores will be released;
- b.13 ensure that test takers are aware of the procedures for making complaints or notifying problems.

The test user will inform test-takers that they are expected to:

- b.14 treat others with courtesy and respect during the testing process;
- b.15 ask questions prior to testing if uncertain about why the test is to be administered, how it will be administered, what they will be required to do and what will be done with the results;
- b.16 inform an appropriate person about any condition that they believe might invalidate the test results or which they would wish to have taken into consideration;
- b.17 follow the instructions of the test administrator;
- b.18 be aware of the consequences of not taking a test if they choose not to take it, and be prepared to accept those consequences;
- b.19 ensure that, if required to pay for any of the testing service(s), payment is made by the agreed date.

Index